THE AGE OF MACDIARMID

"When the political and literary history of the period comes to be written, it may well be known as the Age of MacDiarmid"

The Economist, 22 October 1977

THE AGE OF
MacDIARMID
ESSAYS ON HUGH MacDIARMID
AND HIS INFLUENCE ON CONTEMPORARY SCOTLAND

Edited by
P.H.SCOTT &
A.C.DAVIS

MAINSTREAM
PUBLISHING·EDINBURGH

First published in Great Britain by
MAINSTREAM PUBLISHING COMPANY (EDINBURGH) LTD.,
28 Barony Street, Edinburgh, EH3 6NY.

ISBN 0 906391 12 1

The publisher gratefully acknowledges
financial assistance from the
Scottish Arts Council.

Printed and bound in Great Britain by
Redwood Burn Limited, Trowbridge and Esher

Contents

[continued overleaf]

A Writer

Events got him in a corner
And gave him a bad time of it—
Poverty, people, ill-health
Battered at him from all sides.
So far from being silenced,
He wrote more poems than ever
And all of them different—
Just as a stoned crow
Invents ways of flying
It had never thought of before.

No wonder now he sometimes
Suddenly lurches, stalls, twirls sideways,
Before continuing his effortless level flight
So high over the heads of people
Their stones can't reach him.

NORMAN MacCAIG
Surroundings

7

Introduction

Hugh MacDiarmid was a writer for whom very large claims have been made by many people and over a long time. For about fifty years (for he had a long and productive life) it has been a commonplace to describe him as the greatest Scottish poet since Robert Burns, if not since William Dunbar. More than that, he is often described as transforming the political and social atmosphere in Scotland — the vision which the Scottish people have of themselves. I take some such comments almost at random. In 1962 George Bruce[1] described him as "the poet who now dominates the imagination of Scotland". *The Economist* in October 1977, calling him "a one-man revolution", said that "When the political and literary history of the period comes to be written, it may well be known as the Age of MacDiarmid". David Murison in *Lines Review* of December 1978, a few months after MacDiarmid's death, wrote of him: "There is one other Scot, at first blush an unlikely candidate for comparison, who is his spiritual ancestor — John Knox; in him we have the same uncompromising aggression, the same extremist absolutism, the same unrestrained vituperative argumentativeness. . . . After MacDiarmid, as after Knox, Scotland will never be the same place again."

Even if these claims are seldom questioned or disputed (if only because the usual tactic of the unconvinced is to ignore them) they still require explanation. They are not self-evident. Although Chris Grieve was the kindest and gentlest of men, in his *alter persona* of Hugh MacDiarmid he was so violent in controversy that he was more liable to alienate than convince. He was unashamedly inconsistent. In his lyrical poetry in Scots, he could express a wealth of meaning in a few words, but his prose was often undisciplined, muddled and diffuse. His communism was not of

9

the fashionable 1930s' variety, but stubborn and idiosyncratic, surviving the invasions of Hungary and Czechoslovakia, and this alone might have destroyed his credibility with most people. Those who were tolerant of this might have been offended, with less reason, by his impatience with the common man which was of the kind which it is now usual to condemn as "élitist". His Scottish nationalism was similarly impatient with the inadequacies of contemporary Scotland, and expressed itself more readily in condemnation than in praise. MacDiarmid never sought popularity. He was a life-long campaigner for his own vision and his own ideas, but he was never ready to compromise or accommodate. An unlikely man, one might think, to transform the intellectual climate of a country. Poets, despite Shelley, are not often "unacknowledged legislators". They are more often likely to be read only by a small coterie. MacDiarmid, whose work is linguistically and intellectually demanding, might easily have remained a cult figure of that kind. So in what sense was he a "one-man revolution"? How true is it that "Scotland will never be the same place again"? What, in fact, was the nature and effect of MacDiarmid's influence? The main object of this book is to try to find answers to these questions.

Of course, it is too soon to hope to reach anything approaching a definite conclusion about the permanent or long-term consequences of MacDiarmid's influence; but there are good reasons for making at least a preliminary attempt without any further delay. We are less than two years away from MacDiarmid's death on 9 September 1978, and can therefore still hope to record the attitudes towards him which prevailed in his own lifetime. We can collect the evidence of people who came under his direct influence, from personal contact as well as from his writing. This is something which must be done now while memory is still fresh.

So we approach the subject in this straightforward way by inviting, in the first group, a number of people to describe the impact which MacDiarmid made on them personally. They are all, as it happens, poets, because they are the people most likely to be the first to respond to the influence of a poet. Perhaps some of them only became poets because of the effect on them of

10

MacDiarmid's example. They span some 50 years, from J. K. Annand and Sorley Maclean speaking of the 'twenties and 'thirties, to Alan Bold of the 'sixties and 'seventies. There is abundant evidence that MacDiarmid was invariably helpful, encouraging and stimulating to other writers; but his effect was something much more powerful than this. Perhaps it is summed up most concisely in Sorley Maclean's remarkable essay. He talks of his "instinctive and overpowering" response to MacDiarmid's lyrics, and of the importance to him of the fact that the greatest living Scottish poet was an "uncompromising Socialist and Scottish Nationalist". One feels that the emphasis is on the word "uncompromising", which Maclean repeats and expands. He sees MacDiarmid as "a visionary and an activist, a Scotsman who had his spiritual eye on everything that mattered to Scotland and on the ends of the earth as well". The unbounded ambition of MacDiarmid to expand the intellectual range of poetry, and of Scottish poetry in particular, to embrace all knowledge, all experience and all space, is one of the constant themes of the papers which follow.

If the first group of essays is largely autobiographical in emphasis, they inevitably diverge into criticism of MacDiarmid's poetry and consideration of his politics. Each of the next two groups concentrates on each of these in turn. George Bruce gives a ringside account of MacDiarmid's reaction to Edwin Muir's *Scott and Scotland*, the trigger to one of the central controversies over MacDiarmid's use of Scots. In the next essay, David Murison, who knows more about the language than anyone else now alive, considers MacDiarmid's experiments with it. David Daiches relates him to the Scottish literary tradition; Kenneth Buthlay and Iain Crichton Smith consider some of the long poems in detail, so that we do not lose sight of the trees in considering the whole wood.

MacDiarmid's political influence is less obvious than the literary and much less easy to define or estimate. This is the subject of the third group. Stephen Maxwell at one point seems to come close to denying altogether that he had any political influence: "MacDiarmid's impact on Scottish political opinion has been slight". Maxwell writes as a practising politician (although one of

11

unusual intellectual honesty). From this point of view, it is natural for him to take this position. MacDiarmid, although he helped to found organisations, including the National Party of Scotland, was anything but an organisation-man. This is the reason, I suspect, why few people take his communism seriously, even if it was real enough and important enough to MacDiarmid himself. The party discipline of the true communist was obviously alien to him. He was equally incapable of the constant compromise and adjustment required by the activist in any party if he is to have influence on policy. MacDiarmid, although full of political ideas and several times a parliamentary candidate, was no politician. There is probably no decision on policy by any party which can be directly attributed to him. Neal Ascherson's brilliant account of MacDiarmid's political philosophy shows, I think, that it was consistent within itself, but well beyond the reach of any conceivable party programme.

But does this mean that he had no political influence? Scotland after MacDiarmid is a very different place from the Scotland in which he was born. It is more assertive of its identity, more intellectually alive, more conscious of its past, and more optimistic and self-confident towards the future, even if it had a temporary relapse at the time of the Referendum in 1979. The theatre, literary and artistic endeavour, the publishing of magazines and books, the study of Scottish history and of all aspects of Scottish life, are now all flourishing to a degree that no one would have thought possible when MacDiarmid began to write. We may think that things are still very far from satisfactory, but they were incomparably worse in the 'twenties and 'thirties. How much of this is attributable to his direct and indirect influence, and how much to other causes? This is one of these questions which can be answered only by subjective judgement and is incapable of proof. We think that most people who have considered the matter at all would agree with David Murison. On 11 September 1978, two days after his death, *The Scotsman* said in its first leader, headed simply "MacDiarmid": "Out of his forge came an energy which spread through Scottish cultural life. There is very little written, acted, composed, surmised or demanded in Scotland which does not in some strand descend from the new beginning he made." Even the new consciousness of the gap between the actual and the potential in Scotland, and the refusal to accept it, can be ascribed to MacDiarmid's influence. Perhaps Shelley was right after all.

I cannot close without a word of gratitude to my joint editor, A. C. Davis, a man who for years has been associated with most of the desirable endeavours in Scotland. For good reasons his range of friendship and acquaintance ramifies in all directions. He was therefore the ideal man to persuade our chosen contributors to take part. Even with his persuasive abilities, we had two or three failures — people who should be represented in these pages, but who for one reason or another declined. There are many others who could have made a valuable contribution, but whom we reluctantly had to deny ourselves if the book was to be of manageable length. Our contributors together do, I think, give a rounded and comprehensive view of MacDiarmid and his influence. I have not mentioned all of them, but that is unnecessary. They all speak for themselves and the cross references, agreements and contradictions between them are self-evident. It is not a simple, coherent account; but if it were, it would be false.

May 1980   P.H.S.

References
1 In *Hugh MacDiarmid: A Festschrift,* ed. K. D. Duval and Sidney Goodsir Smith (Edinburgh 1962), p. 57.

Part I

MacDiarmid 1933-1944

SORLEY MACLEAN

It was in the spring or early summer of 1933, when I was in my twenty-second year, and just before I sat my finals in English Literature at Edinburgh University, that I first read any of the poetry of Hugh MacDiarmid, and it was with *Sangschaw, Penny Wheep* and *A Drunk Man Looks at the Thistle* that I started. A Gaelic-speaking West Highlander, obsessed with the musical and poetic glories of some kinds of Gaelic song then practically never heard on radio or platform except in the "versions" of Mrs Kennedy-Fraser, I had hitherto been rather lukewarm towards Lowland Scots poetry except the Ballads and Burns and some of Henryson, Dunbar and their contemporaries and successors. My introduction to the poetry of MacDiarmid was peculiarly fortunate for me because it came from two outstanding undergraduates, George E. Davie and James B. Caird. Davie was then in his third year in Classics and already a legend in Edinburgh University for his colossal knowledge of all things Scottish. Caird was only in his second year in English Literature but he was exceptionally well read in Latin, Greek, Scots, French and Russian literatures, and his knowledge and sensibility astounded me. Davie's incessant intellectual activity and his memory for ideas, and Caird's literary sensitivity and sheer knowledge of literature had a great influence on me. When I now try to recall MacDiarmid's first impact on me, it is difficult for me to say what it would have been like without Caird and Davie as intermediaries, and it is also difficult for me to say how much of theirs I passed on to Sydney Goodsir Smith and others from 1939 onwards.

Before I read any of MacDiarmid's poetry I myself had written a fair amount of verse in Gaelic and in English, but by the age of

15

twenty I had destroyed almost all my English verse and most of my Gaelic verse as well and was now writing verse only in Gaelic, and perhaps only because I could not sing. Before I was twenty I had discovered Croce's doctrine of the primacy of the lyric and the lyrical quality of all poetry that is intrinsically poetry. My upbringing in a family of Gaelic tradition-bearers, especially of song, had made me never question that the primary sensuousness of poetry is of the ear, Verlaine's "de la musique avant tout chose", and I found then, and still find, a new and breathtaking music in MacDiarmid's lyrics, and that long before I heard any of Francis George Scott's settings of them. I think that the rhythmic marvels of many of MacDiarmid's lyrics consist in the uncanny juxtapositions within single lines and within whole poems of "feet" of two, three, four, and sometimes even five syllables, and often of one single stressed syllable alone; and though I have never fully and properly analysed it, I think that his coincidences and juxtapositions of quantity and stress are extraordinary and magnificent. I am not implying that this is self-conscious and deliberate art. I remember his telling me that one of his great lyrics came to him suddenly and whole as he was standing at a bar waiting for a half-pint of beer. I think that there is a great kinship between those triumphant rhythms and his triumphant use of "Synthetic" Scots, a love of words and the rhythms of words and phrases indissolubly linked in artistic wholes. I do not know to what extent Gestalt psychology has been applied to art, but I feel it must have something relevant to say on this.

Away back in 1933, my response to the music of MacDiarmid's lyrics was instinctive and overpowering. But from the very first encounter I was very conscious of the other qualities that, with their music, make them for me some of the very greatest poetry that I know, but they would not be that without their music. For me no one reaches in poetry valid, credible, unmistakable frontiers of consciousness unless the very sound of the poetry is proof of it, perhaps only one proof, but one that is indispensable. In MacDiarmid's lyrics there is a sensitivity to certain impressions from external nature that excel even the very greatest of the great Nature passages of Wordworth's "Prelude", "Tintern Abbey" and the "Immortality Ode": they approach nearly the expression of the inexpressible complex of physical sensation and emotion. Some of the Moon poems especially send "a shiver down my spine", and they are at the same time instinct with what Dr George Kitchin long ago recognised as the "high seriousness" of Arnold's critical gropings, a "high seriousness" that is so unobtrusive as to seem almost implicit. I am not at all suggesting that MacDiarmid owed something special to Wordworth, only that I can think of no other poet who can set a human situation, or the human situation, against the background of the great Universe as Wordsworth or MacDiarmid can. The "high seriousness" of MacDiarmid's lyrics is not to be inferred by ingenious inferences; it is ineluctable: in other words it has power as well as delicacy and subtlety, and the originality of the whole individual lyric is supreme.

Some years ago I expressed the opinion that MacDiarmid's turning to Scots in 1925-26 was a safety-valve against the excessively ambitious intellectuality of his nature, of which one result was the clotted English verse he was writing before 1924 or 1925. I had read nothing at all of this verse in 1933 and not much of it since.

Situations in human life, sometimes even marginal situations, set against the Universe, with huge intellectual and psychological resonances, poems of magical form, made the lyrics of *Sangschaw, Penny wheep* and *A Drunk Man* miracles to me before I knew the passion of MacDiarmid's involvement in the most significant spiritual conflicts of his age in philosophy and politics. I say politics as well as philosophy, for politics is surely a most important part of moral philosophy. The period of the great industrial depression in Europe and America was one in which the Ivory Tower was specially repugnant to people like myself, as it is today in the age of the atomic bomb and the fuller consciousness of the terrible poverty of so much of the world; and though politics was only "bairns' play" to the MacDiarmid of the "Second Hymn to Lenin", it was a "bairns' play" that was an imperative of imperatives. I do not pretend now that it was not of very great importance to me, and to people like me, in the early thirties that by far the greatest living Scottish poet was an uncompromising Socialist and Scottish Nationalist. On the strength of the three

17

volumes of 1925-26 he was a much greater poet than Eliot, Yeats and Pound; and whatever he might say of élitism (I cannot remember that he said much then) he was "assuming the burden of the doom" of the Scottish people, and in those years that was the burden of the masses of humankind. I do not remember that he made much of his "Anglophobia" in those days, but if he did, it meant to most of us only a hatred of the capitalist imperialism of which England was the dominant partner, and of the Anglicised Scottish landlord-capitalists who were the hirelings of that system.

It is true that by 1935, the year of the publication of the volume containing "Second Hymn to Lenin", I was seeing inconsistencies in MacDiarmid's politics. In July and August of that year I spent a week in Whalsay, and I remember arguing with him about his belief that Major Douglas's Social Credit could solve man's economic problems. My point was that if Social Credit could do that, then the Social Revolution was unnecessary. His answer was to the effect that the bourgeoisie must be liquidated. I am not at all sure that "liquidated" was the word he used but I took his answer to mean that the ethos of the bourgeoisie must be psychologically or morally destroyed. I do not think he would then have used the word "morally", but in the context "psychologically" implied "morally" to me. Nowadays this seems to me a cavilling on my own part, for his union of poetic sensibility and spiritual and practical commitment was then to me, and still is, above all admiration. His very poverty was itself a proof of the greatness of his uncompromising commitment. The only great poet I had heard of who could be compared with him was William Blake, and to me MacDiarmid's greatness was all the greater because he was a materialist in philosophy and in practice an idealist of idealists. It mattered very little to me that I thought him mistaken about Social Credit or that I thought him hard on Auden, or that I disagreed with him profoundly on what is called "folk poetry", or that he published his translations of MacDonald's *Birlinn* and Macintyre's *Ben Dòrain* without first showing them to me.

MacDiarmid regretted very much that he was not a Gaelic speaker but he had some valid intuitions about some Gaelic poetry, especially the poetry of Alexander MacDonald and, to a lesser extent, the poetry of Duncan Macintyre, for Macintyre's quietism could not strike chords in him as MacDonald's activism did, and, of course, *Ben Dórain* is because of its metrics infinitely more difficult to translate then most of the *Birlinn* is. MacDiarmid was given to honour the learned, highly self-conscious poetry of the Bardic schools and their sixteenth- and seventeenth-century successors, while I myself was even obsessed with the organic fusion of poetry and music in the great anonymous songs and the great songs of obscure authorship; but whatever reservations I had about his attitude to Gaelic poetry, I had no reservations about his own supremely great lyrics and I believed that in *A Drunk Man Looks at the Thistle* he had achieved the impossible in a long poem and that in a language that I considered inferior to Gaelic.

My own admiration for MacDiarmid's lyrics and my lesser, but still great, admiration for *A Drunk Man Looks at the Thistle* had for many years an ambivalent effect on my own poetry. In some ways MacDiarmid's poetry and personality were the strongest of stimulants, but MacDiarmid's lyrics, with the old reinforcement of the supreme union of poetry and music in certain Gaelic songs, made me despair of any poetry that either I or anyone else could produce. The best of Eliot or Yeats and *A Drunk Man* itself was accessible as those lyrics were not. I could imagine myself writing poetry that in some way or ways could compare with those others, but not with MacDiarmid's lyrics. Indeed I think that for many years those lyrics (and some Gaelic songs) were red lights stopping my way of poetry. Some nine years after 1935, when I was invalided back from North Africa, Christopher and I argued through most of the night and early hours of the morning about his lyrics, and I remember asking him who he thought he was or what did he think had been given to him when he hoped to write greater poetry than those lyrics. I think I wore him down. That night was in 1944, at least nine years after the time of which I am writing, but it reminds me of the force of the first impact his poetry made on me and of its permanence.

I am writing primarily of the years 1933-34 and to a lesser extent of 1935. It was not till 1936 that a Fascist conquest of Europe became likely and not till 1938 that it became far more than likely. People like myself, who were convinced Socialists and Scottish

19

Nationalists, came to believe that the immediate task was to make a United Front against Fascism even if that meant the defence of what was bad against what was far worse, for Fascism meant a dictatorship in the interests of landlord-capitalism using a ballyhoo of nationalist propaganda; war; and the enslavement of the human spirit by those who were most successful in producing and controlling the means of destruction. For the Scottish Nationalist there was the additional perplexity, even if he cared little for social justice, that he could hardly shut his ears to the loudly repeated implication of the Nazi theorists that the English were more Teutonic than the Scots, and the inevitable inference was that if the English were to become second-class citizens, the Scots would be third-class.

I would not care to say how much MacDiarmid was sustained during those years, 1936 to 1939, by the Communist belief that Fascism was just the last kicks of Capitalism and that its triumph would be short-lived; and that therefore one ought not to be greatly concerned with the defence of a rotten pluto-democracy against a more brutal but a more short-lived kind of Capitalism. At any rate, this Communist doctrine was made irrelevant by the heroic examples of so many Communists in Spain and their devotion to a United Front with Social Democrats, Liberals and even Anti-fascist Conservatives. As far as I know, MacDiarmid was no pacifist at any time in his life, and in September 1939 I was not in close touch with him and I just do not know how much he accepted the Communist Party line between September 1939 and the Nazi invasion of Russia in June 1941. Nor do I know how much he approved of the stand made in 1939 by certain very fine Scottish Nationalists, whom I myself greatly liked and admired as men although I could not agree with them even during the time in 1939 and 1940 when the war seemed a Phoney War. However much one disagreed with MacDiarmid at any time, one felt that he would never compromise with any Establishment, and if he were mistaken, it was because of his refusal to countenance the art of the possible and the necessity for choice between two evils even if one was immeasurably greater than the other.

Although the great economic depression was terrible in 1933, 1934 and 1935, the political urgency for the whole of Europe was not then quite as demanding as it became in 1936 with the Spanish Civil War, and people like myself could still give most of their political and literary thought to Scotland and Gaelic Scotland in particular, and to us Hugh MacDiarmid was the champion, the leader who would not leave us for "a handful of silver" or for tons of pure gold. Even though he sometimes scarified people who did not deserve it, he was a ruthless hunter of shams and humbugs who stood in the way of what we knew was for the material and cultural good of the Scottish people. That he was a very great poet was beyond a shadow of a doubt; that he was an intellectual dynamo with a passion for seeing Scotland in the intellectual forefront of Europe and not just a poor intellectual pensioner of England was clear to all of us, as was his immense moral courage and passion for social justice and disregard of his own material welfare. He was a visionary and an activist, a Scotsman who had his spiritual eye on everything that mattered to Scotland and on the ends of the earth as well. It was, however, inevitable that his power over us should temporarily lessen with the great acceleration of material urgencies from the beginning of the Spanish War in 1936 and through 1937, 1938 and 1939, when almost every month made it more likely that Fascism was going to conquer Europe and hold it down for generations. In the face of those probabilities both the golden lyric and the castle walls of the most impassioned and comprehensive philosophical poetry seemed frail defences not much stronger than the Ivory Towers of the most self-indulgent escapists.

MacDiarmid at Broughton

J. K. ANNAND

I had the great good fortune to come under the influence of the same teacher of English as Christopher Murray Grieve. Ten years after Grieve left Broughton Higher Grade School, as it was then called, I enrolled there. In my first year at the school, George Ogilvie, Principal Teacher of English, who had early recognised the literary potential of Grieve, wrote an article in the Christmas 1920 issue of *The Broughton Magazine*, paying tribute to two of his former pupils, C. M. Grieve and R. W. Kerr, who were represented in the then recently published anthology *Northern Numbers* which was edited by Grieve. Thus at the age of twelve I was made aware of the existence of the poetry of C. M. Grieve who was to become two years later, Hugh M'Diarmid (as he then spelt it).

George Ogilvie described Grieve on his arrival in Edinburgh in September 1908 at the age of sixteen. He saw the "little slimly-built figure in hodden grey, the small sharp-featured face with its piercing eyes, the striking head with its broad brow and great mass of flaxen curly hair". He was "the life and soul of the Literary Society and ready at a moment's notice to write a poem or make a speech". He "had a most engaging ingenuousness", and Ogilvie had yet to meet the infant who could look as innocent as Grieve.

In 1910-11 the joint-editors of *The Broughton Magazine* were John Gould and Roderick Watson Kerr, who were later to join with George Malcolm Thomson in founding The Porpoise Press. John Gould remembered Grieve as a great character who was very popular with his fellows. He had a lilting Border accent and his hair stood out like a halo round his large head. In adult life Gould and Grieve had differences of opinion and drew apart, but while at school Gould liked C.M.G. immensely and he has vivid memories of his "blatant and brash exuberance" at the Literary Society where he vied with Kerr in their extravagances. They often argued over literature and politics and though Grieve was not the "red" he later became, he was a "natural rebel". Gould was of the opinion that if Grieve had stuck it out and become a schoolmaster he would have been another A. S. Neill. Another contemporary was Thomas G. P. Walker, who predeceased Grieve by about a year. He wrote: "Chris, as I knew him at Broughton, was quite a boy with a mass of rough hair and a light of humour in his eyes. He was ever ready to see and appreciate the funny side of any situation."

As noted above, Ogilvie declared that Grieve was the life and soul of the Literary Society. During session 1909-10 he served on the committee. He spoke regularly in debates, delivered papers on a variety of topics, and was no less active in the more frivolous and social evenings at the Lit. Then, as in later life, he championed the unpopular and minority views. Even in literary matters he was the devil's advocate, moving the negative to a motion that "Blood and thunder in literature is pernicious". In a mock election at the beginning of 1911 he stood as an Independent Women's Suffrage candidate. On the evening of the Literary Tournament he scored heavily for his year with a sonnet, a parody, and a stump speech. The latter was described as a remarkable effort on an intractable subject — "Vegetation in Morocco". For effect he grabbed a large tablecloth and robed himself in it. When Goldsmith's *Good Natured Man* was performed he played the part of Jarvis.

It was in the school magazine, however, that he really left his mark. He was the editor in 1909-10, producing three issues. During his year as editor, his contributions were many, though he never signed his name to anything, writing either anonymously or over a pseudonym, but his various writings have been identified by Ogilvie. In his first issue he started off with an outstanding editorial, written with fantastic humour and poetic phrasing. In the course of his editorship he wrote short stories, gruesome as in "The Black Monkey" and hilarious and preposterous as in "The Lighthouse Mystery" and "A Dog's Day". Poems, too, appeared, humorously in "The Land Beyond Quadratics" and lightheartedly

23

in some of his verses on school social occasions. His great expertise in verse, however, appears in his last issue in summer 1910. Like many an editor he was short of material to fill the magazine, and asked Ogilvie for something. Ogilvie wrote "Two valedictory poems by any teacher to any pupil leaving Broughton", one grave, and one gay. He tells how Grieve read them, sat down, and in an incredibly short space of time ran off "Two valedictory poems to any teacher from any pupil leaving Broughton". Both sets appeared in the magazine, and Grieve's can be seen in facsimile in the catalogue produced by the National Library of Scotland for the MacDiarmid Exhibition in 1967. He also wrote elegant, witty and entertaining comment on school affairs in a mixture of prose and verse. In those early days, too, he had already begun his habit of writing about himself over a nom-de-plume.

My own connection with Grieve began in 1925. *Sangschaw* was published in September of that year, and I obtained a review copy for *The Broughton Magazine* which I was editing in 1925-26. The Christmas issue featured a display of the poem "O Jesu Parvule". The editorial hailed the publication of *Sangschaw* as a "crowning triumph" and in a review of the book I wrote that "M'Diarmid's work, though an experiment in a new type of Scots poetry, is a complete success at the first venture. He has shown us that Scots is still a suitable, and a highly successful, medium of expression for all kinds of verse." I should think that I am probably the only person now alive who reviewed *Sangschaw* when it first appeared.

Grieve was very pleased with the welcome which his old school magazine gave to his first volume of poetry, and he proved very helpful when, with the ready encouragement of George Ogilvie, I decided that the next issue of *The Broughton Magazine* should be a Braid Scots number in recognition of the work which our former editor was doing for what he called the Scots Literary Movement. There began a correspondence between us, and his letters to me are valuable for the light they throw on Grieve's attitude in general to the development of Scots, and in particular on the progress he was making towards the completion of his masterpiece, *A Drunk Man Looks at the Thistle*. At the time, I did not fully appreciate the amount of time and trouble the poet devoted to helping an untried schoolboy to produce a magazine, but looking back more than half-a-century later, I realise how lucky I was. Here was a man holding down a full-time job as a journalist, who was also producing great quantities of poetry of the finest quality, not to mention being actively engaged in local government and in nationalist political propaganda, yet he could find time to write me six-page letters of advice, and send me manuscripts of his poems for the use of the magazine.

To illustrate the trouble he took, it may be of interest to mention two of the subjects dealt with in these early letters. I wanted to write an editorial on "The Scottish Renaissance" but my difficulty was to find the necessary vocabulary of Scots words for a literary subject — a problem not unknown to writers of Scots prose today. I asked Grieve if he could suggest a source for such terms. There is of course no such source, but Grieve generously suggested that either I write the editorial in English and he would translate it into Scots, or that I should write it in Scots and he would correct it. I chose the first alternative. The translation arrived in good time for publication, and the accompanying letter gave the impression that I had done him a favour instead of my being very much in his debt.

Secondly, I had sent him a couple of translations into Scots verse which I had made of German poems. He devoted a couple of pages to advice on translations and writing in Scots. His criticism was kindly and helpful, but he was honest enough to tell me that my translations were "not *really* good".

Grieve told me that he believed that no one should attempt to write in Scots unless he found English incapable of expressing what he wished to express. This pre-supposed that the writer should have a fluency in spoken Scots, but he did not preclude the use of obsolete or little-known words which were capable of re-adaptation to vital modern uses. But he condemned the inartistic employment of such words. Their use could only be justified in the result, making them somehow the inevitable media of whatever was effected through them.

Many years later, when the first issue of *Lallans* appeared, Grieve wrote me a congratulatory letter, but took exception to one contribution which he thought was an attack on his own use of Scots, because of the writer's insistence on Scots as it is spoken at the grass roots. Grieve maintained his position that all literature evolved by moving away from the grass roots and evolving higher forms of literary expression. He continued: "I know no literature of any value that uses the language in which it is written, as that language is used by the man in the street. All living languages add to their vocabularies by importing words from other languages . . . or by inventing new words. . . . Certainly I myself have no interest whatever in writing for the minimally literate."

Lines of Communication with Hugh MacDiarmid

DUNCAN GLEN

I left school at fifteen (I could have left at fourteen) in March 1948 with no knowledge of Scottish literature as a separate entity. After I left school I read a lot of Sir Walter Scott, just as I read Dostoevsky or George Eliot, as part of the line of great novelists. I did not read Scott's poetry and the only Burns I remember reading — and this at school — was "The Cotter's Saturday Night" which I had no time for and which put me off Burns for years and years. Although ignorant of the native Scottish cultural traditions, I was something of a natural Scottish nationalist, and I began to read Scottish history books, including what I thought was the history of Scottish literature — in other words Henry Grey Graham's *Scottish Men of Letters in the Eighteenth Century* which I admired a lot, accepting quite naturally that Scottish literature was a part of English literature. I still have a notebook in which at this time I listed the important figures of English literature — they were all novelists from Richardson to Virginia Woolf. The only Scots in the list are Smollett, Scott and Stevenson. I was at that time writing short stories and contemplating a novel. Very soon after that I discovered modern Scottish literature through, I think, buying the Saltire pamphlet *Modern Scottish Literature* by J. M. Reid. I wrote out a list of Scottish writers beginning with Macpherson (Ossian) and Sir Walter Scott and ending with Sydney Goodsir Smith. I had already read the popular modern Scottish novelists — Stevenson, Neil Munro, Compton Mackenzie, George Blake and Eric Linklater — but now I discovered the novelist who changed my whole way of thinking about the Scottish novel, Lewis Grassic Gibbon. It was *Sunset Song* that did it, but soon I was reading everything I could find by Gibbon and his other self, J. L. Mitchell.

And then I was reading the prose works of C. M. Grieve and Hugh MacDiarmid and here, indeed, was another hero for a young man.

Soon I was no longer content with just borrowing the books from the public library and I began to look for the works of Gibbon and MacDiarmid in second-hand bookshops which I had haunted ever since I left school and started work in Glasgow. The first book of poems that I bought by MacDiarmid was his *Selected Poems* edited by Crombie Saunders. Having really read only novelists, apart from anthology poetry at school which I had rejected, I did not know enough about poetry to be bowled over by MacDiarmid's poetry in this selection. At this time I was really attracted to him as a rebel and nationalist rather than as a poet. I was all for the novel and thought poetry played out. But quite soon after finding the *Selected Poems* I was fortunate enough to get a second-hand copy of *A Drunk Man Looks at the Thistle* in Glen's shop when it was in Parliamentary Road, Glasgow — it was the first edition and cost me five shillings. The man who ran Glen's kept books like that hidden away in the back shop and I had been pestering him for some time before he brought out anything by MacDiarmid from the back. Not that there was any great demand for MacDiarmid at this time, as the price indicated. Another shop I kept visiting, opposite the Mitchell Library, had a most knowledgeable owner, but to him MacDiarmid was a socialist poet of the thirties whom he linked with Auden. Anyway, I had a copy of *A Drunk Man* and I can say that it changed my life. I was bowled over. Never had I thought that poetry like this existed; a poetry which spoke to me directly and yet was also beyond me in many places. A new world was opened up for me just as it had been (although to a lesser extent as I knew what the novel could do) when I first read *Sunset Song*.

I was lucky enough to get a copy of *Sangschaw* — also in Glen's and also for five shillings — and again my whole concept of what poetry could do was changed. I do not remember having any difficulty with the Scots and took it just as part of the revelation I had experienced with regard to poetry. My notebook gives a checklist, compiled at this time, of the works of both Gibbon and MacDiarmid. The books by MacDiarmid that are ticked, indicating I owned them, are *Sangschaw, A Drunk Man, Selected*

Poems (Saunders), *Contemporary Scottish Studies* and *Scottish Eccentrics*. But by this time I was reading everything by MacDiarmid that I could find in libraries. I had also discovered Sydney Goodsir Smith's poetry and in my notebook there is a checklist of works by him that I knew. The first list consisted only of *Under the Eildon Tree* but at a later date, judging by the change of ink, I added *So Late into the Night*.

Soon I had moved to Fife and was working in Kirkcaldy and attending evening classes in Edinburgh, and another source of contact for me with MacDiarmid's writings was the *Scottish Journal* which I bought at the bookstall in Kirkcaldy station. This was published and edited by William McLellan, but for me it was dominated by the writings in verse and prose of Hugh MacDiarmid. Heady days for a young man. There was also, soon, the revived *Voice of Scotland*, edited by MacDiarmid of course. And then I was reading *Lines Review* and visiting Callum Macdonald in his newagent's and printing shop in Marchmont Road to get a copy of the Edinburgh University publication *Jabberwock* which he had printed. I wanted *Jabberwock* because it had included a radio talk by MacDiarmid as well as reproducing a photograph of the Benno Schotz head of MacDiarmid — that was in 1955. By then I was well and truly involved, as a reader, in the modern Scottish literary movement with its nationalistic supports. I never thought of getting to know any of the writers although I was still writing short stories and an attempted novel. By 1955 I was also quite well educated in the whole history of Scottish literature, having read a lot of the works and also the histories old and new, including *Scottish Poetry, A Critical Survey*, edited by James Kinsley, when it was published in 1955. The bibliography published in Sydney Goodsir Smith's *A Short Introduction to Scottish Literature* (1951) was very useful to me in my studies and the book itself was an excellent counterbalance to all the books which see Scottish literature as an appendage to English literature. Goodsir Smith's book was written under the influence of MacDiarmid's advocacy of the "Caledonian Antisyzygy". By 1956, when I was a full-time student at Edinburgh College of Art, I was fully under the spell of MacDiarmid's poetry and theories of literature. I set some of his poetry in type in the Art College but pulled only a few proofs.

29

My first meeting with MacDiarmid was also whilst I was at the College. He came one evening to give a talk to what was only a handful of students. He had copies of the *Scottish Journal* with him and pulled them out of his old attaché case as he spoke. But for me the highlight of the evening was the long session of questions and discussion afterwards. I well believe we would still be there imposing on our generous speaker if the caretakers had not evicted us from the College at locking-up time. I went to that talk expecting to meet the firebrand of his prose works and, indeed, in his talk he was most forceful. In the question time, despite some very ignorant English imperialistic attitudes from an English questioner, the poet was very kind and gentle in his replies. This I was a little disappointed in, although I enjoyed the way he still effectively replied for all his kind politeness. I exchanged a few words with our speaker afterwards — in the gent's toilet in the basement of the building!

In May 1956 I started my National Service in the RAF and whilst home on leave that same year I picked up a copy of the first issue of the bibliographical magazine *The Bibliotheck* with Geoffrey Wagner's checklist of the writings of Lewis Grassic Gibbon. I was absolutely bowled over by this checklist which gave a lot of critical references in periodicals as well as Mitchell/Gibbon's books, etc. Within days I was in the Mitchell Library making tentative beginnings for a decent checklist of MacDiarmid's works. I spoke to the librarian there, Mr Hepburn, and he already had the beginnings of a list in card index form which he showed me. *The Bibliotheck* was published from Glasgow University Library and I went to see the editor, but he was not available. Not that he would have encouraged a young amateur like myself, I imagine. But I was obsessed by this need for more knowledge of MacDiarmid's writings and the surrounding literature, so I got a ticket for the Reading Room of the British Museum, and on those Saturdays when I had the necessary money for the fare I travelled up to London from Huntingdon where I was stationed. This was the beginning of a long period of a mad and total obsession with MacDiarmid's writings. By the time I came out of the RAF in May 1958 I can say, looking back, that I knew his writings well and was completely under his influence. I never thought to approach the great man himself. The complete work — in all its vast extent in uncollected poems and essays — was what I was after. By now I was writing up my own findings and during my holiday following demob, which I theoretically spent with my wife at her parents' home in Fife, I lived in the Edinburgh Public Library, George IV Bridge, where I was greatly helped by Miss Catherine Dickson.

I got a job in London quite close to the British Museum and throughout 1958 and 1959 I spent my lunchbreaks and many Saturdays in the Reading Room. In autumn 1958 came a blow to me — the publication of W. R. Aitken's excellent checklist of the books and pamphlets of MacDiarmid in *The Bibliotheck* — a professional had beaten me to the bibliographical side so far as the books and pamphlets were concerned, but I was by now well into writing a book of which the bibliography was only a part. Also I had researched the poetry and prose uncollected in books and available only in magazines and newspapers. This periodical research gave my work a lot of its strength and uniqueness. So I did not feel too discouraged.

By the end of 1959 I had finished the first version of *Hugh MacDiarmid and the Scottish Renaissance* but I kept finding new facts and my wife had to type this massive work a second time. I let the book lie for some reason — being perhaps too exhausted and too involved in a new job at Watford College of Technology. At any rate it was not until early in 1962 that I wrote to Hugh MacDiarmid sending him my bibliography to my book and asking him some questions. I got a very kind letter in reply, but I decided that my own research was more accurate than Dr Grieve's memory of exact dates and sequences of his life and work — understandably enough. This led to my going to visit him at Brownsbank for the first time. I went by bus which arrived at lunchtime and as this seemed an inconvenient time I explored the immediate area of Candymill village. Then I walked up that farm track for the first time and knocked on Brownsbank's door with its thistle knocker. MacDiarmid appeared at the door and it was obvious that he had no idea who I was although I was expected — but I was not what he had expected; I think my youthfulness surprised him. I will never, of course, forget that first visit with the great man in his customary chair before the tall pigeon-holed unit which he told me came from a lawyer's office. I wrote a poem about him sitting before these pigeon holes, or grid, and it was eventually printed in *Poems addressed to Hugh MacDiarmid* which I edited and published in 1967 for his seventy-fifth birthday:

TO HUGH MACDIARMID
(AT BROWNSBANK)

Aside the bleezin fire I see you a movin heid
Afore a muckle daurk grid
Haudin fechtin petterns I glint within
Thae great lines
Risin frae your heid.

I see you a sma still haun lying in the shadows
O that aye movin heid
But fremit lookin wi it and aa
Thae great lines
Risin frae your heid.

But that fine still haun moves to your heid
And baith are ane
Afore the movin petterns hail in
Thae great lines
Risin frae your heid.

I now began to correspond with MacDiarmid and another result of my visit was that he gave me permission to print and publish in pamphlet form forgotten or lost poems that I had found in my researches for my book. I have told the story of my publishing of MacDiarmid elsewhere — *A Small Press and Hugh MacDiarmid*, 1970 — but this publishing gave me great pleasure and I was especially pleased when the poems that I had put back into circulation were collected in *A Lap of Honour*, 1967.

I sent my synopsis of *Hugh MacDiarmid and the Scottish Renaissance* to two publishers who were not interested, but the third one I sent it to — Chambers — asked to see it and, after long delays, it was published in November 1964. Chambers gave a launching party for it in the coffee room above the Edinburgh Bookshop in George Street, Edinburgh. There were gathered many poets and artists and others of the modern Scottish cultural scene. MacDiarmid, who had been entertained all afternoon by American journalists, was at his most mischievous there and afterwards at dinner in the George Hotel, although he spoke most kindly at the party of my work — "a labour of love" he called it — and my book.

In 1965 I launched *Akros* magazine and in a very real sense I saw this — and still see it — as a continuance of the Scottish Renaissance of poetry which MacDiarmid instigated and led. Of course I saw it as a developing revival opening up new paths and new ideas and new theories of literature and art generally. I am sure MacDiarmid disapproved of a lot of what I have done in *Akros* and in my other publishing — books and pamphlets — but I still saw it as a continuance of his work. The fact that he might disapprove I saw as a tribute to his ideas—an ever-open mind and ever-new advances in art.

Being a born maker of books and with my training in printing and publishing, I would probably have published books and maybe also a magazine even without the spur of admiration for the work and ideas of Hugh MacDiarmid, but what is less likely, without his influence, is that I would have written or published poetry. Until I came under the influence of Hugh MacDiarmid's writings I had confined myself to short stories and attempts at novels — in English of course. Through his influence I became a poet — and a poet in Scots. As with editing *Akros*, I have always believed that the best way I can show my admiration for MacDiarmid's poetry is by going my own way in my poetry. One can learn from one's predecessors and contemporaries but to be of any worth as a poet one has to create one's own forms. But the achievement of MacDiarmid was, and is, an inspiration to me. He showed what could be done by a Scots poet, given high aim as well as talent or genius, and if he could do it perhaps it would also be possible for us who came after him. His theories of language I at first took over almost whole, but gradually I have moved away from him in this and this independence is, I am sure, a greater tribute to his teaching than imitation of his style and unprogressive acceptance of his literary theories. Of course I have not rejected all his theories. I still accept Scots as my mother tongue and therefore, as he taught me, my primary literary language. But MacDiarmid seemed to abandon this in his own practice if not in his theory when he turned, mostly, to writing in English. However, there can be no doubt that there would have been very little likelihood of a revival of writing in Scots without the example and the achievement of Hugh MacDiarmid. We are all in his debt. He showed what could be achieved, and fought long in the isolation and neglect of the literary wilderness for his beliefs, which I absorbed in the late fifties and which I work to develop and to keep abreast of recent developments in world literature. Hugh MacDiarmid destroyed the parochial in Scottish literature whilst not losing touch with Scottish roots. It is our task to be true to his example by a similar Scottish internationalism, which can keep Scotland a part of the world rather than of its own kailyard, or of a fake internationalism without the local of Scotland being a part of these internationalisms. But above all, for me MacDiarmid achieved a poetry which can speak to me in my own language in a way that no other language can, and yet his poetry speaks also to the whole world; a great poetry which rises above all creeds whether political or religious or philosophical. His work and life are an example to us all. He tells us to be true to ourselves and to our own vision, to keep a mind as open as the grave, and to aim high without fear of failure. The good, he tells us, is the enemy of the best. I have been fortunate enough to know both the poetry (and the prose) and the man who is the greatest of Scottish poets.

Dr Grieve and Mr MacDiarmid

ALAN BOLD

In The Auld Symie (Preston 1971), my only booklength venture into Scots so far, I wrote a little poem called "Notice on MacParnassus" which was intended as a tribute to two aspects of a poetic mountain:

> The hill was high, I really wouldnae hairm it
> Yet had to leave;
> It said, "Reserved for Hugh MacDiarmid
> (Signed) C. M. Grieve."

Scotland is a divided land, geographically and linguistically, and it is hardly surprising that the cultural dichotomy has been reflected by writers who habitually adopt literary pseudonyms. Think of Fiona MacLeod (William Sharp), Lewis Grassic Gibbon (Leslie Mitchell), James Bridie (O. H. Mavor), Fion Mac Colla (Tom MacDonald); even, in the most profound analysis of Scottish psychology, Edward Hyde (Henry Jekyll). In most of these examples the assumed name was a strategy to conceal artistic doubts experienced by the private citizen saddled with a paternal label; in the case of Christopher Murray Grieve the pseudonym revealed the real man as a single-minded personality who wanted to give himself the benefit of the creative doubt by entering a more extreme dimension. MacDiarmid loved contradictions. His favourite quotation was from Whitman's "Song of Myself":

> Do I contradict myself?
> Very well then I contradict myself,
> (I am large, I contain multitudes).

MacDiarmid liked to confuse his followers by a series of dramatic shifts: from Scots to English, from nationalism to internationalism, from the lyric to the epic, from poetic sensuality to prosaic common sense. What attracted him to Marxism was, I believe, the Hegelian dialectic that produced a synthesis out of thesis and antithesis. That sort of intellectual abstraction suited him down to the ground. As he put it in *A Drunk Man Looks at the Thistle*:

> I'll ha'e nae hauf-way hoose, but aye be whaur
> Extremes meet — it's the only way I ken
> To dodge the curst conceit o' bein' richt
> That damns the vast majority o' men.

MacDiarmid was no liberal egalitarian who wanted to see "the vast majority" conforming to a democratic norm; as a Scotsman he wanted to be, and was, a man in five million.

I first made contact with Hugh MacDiarmid in 1962 when I was nineteen and he was seventy. I remember the circumstances well as they played a crucial part in my development as a writer and gave me the opportunity to know a man whose artistic integrity was so complete that he shared his extraordinary gifts with all and sundry without the slightest thought of personal gain or aggrandisement. Considering MacDiarmid's talent for polemic and publicity, this mention of his modesty may be hard for some to swallow; he was, I assure them, no narcissist but a poet who held himself up as a mirror to Scotland's truest nature. As an adolescent I had no idea that such a man might exist, far less exist in Scotland. Until the age of fifteen I had never seriously read a book and the notion of writing for a living would have, if I ever considered it, seemed like a grotesque fantasy. I left school at fifteen and became an apprentice baker. Then, in a Pauline moment, I suddenly decided to take the high road to what I vaguely thought of as the visionary life; as a first step along this road I hitched back to my old school, Broughton (where, co-incidentally, MacDiarmid had trained as a teacher). To cut a long story short, I took an instant like to literature.[1] Fortunately I was encouraged in my new-found interest by Ronald Stevenson who was then a music teacher at Broughton and is now recognised as a brilliant composer. Ronald had his own personal pantheon of artistic heroes (Blake, Busoni, Gordon Craig, Whitman, Sorabji) and constantly sung the praises of an unholy trinity of modern writers: Joyce, Pound and MacDiarmid. As my first love was for

36

ambitious works that confronted the challenge of the twentieth century I devoured *Ulysses, The Cantos* and *In Memoriam James Joyce* in that order. When I had duly responded to MacDiarmid's Joyce poem, Ronald (who lived at West Linton) suggested that I might meet the great man (who lived at Biggar). I wrote to MacDiarmid and was invited to his home. It was the beginning of a vigorously stimulating friendship.

Throughout my fits and starts as a writer, MacDiarmid constantly backed me and kept on doing this until the end. Reading through the many letters he sent me, from 1962 onwards, I am reminded of how frequently one of his letters would pop up out of the blue and provide a much-needed lift at just the right moment. A few examples will suffice to show what I mean:

> *1 March 1964:* I am delighted to know you are likely to be having a book of poems [*Society Inebrious*, Edinburgh 1965] out this year, and I will certainly be pleased to write an introduction.
> *12 February 1965:* Delighted to receive your book. It is excellently printed and produced. It is indeed a "bold beginning" and I have great hopes of subsequent books of yours.
> *19 March 1971:* I've just been re-reading your Introductory Essay to the anthology of Socialist Poetry [*The Penguin Book of Socialist Verse*, Harmondsworth 1970]. It is a masterly bit of work. The Anthology has of course met the usual criticisms incurred by all anthologies, and then some! But it is withal a splendid selection and I hope it sold well.
> *30 January 1976:* I've just received — and read — the C.U.P. anthology [the *Cambridge Book of English Verse 1939-1975*, Cambridge 1976] and hasten to congratulate you most heartily. It is a really splendid production. The notes on the various poets are blessedly succinct and free of reviewers' clichés and blah-blah generally and the extensive notes on the poems are wonderfully informative and helpful. . . . You have certainly added to your laurels with this C.U.P. one. Bless you.

Then, a few months before his death, MacDiarmid noticed that I was being subjected, in *The Scotsman*, to a barrage of abusive letters from readers outraged by the tone of my football poems in

Scotland, Yes (Edinburgh 1978). In a letter published in the paper on 8 May 1978 he defended the poems generally then astonished me by writing this remarkable third paragraph:

> Years ago I said that Scotland had had in Burns a grand popular poet, and I thought it was time it had a great unpopular one, a role I thought might be mine. Unlike Bold, I have no use whatever for anything that commands a great public following, but with his qualifications it now seems that Bold will assume the role I had thought might be mine.

So from my first book to the last book I published before his death, I was consistently driven on by MacDiarmid's apparent belief in me. Anyone who has the temerity to set up shop as a writer in Scotland is bound to attract hostility; in my case the criticism was intensified because I belonged to no poetic school and had no safe university seat. With my non-literary background I had few resources to enable me to survive the tidal waves of verbal assault and I might have been persuaded to conform, rather than continue, had it not been for MacDiarmid's vocal support. His inspiration enabled me to survive and gave me a sense of purpose. In writing about him, therefore, I cannot pretend to be entirely objective. I loved the man and adored his work and it is still difficult for me to think of him in the past tense.

Those who know MacDiarmid only from his published work might have expected the man to be, on the evidence of his public anger, a fiercely combative individual who never relaxed his grip on Scotland. Yet he was a perfectly gentle man in private. In an article I contributed to *The Scotsman* shortly after his death, I tried to indicate his internal dialectic by examining the two sides of the man who was both Hugh MacDiarmid (public personality) and Chris Grieve (private person). All who had the privilege to know him were amazed by the difference. One moment he would be Chris, contentedly discussing the day-to-day matters that occupy all of us most of the time. He would ask after family and friends, politely enquire how so-and-so was getting on, and would relish the opportunity of topping a fine story with an even finer flash of wit. He would chuckle at some amusing or absurd incident, his eyes would twinkle, and the sheer warmth of his personality would flood out. At such times the world seemed a good place to be in and it was invariably a Scotocentric world. Then, if a matter of principle came up, he would literally rise to the occasion. His face would harden into features of sheer determination and he would display all the eloquence of a man addressing a multitude, speaking to humanity itself. That was Hugh MacDiarmid, not Chris, and when that serious mood took him you were acutely aware you were face to face with the indomitable quality of Scotland. His ability to switch from a cosy chat to a shatteringly incisive discourse never ceased to amaze me, but then he was an amazing man.

And I remember some amazing moments with MacDiarmid. How he came to my wedding and behaved impeccably as the life-and-soul of the party while getting up to all sorts of high-jinks. MacDiarmid was not a man who carried his greatness like a laborious burden; he was full of fun, activated by panache, and his sense of joy at my wedding was conveyed with all the energy of a teenager out for his first Big Night. At one stage of the ongoings, I retired to bed prematurely, somewhat the worse for drink. MacDiarmid would have none of that. He came into my bedroom, yanked the covers off me, and insisted I carry on. I did as I was telt. I remember too how he and Norman MacCaig and John Cairney came to read at an exhibition of my "Illuminated Poems" in Kirkcaldy. He had been ill shortly before but mere intimations of mortality were not enough to stand in his way. He came and read beautifully — giving a magical rendering of "Water Music" — and afterwards we retired to a hotel room for a post-performance drink. When we were all talking about this and that, MacDiarmid suddenly rose to his feet. We waited and he launched into an impromptu address on the necessity of a Gaelic revival in Scotland. He was full of such surprises. Then there was the last meeting. Henry Stamper, who had brilliantly acted the part of the young MacDiarmid in his monologue *Between the Wars* (a redaction of *Lucky Poet*), suggested I accompany him to Biggar as he wanted to discuss the show with Chris. MacDiarmid was clearly ill but showed no mental fatigue whatsoever. He laughed and cracked jokes; suddenly, cosy in his armchair, he talked at length about *A Drunk Man Looks at the Thistle*. He had his priorities right there in his inventive mind.

It always fascinated me to imagine the man at the moment of transition when he turned Chris Grieve into Hugh MacDiarmid. I knew the mature man who had the achievement of the MacDiarmid poems behind him; I could only speculate on his earlier metamorphosis. Yet there was a point, in the 1920s, when Christopher Murray Grieve saw beyond his own circumstances and decided to remake Scotland in the image he called Hugh MacDiarmid. That point in time is crucial in Scottish literary history and it deserves examination. On the death of his father, Chris Grieve — would-be schoolteacher — had abandoned all idea of a steady career. In the First World War, he served with the Royal Army Medical Corps and was invalided home from Salonika suffering from cerebral malaria. In 1918 he married Margaret Skinner and the couple moved to Montrose where Grieve became the chief reporter to the weekly *Montrose Review*, the father of two children, a Labour member of the town council, a Justice of the Peace; and a founder of the Scottish Centre of P.E.N., the National Party of Scotland, and two magazines. The first of these magazines, *Northern Numbers*, was a fairly conventional Georgian publication and Grieve used it systematically to establish himself. The first issue appeared in 1920, the third and last in 1922. In those two years Grieve used his editorial prerogative to oust the lesser lights and concentrate on his own work. As he explained:

> I began, when I issued my *Northern Numbers* anthology, by displaying the best of the work available by living Scottish poets; and side by side with it introduced work by other and then quite unknown poets, including myself, who had very different ideas from those prevalent. . . . The well-known poets represented alongside *les jeunes* in the earlier issues — Neil Munro, John Buchan, General Sir Ian Hamilton, Violet Jacob, Charles Murray, Lewis Spence, Donald A. Mackenzie — were speedily, and no doubt a trifle unceremoniously, 'dropped'; and the field was left to the rising school.[2]

Among those "well-known poets", the most significant for MacDiarmid's career was Lewis Spence (1874-1955). Spence was no ivory-tower poet but a man who put his ideas to a political test. He was born in Broughty Ferry and worked as a journalist with *The Scotsman*, the *Edinburgh Magazine* and the *British Weekly*; in 1926 he founded the Scottish National Movement, in 1928 he helped found the National Party of Scotland and became its first vice-president, and in 1929 he became the first Scottish Nationalist to stand for Parliament. Spence's patriotic energies were applied to the current state of Scots poetry and it seemed to him that the range of the medium had to be extended by returning to the linguistic virtuosity of the great Makars:

> [in 1898] I had begun to make a serious study of Middle Scots literature, which appealed to me as the only trustworthy basis on which the rehabilitation of the Scots tongue could well be essayed. My main intention was to modernize that phase of Scots in such a manner as would make it serviceable for use at the present time in prose and verse by following the analogous process by which Chaucerian English had developed into modern English, this indeed being the simplest and most efficacious means to my hand.
>
> This process, indeed, occupied many years of labour in my spare time. By the late twenties I had completed perhaps half of my task when Mr MacDiarmid (who had applauded my endeavours and was fully knowledgeable concerning them) ventured upon his scheme for the formation of a generalised Scots drawn from all the known phrases and dialects of that tongue and which he described as 'Synthetic Scots'. Of course Mr MacDiarmid had a perfect right to formulate any such system as seemed good to him. This withstanding, I cannot believe that his efforts were founded on any tolerably scientific or rational basis.[3]

Spence had apparently become bitter enough to get it wrong on two counts: first, MacDiarmid's linguistically synthetic Scots (an almost Hegelian coalescence of an oral thesis and a literary antithesis) appeared in the early, not the late, twenties; second, MacDiarmid's principles were not intended to be scientific or rational but imaginative. MacDiarmid was, though, enthusiastically aware of Spence's linguistic innovations; in 1926 he saluted Spence as "the first Scot for five hundred years to write 'pure poetry' in the vernacular".[4] Spence's example undoubtedly

41

influenced Grieve at a time when he was writing in English and taking an antagonistic attitude to the attempts of the Vernacular Circle of the London Burns Club to preserve the Doric. Pseudo-Burnsian poetry was anathema to Grieve in 1922; Spence's return to the basic principles of pre-Burnsian vernacular verse was a different matter (and manner), for the Makars were ripe for a revolutionary revival. Grieve's mind, then, held two distinct possibilities: that the potential of Scotland could be expressed in poetry written in English with European terms of reference; or that Scotland could best parade her possibilities by exploring all the nuances of Scots, so that words floating around in the oral atmosphere could be allied to the literary vocabulary preserved in Jamieson's *Etymological Dictionary of the Scottish Language*. Never a man to limit himself to one *via media*, Grieve managed to get the best of both worlds by adopting Hugh MacDiarmid as his *alter ego*. Hence MacDiarmid was launched by Grieve in his new periodical *Scottish Chapbook* which bore the relevant motto "Not Traditions — Precedents". The first number appeared on 26 August 1922 and the third number (October 1922) included a poem by Hugh MacDiarmid. This was "The Watergaw", which has since become recognised as one of the greatest lyrics in Scots and the quintessence of MacDiarmid's early style.

It is as well, at the outset, to establish that MacDiarmid's Scots was not quite so dictionary-based as his propaganda suggested. He did, after all, grow up in the Borders where many of the great traditional ballads had been preserved in oral transmission thus ensuring that spoken Scots was still strong. MacDiarmid's educational platform — which insisted on the teaching of Scots, or at least Scots poetry, in schools — led him to condemn bitterly the reliance on English in schools (and before MacDiarmid's achievements made educationists rethink the matter, English *was* used rather exclusively in the classroom while Scots was tasted, with the flavour of forbidden fruit, outside school hours). MacDiarmid thought his native Langholm was "the bonniest place I know"[5] and it was natural that his treatment of it should have been in Scots of a sort. Border Scots was unusually rich, perhaps because the Borderers like to underline their differences with their English neighbours. Another Scottish writer, Lavinia Derwent, had good cause to remember her Border childhood and the earthy vocabulary of a farmworker:

> Some of Jessie's words were difficult to translate into plain English, but they were so expressive that their meaning was easily guessed. A chatterbox was a bletherskite, a tell-tale a clype, a round-shouldered person was humphy-backit, a throat was a thrapple, a turkey-cock a bubblyjock, upside-down was tapsulteerie, and dumfoonert meant astonished. It was far better fun than a dead language like Latin.[6]

Later in the book Jessie uses the phrase "The hale clamjamfry"[7] and there, used without artifice, is the last line of the first lyric in *Sangschaw*, "The Bonnie Broukit Bairn" with its memorable image of the weeping earth:

> — But greet, an' in your tears ye'll droun
> The haill clanjamfrie!

So MacDiarmid began with a reservoir of Scots words he had absorbed from his Border childhood; his development of this familiar speech into synthetic Scots was motivated by a desire to make Scottish culture into the mainstream of contemporary modernism. Helping him along the way was the precedent of Lewis Spence's poetic imitations for the Middle Scots style. Spence, however, did not go far enough for MacDiarmid's liking.

In the "Hitherto Uncollected" section of MacDiarmid's posthumously published *Complete Poems 1920-1976* (ed. Michael Grieve and W. R. Aitken, London 1978) there is an early poem in conventional Scots, "The Blaward and the Skelly", which has some similarities with Burns's first poem "O, Once I Lov'd a Bonnie Lass". Both heroines are called Nelly (Burns's song was written for Nelly Kilpatrick) and both have their virtues recounted in lilting quatrains. Burns's Nelly is exceptionally delicate:

> As bonnie lasses I hae seen,
> And mony full as braw,
> But for a modest gracefu' mien
> The like I never saw.

Grieve's Nelly is more robust:

> The gowden hair that glamoured
> To wan weeds turned the skelly
> And bluer than the blaward
> Were your eyes, Nelly.

On internal evidence we could safely assume that the Grieve poem, though dated 1922, stylistically predates the first MacDiarmid poems. It is derivative and derives mainly from the Burns tradition and the oral Scots of Grieve's youth. If, as he claimed, his earliest poetry was in Scots then it was in a Scots similar to that employed in "The Blaward and the Skelly":

> the fact is that Scots was my native tongue. . . . And, above all, it should be understood that my earliest literary efforts were all in Scots, for in those days many Scottish papers ran a 'Doric' (i.e. Scots vernacular) column, and the influence of Sir J. M. Barrie . . . and the other writers of the Kailyard school was in the land, and more people spoke Scots — or spoke more (i.e. richer) Scots than do so today.[8]

Grieve was not, then, converted to Scots; he had been converted to English because of a desire to dismiss Kailyardism and to avail himself of the international range of poetry in English (a theme he returned to in his "Mature Art" sequence comprising *In Memoriam James Joyce, The Kind of Poetry I Want* and the eventually abandoned *Impavidi Progrediamur*). What persuaded him to return to Scots was the realisation that the language could be shaken to its linguistic roots by an application of modernist theory. Taking as his poetic ingredients oral Scots, literary Scots and a shrewd contemporary mentality he self-consciously constructed an idiom that would be so alive with modern thought that it could not be construed as either reactionary or escapist. The distance between "The Blaward and the Skelly" to "The Watergaw" is an imaginative leap of unimaginable proportions. MacDiarmid was, at a bound, on a par with the pioneers of modernism. It should never be forgotten that "The Watergaw" first appeared in 1922, the *annus mirabilis* of modernism: the year of *Ulysses* and *The Waste Land*. MacDiarmid followed the careers of Joyce and Eliot closely. He emulated Joyce's liquid verbosity in "Water Music" and wrote *In Memoriam James Joyce* as a tribute to the Irish master. Eliot never fascinated him in quite the way Joyce did, but he respected him enough to refer to him with affectionate humour in *A Drunk Man Looks at the Thistle*:

> T. S. Eliot — it's a Scottish name —
> Afore he wrote 'The Waste Lnad' su'd ha'e come
> To Scotland here. he wad ha'e written
> A better poem syne — like this, by gum!

A scientific experiment is an exploration of a possible world; a literary experiment is a tentative research into life. MacDiarmid's "The Watergaw" was an experiment that succeeded triumphantly enough to look like the pinnacle of a long tradition rather than the renewal of a lost language. Thematically the poem is a memory of the death of the poet's father, an instant that is also alluded to in the poem "Kinsfolk" (from *Work in Progress*):

> Afore he dee'd he turned and gied a lang
> Last look at pictures o' my brither and me
> Hung on the wa' aside the bed, I've heard
> My mither say. I wonder then what he
> Foresaw or hoped and hoo—or gin—it squares
>   Wi' subsequent affairs.

However synthetic the language the experience was a basic one, and it is MacDiarmid's evocation of the mystery of reality that makes the poem so memorable. It uses imagery for philosophical purposes; it takes a symbol and invests it with an other-worldly significance. In the second stanza MacDiarmid refuses to spell out the vital light that is both watergaw and life itself. Instead he let the conclusion, like the symbol, hang in the air:

> There was nae reek i' the laverock's hoose
> That nicht — an' nane i' mine;
> But I hae thocht o' that foolish licht
> Ever sin' syne;
> An' I think that mebbe at last I ken
> What your look meant then.

That "mebbe" is not inserted in the interests of prosodic regularity; it is there to stress human fallibility and the possibility that there might be a perspective that transcends the three-dimensional human outlook. Stylistically, MacDiarmid had introduced a new note to Scots poetry. He had abandoned both the rigid quatrain and the Standard Habbie measure (which had been *de rigeur* in Scots poetry since Burns popularised it in the eighteenth century) in favour of a more fluid stanza which concluded with a clinching couplet. Finally, MacDiarmid had intellectualised Scots poetry by isolating a particular image and then seeking out its cosmic implications.

Again and again in the lyrics in *Sangschaw* (1925) and *Penny Wheep* (1926), MacDiarmid suggests a multidimensional view of reality by contrasting our usual viewpoint with a God's-eye-view of the universe; this cosmic outlook simultaneously shrinks the world to socially manageable proportions and suggests the imaginative majesty of man who is capable of possessing the cosmos through creativity alone. MacDiarmid used God as an instantly accessible image of a meaningful universe and avoided the theological stereotype. For example, the God of "Crowdieknowe" is no awesome patriarch but an odious observer who has to contend with the truculent force of humanity in the shape of the Langholm locals who are unwillingly resurrected:

> An' glower at God an' a' his gang
> O' angels i' the lift
> —Thae trashy bleezin' French-like folk
> Wha gar'd them shift!

The faith that the mature MacDiarmid put in scientific insights was already present in the early lyrics. In "The Eemis Stane" he saw a poignancy in the spectacle of the planet earth trembling in space:

> I' the how-dumb-deid o' the cauld hairst nicht
> The warl' like an eemis stane
> Wags i' the lift;
> An' my eerie memories fa'
> Like a yowdendrift.

That visionary approach could be extended to almost mystical levels, but for MacDiarmid even the most puzzling elements of existence still deserved a human solution. He saw no point in genuflecting before an abstract deity. Instead he suggested the human predicament in his poem "Empty Vessel" by comparing a girl crooning over a dead child to the intergalactic light that unfeelingly illuminates the universe:

> Wunds wi' warlds to swing
> Dinna sing saw sweet,
> The licht that bends owre a' thing
> Is less ta'en up wi't.

"Empty Vessel" demonstrates that MacDiarmid's originality is always rooted in tradition for the poem is, technically, an expansion of a folk fragment.

Because MacDiarmid had always made himself *au fait* (to use one of his favourite expressions) with verbal advances in contemporary poetry, he was able to invest his early lyrics with the electrifying shock-effect of the new. His range of reference was remarkable and few poets have been able to command such a diversity of stylistic mannerisms. Moreover, no nationalist was ever more internationally minded, and MacDiarmid, though pugnaciously Scottish, usually confined his interest in Scottish poetry to the work of the great Makars, to a few poems by Burns (whom he regarded as a great songwriter rather than a great poet) and to the neglected genius of John Davidson. In the early 1920s he was more interested in the state of European poetry in general than in the facetious tone of contemporary Scottish poetry. MacDiarmid felt that his fellow Scottish poets merely wished to *conserve* the Scots language for antiquarian purposes and there was nothing conservative about his own thinking. He was, in 1922, working in isolation in Scotland but could not resist the temptation of thinking in the royal plural and hinting that there was a movement when there was really just one man making a new beginning. In 1923 he spoke of:

> the possibility of a great Scottish Literary Renaissance, deriving its strength from the resources that lie latent and almost unsuspected in the Vernacular.[9]

What MacDiarmid omitted to mention was that, in 1923, he *was* this "great Scottish Literary Renaissance". Later he attracted disciples who wrote outstanding poems in the MacDiarmid manner — I think of Soutar, Goodsir Smith, Garioch and others — but he remained unique because he could never be contained by a movement. He was too large for that. He was certainly not content to rest on his laurels as a lyric poet and decided to move on to bigger things. Yet the MacDiarmid who first set the heather on fire *was* a lyric poet, the author of *Sangschaw* and *Penny Wheep*. That his break with the past took the form of renewing it, was not, basically, different from the method adopted by the three most celebrated modernists: Joyce based his *Ulysses* on the pattern of Homer's *Odyssey*; Eliot's post-war world was a wasteland because, according to Eliot, contemporary reality was aesthetically inferior to the Elizabethan age; Pound's poetry was shot through with archaism and abstraction and what he called the Spirit of Romance. MacDiarmid used tradition to draw up a reliable map of the modern world, a map on which Scotland was coloured in red. Lewis Spence, MacDiarmid's predecessor in the experimental use of Scots, wrote that "no poetry for a century and a half has reflected so much of the authentic Scotland as the poems in Mr MacDiarmid's recent book *Sangschaw*"[10] but MacDiarmid's notion of "the authentic Scotland" involved a small country whose great past was about to be overshadowed by a brilliant future. In the 1920s MacDiarmid was a revolutionary poet in love with tradition; an explosive talent who was often unsure of what direction his genius would take him in. In *Penny Wheep* he wrote a riposte "To One Who Urges More Ambitious Flights" and concluded:

> Wee bit sangs are a' I need,
> Wee bit sangs for auld times' sake!
> Here are ferlies nae yin sees
> In a bensil o' a bleeze.

Five months after the publication of *Penny Wheep*, MacDiarmid published *A Drunk Man Looks at the Thistle* (1926). Obviously enough he had decided "wee bit sangs" were not enough and that Scotland needed the full treatment.

A Drunk Man Looks at the Thistle is, despite the excellence of his other books, MacDiarmid's masterpiece. He was never again able, or inclined, to organise his material with such consummate skill. The narrative was, fundamentally, a vehicle for MacDiarmid's views on the rejuvenated Scotland. A drunk man, during his unsteady odyssey home to the bed of his beloved Jean (a folk equivalent of Homer's Penelope), stumbles on a hillside and there, by the light of the full moon, considers the thistle as a rugged symbol of Scotland's past and potential. As the alocholic spirit wears off, it is replaced by a deep psychological spirituality and the drunk man's increasing sobriety is expressed in penetrating verse of great dignity. Scotland is no longer condemned as a country with defeatist obsessions, but addressed as a nation with a glorious future:

> The thistle rises and forever will
> Getherin' the generations under't.
> This is the monument o' a' they were,
> And a' they hoped and wondered.

In the space of a few years MacDiarmid had moved from the lyric to the epic (and though there are seemingly autonomous passages in *A Drunk Man*, they operate best in the narrative context). MacDiarmid had written great poetry and had served notice on Scotland that it was far from finished as a force in the world. MacDiarmid, too, was far from finished and he went on to initiate the political poetry of the 1930s with *First Hymn to Lenin* (1931) and to create the dazzling intellectual world of his later scientifically-orientated poetry. Chris Grieve had become Hugh MacDiarmid, and MacDiarmid — in the words of Auden's "In Memory of W. B. Yeats — "became his admirers". I, as one of them, looked backwards through MacDiarmid's work, appreciating the long poems first and the lyrics much later. Yet the lyrics contain the source of all MacDiarmid's work: the passion, the cosmic viewpoint, the linguistic wizardry, the fascination with the dialectic process, the concern with humanity. It is all there. MacDiarmid's old favourite Whitman would have approved, for MacDiarmid's lyrics are large and, yes, they contain multitudes.

References

1 For the full story, see my essay "Confessions of an Escapologist" in *Jock Tamson's Bairns*, London 1977, ed. Trevor Royle.
2 Hugh MacDiarmid, *Lucky Poet*, London 1943, reissued London 1972, pp. 178-9.
3 Lewis Spence, "Poets at Loggerheads", *Scotland's Magazine*, August 1954. p. 34.

4 C. M. Grieve, *Contemporary Scottish Studies*, London 1926, p. 196.
5 Ed. Duncan Glen, *Selected Essays of Hugh MacDiarmid*, London 1969, p. 53.
6 Lavinia Derwent, *A Border Bairn*, London 1979, pp. 13-14.
7 Lavinia Derwent, *A Border Bairn*, London 1979, p. 126.
8 *Lucky Poet*, p. 17.
9 *Scottish Chapbook*, February 1923.
10 Lewis Spence, "The Scottish Literary Renaissance" in *The Nineteenth Century and After*, vol. 100, no. 593, July 1926, p. 127.

The Influence of Hugh MacDiarmid

TOM SCOTT

The Oxford Dictionary tells us that *influence* means an emanation from the stars, the flow of an etherial fluid from them acting upon the character and destiny of men, an occult power. MacDiarmid is certainly a star of poets but his influence is a bit dubiously thought of as etherial or occult: as well apply such terms to a punch in the solar plexus or a kick from a wild horse, or the blast of a hurricane. Yet spiritual it certainly is, and complex rather than simple in nature. It can be a bad as well as a good influence, a negative as well as a positive. It can be a general cultural climate and it can be specific in particular areas of life, thought, literature, and on individual writers. There is, for instance, his good influence in general on Scottish poetry and poets in Scots and Gaelic, usually positive and salutary. But there is his influence on Edwin Muir and other writers of English which is mostly bad and negative, provoking hostility and resistance. There is his influence on literary Scots, on Gaelic culture by encouragement and furtherance, his support of the modernist movement associated mainly with the poetic revolution of Pound and Eliot in verse and of Joyce and others in prose — specific influences. There is his general avant-garde stance, not to be confused with phoney avant-gardism, craze-mongering, by people who don't know what poetry is. There is his influence on politics, his republicanism, his avowed Marxism (he was no "ist" of any sort), his belief in Douglas's Social Credit as an interim solution, his nationalism. One should be mindful too that the influence he aimed at having is not necessarily the influence he in fact has: clearly he did not "aim" to antagonise Muir, but having done so he kept it up. There is his influence on the Burns cult and other kailyairdie diseases of the body literary, on all kinds of anglicisation on the one hand and of Scotch comic caricaturing on the other. I cannot say whether his materialist philosophy has any philosophic influence at all: probably not, except perhaps on non-philosophers. There is his fiercely intellectual patriotism, advocating the best and damning the worst in Scottish life and culture. I suppose through F. G. Scott he must have had an influence on music, if only on songs. All that adds up to one hell of a lot of influence, and even that is by no means exhaustive. There is his negative influence on the folk song revival, led by Hamish Henderson: his unpopular, élitist intellectualism was incompatible with Hamish's revival of the basic folk idiom, the perennially human, and his Herculean labours at rescuing hundreds and hundreds of songs in oral tradition from possible loss, many tales and other items of folklore. That their attitudes were incompatible is one thing, but they need not have led to such desperate enmity as in fact occurred and in which, as usual, nobody gained and Scotland lost. There was plenty of room for both MacDiarmid and Henderson, not to say Muir, and for many other attitudes and fields of work.

For me personally, perhaps his most significant influence is his practice and championship of the long poem. I'm not aware of being influenced by his Scots, except in the general sense that all of us owe much to his being there at all, the man who made it possible again to write a serious poetry in Scots. I came to Scots my own way, and after a few experiments in what I call muscle-bound Scots, hammered out a Scots style of my own in which Scots and English easily intermell in such a way as to express my own mind and nature. I have always had much to say, aiming at an integrated vision of life (and that means length), am geared rather for the mile or the marathon than the sprint: lang-windit, if ye like, rather than fast. Scots poetry has always been rowth of lyrics, and since the Reformation, of damn little else. To go on doing the same thing is moribund, useless. But MacDiarmid, after his superb early lyrics, became increasingly a marathon runner, he went for the sustained meditation, long view, the poem of some length. In this he owed much to and was influenced by Ezra Pound, probably the one poet of his time who was his equal if not his superior in some ways — technically, for instance. It is in this that MacDiarmid is most admirable as a poet, and is of course in benighted Scotland least admired, even by fellow-poets. Goodsir Smith is one of very few who could follow Pound and MacDiarmid into sustained work, and did so in his finest work — *Under the Eildon Tree*, heavily indebted to them both.

Precisely where he is least respected, therefore, is where I most respect him, where he was most a pioneer loner. The tyranny of fashion and fashion-mongering allied to criticasting theorising has done as much damage in poetry as elsewhere. The staple of poetry has always been the epic and the drama, which can use lyric poetry *en passant*, but the sheer lack of weight of the lyric had made it the only possible form for the amateurs, hobbyists and spare-time writers of little talent and less time, so that poetry has come to be identified with lyrics, short forms, and even poets rarely have the knowledge, taste and judgment to see and enjoy the superior major forms. For one who can enjoy Wordsworth's "Prelude", there are thousands who can enjoy his "Daffodils"; but any critic who would dare assert the superiority of the latter over the former would publish his incompetence to comment on poetry at all. Yet Scottish poetry has little but lyrics to show, and most poets today are in the category of the "Daffodil"-lovers: a fact which MacDiarmid had to live with, as his best work was regarded by the polloi as an aberration by a good lyric poet. The theorists aver of course that prose can do better what the epic used to do and go on mouthing the stupid platitude that what can be done in prose is better done as prose. On the contrary, prose cannot do what the epic does nor the true poetic drama, and that which can be done as verse is best done as verse. There is no alternative to the heroic song, and no prose can sing at all. Those who really believe in, like, poetry, must want to see it win back as much ground lost to prose as possible.

The rot, I suppose, set in in Alexandria, a school of academics who, having no stamina for the sustained work, preached against it, thus helping to undermine the very art they professed to advance. No long poem can of course be judged by lyric intensity or be "poetic" all the time: and no fit reader would expect it to. Much of MacDiarmid's longer poems is chopped-up prose, I agree, and simply not good enough: matter of any sort has to be digested into verse. But that is precisely what happens in MacDiarmid's best long poems, whether in Scots or English. They are the peak of his achievement and for that reason are the least influential: few have the poetic stamina to take up this aspect of his work; the mini-singers have taken over again, reduced the standards from his height to their own mediocrity, and miscall the few who aim above their own depressed and depressing standards.

This raised another aspect of the influence question: the influence he has *not* had so far and might have been expected to have. As with Burns, there grew up around him a cult of MacDiarmid, a horde of hangers-on, of great-man worshippers, relationship-claimers, Dear-auld-Chrissers, sycophants, flatterers, personality-sunbathers, a haill clekkin o scunnersome bumsuckers who had no critical awareness of his worth and cared less. Among them were a few writers who associated with him as personal friends and were the enemies of all he stood for: and for one man who would "do his work" there were thousands of these stuffed-lionisers. I could never understand how he could put up with them: or if I did I put it down to his inordinate vanity and the rough time he got from the Establishment, especially in his younger and middle years. He had no influence on them at all, for there was nothing there to influence ae way or tither. Most of them were paper pokes wi' a hole in the bottom. It's not merely that they wouldn't stand and slog it out with him (work for the brave or reckless, but at any rate the serious): most of them couldn't have gone a single round with him on anything that mattered. That is why, only a few months after his death, there is almost nobody doing work that shows any influence at all of his best work, of trying to go a bit further, clear a bit more of the forest of the inarticulate, while the symptoms of a return to kailyairdie vacuity and Whistlebinkie slop, tripe and onions, are now almost terminal — especially in Scots. If one challenged him about these people he merely shrugged and agreed, with the air of one who willy-nilly has to pass his time among inferiors. He had no illusions about them, but he needed them as an actor needs an audience. I never heard him say a good word, in private as distinct from public, about any poet close to him except Sorley Maclean: the others he patronised as the best goodish little poets doing what little they could. Maclean he regarded as a major poet, on his own level. He wasn't two-faced about it: I've heard him say it to more than one face, and even to many of us at once: "You're all a lot o tryers". This wouldn't stop him writing a fulsome introduction to a book of poems if almost anybody asked him: mostly self-advertisement.

The whole question of influence therefore is a very complex one. His early lyrics probably influenced anybody who wrote short poems and was young enough to learn: his own age-group were unaffected, unless one thinks of Willie Soutar as his own age-group, and who benefitted a good deal from the lyrics. Goodsir Smith's finest work, *Under the Eildon Tree*, owes something to the MacDiarmid of *A Drunk Man*, but as much to Pound and many others. If it can be said he had many followers, he had no disciples. It's as well in some ways: a good poet should be indebted to all but disciple of none. Unfortunately the bad poets are also seldom disciples of one, but neither are they indebted to all, or to anything but a fashion, usually bad, which they imitate to death. I do not want to suggest, of course, that all of the people round him were mere hangers-on: he had some genuine friends too, however deprecating he may have been about their work: half-fun, whole-earnest.

One doesn't mind, of course, that so many pay lip-service to MacDiarmid but can't even try to follow up his work on the long poem, his attempt to digest his own age and its ideas and themes into major poetry: one does mind the pooh-pahing of his major work in favour of that which lesser people unwilling to make the sacrifices demanded by major work (or by society of those who dare to attempt such work) have, or seem to have, more chance of approximating to. One objects to those Dear-auld-Chrissers who slap him on the back with an open gully. Genius does what it must, talent what it can: but one of the things talent can do is acclaim the higher values and aims. It may not be possible for him to get the kind of poetry he wants, nor even in all reaches desirable: but he leads on a way that even talent might follow, in its own way. Indeed, it is more usual for men of talent to prepare the way for genius than the other way round: think of Ramsay to Burns,

Surrey to Marlowe and Shakespeare, Gray and Collins to John Keats.

In the forty years or so of my own life as a minor poet, I have met many people of talent in various arts and a handful of men of genius. Of the latter, four are particularly outstanding in memory: T. S. Eliot, Jacob Epstein, Tyrone Guthrie and Hugh MacDiarmid. They all had one thing in common, viewed subjectively: in their presence we lesser mortals felt as if delivered from bonds and fetters we scarcely knew bound us. They inspired with their own freedom and self-confidence, so that in their presence one felt one's problems become mere ghosts, devils of negation we mistook for "conscience", the terrible nay-sayer to whom nothing we do is good enough, that jeers the most at our best achievements. I remember Eliot going through a pile of French translations of mine, smiling at the only four lines I'd done of Villon, and turning to me with pleasure. When I objected to the suggestion that I should do more Villon because of my ignorance of medieval French, he simply said something like "with your feeling for the man, and your Scots, you can easily get up the little bit you need for this task". And he made the mountain seem a molehill. Within a week or two I had done good translations of some of the greatest and most intricate poems ever written. To hear Epstein talk about his work in his curious Bowery accent (but powerful command of English) was to enter a larger, freer world: "Adam is my best woik: that expresses the soul of a people, not the poor bloody little ahtist". Tyrone Guthrie had the same liberating effect on talent, and I'm sure every actor who worked under him, or playwright who had the luck to have him as director, must have felt inspired to his best possible by that great spirit. MacDiarmid too could have that effect, but he could also be utterly destructive and oppressive in certain moods, or if one crossed him — he tended to be very dictatorial. I was never one of his entourage, but of course I saw much more of him than of these others, so perhaps they too had a destructive side. He could damn a talent for totally non-poetic reasons, ideological reasons, or personal or political reasons: I needn't enlarge on it, you need only read his prose. But the inspiring, confidence-giving power he certainly had too, and if he took your side, you had an all-out supporter. Some of the best things I have ever read in *The Scotsman* were letters from him in defence and/or attack: rooting for a cause, attacking its enemies. And of course some of his best essays and articles are of this nature. On occasion, too, when he was addressing a meeting and warmed to his subject, he seemed to take fire and light up inside (and I do not mean whisky) by an inspiration which brought out the stature of his mind for all to see and feel. Those who have experienced it will know what I mean: an unforgettable experience.

I don't think I can say more on the subject at this stage. Who knows how his influence will look a hundred, even fifty years from now, if the race still survives (an unlikely survival, on present evidence)? His influence certainly is still at work. This note of mine has turned out rather differently from my own expectations, and that's as it should be. Who knows, maybe he gied my elbuck a dunt here and there.

Part II

Hugh MacDiarmid and the Scottish Literary Tradition

DAVID DAICHES

In Hugh MacDiarmid's collection of poems entitled *Penny Wheep*, published in 1926, there is a little poem of six lines entitled "To one who urges more ambitious flights". "Dinna come tae bauld my glead," it begins: "Don't come to stir up my fire". "It'll be a bear-meal-raik" — "It will be a fruitless errand". The poem goes on:

> Wee bit sangs are a' I need,
> Wee bit sangs for auld times' sake!
> Here are ferlies nae yin sees
> In a bensil o' a bleeze.   (a big fire)

Many years later he dreamt

> of poems like the bread-knife
> Which cuts three slices at once;
> Of poems concerned with technical matters . . .
> Which, as masterpieces of intricate lucidity . . .
> Or in cut-gem clearness surpass even Huxley's
> Prose account of the endophragmal system of the crayfish . . .

He defined as his kind of poetry

> Poetry of such an integration as cannot be effected
> Until a new and conscious organisation of society
> Generates a new view
> Of the world as a whole
> As the integration of all the rich parts
> Uncovered by the separate disciplines.

And in the 1960s in a discussion of the composer Kaikosru Shapurji Sorabji, whose works include the *Opus Clavicembalisticum* which takes two hours to perform, he exclaimed: "I am all for

59

GIANTISM in the arts" and stressed the importance of artists of all kinds producing "bigger and bigger works" that would not aim at any facile mass appeal but would be understood by the perceptive few. Wee bit sangs for auld times' sake, indeed!

Of course it isn't difficult to quote contradictory views from MacDiarmid, especially if these are separated by many years. He might well say, with Walt Whitman

> Do I contradict myself?
> Very well then I contradict myself,
> (I am large, I contain multitudes).

But in MacDiarmid's case it isn't simply a question of his changing his mind from time to time, though of course he has done that like everybody else, nor — in spite of some important similarities with Whitman that I discuss later — is it a question of Whitmanesque largeness. Self-contradiction is for him a mode of poetic awareness. This fact is easily obscured if we look at his work chronologically and chart carefully the different phases in his career. If we do that we will talk of his earliest quasi-mystical poetry in English, his perfectly wrought little lyrics in Scots, and his later massively discursive poems in what might be called a lexicographical English. We will distinguish between these, and say which we prefer and why. But if we take a comprehensive, synchronistic view of MacDiarmid's work we begin to see certain kinds of unity amid all this diversity. And two things will emerge. The first is that the counterpointing of unity and diversity is central to his poetic character. And the second is that such a counterpointing is bound up with MacDiarmid's view of the nature of the Scottish literary character.

You remember the end of *A Drunk Man Looks At The Thistle*, where, concluding the ordered loquacity of the drunk man's meditations, we find the marvellous lyric, "Yet hae I Silence left, the croon o' a'." And just as we imagine that we are being led to the ultimate eloquence of silence, we are jerked out of it again in the nagging everyday prose of Jean's comment with which the poem actually ends.

> "And weel ye micht,"
> Sae Jean 'll say, "eftir sic a nicht!"

Solutions are never final in MacDiarmid's poetry: the commonplace invades the mystical trance. The guttering candle is as likely as the stars to suggest eternity:

> The talla spales
> And the licht loups oot,
> Fegs, it's your ain creesh
> Lassie, I doot,
> And the licht that reeled
> Loose on't a wee
> Was the bonny lowe
> O' Eternity.

This little poem is called "Servant Girl's Bed". The poem that precedes it in *Penny Wheep* is a sort of love poem; but its title is "Scunner"; it identifies "the skinklan' stars" with "distant dirt", and it ends

> And I lo'e Love
> Wi' a scunner in't.

For MacDiarmid, the mystic trance always has a scunner in it, thus anchoring it to the mundane particularities of gritty experience and the realised apprehension of physical things. Similarly, the ultimate reach of what he himself calls his "Ecclefechan Gongorism" is

> Silence supervening at poetry's height
> Like the haemolytic streptococcus
> In the sore throat preceding rheumatic fever
> But which, at the height of the sickness,
> Is no longer there, but has been and gone!

These lines come from *In Memoriam James Joyce*, which in the poem itself he calls "this rag-bag, this Loch Ness Monster, this impact/Of the whole range of *welt literatur* on one man's brain", which at the same time seeks to speak "in the uncanny mode of silence". Joyce is indeed relevant here, and MacDiarmid's instinct was right to link his dual concern with language and silence with Joyce. For Joyce was caught up in a similar paradox: he would have liked to encapsulate all that could be said about human psychology and history in one great reverberating pun which would say everything at once, echoing away in an infinity of meanings and suggestions and associations. But in his attempt to do this he was led to produce the enormous *Finnegans Wake*. Joyce was also fascinated with the authoritative testimony of the senses in revealing the "quiddity" of the physical world. Stephen Dedalus meditates on Sandymount Beach on the "ineluctable modality of the visible", then closes his eyes to receive the physical world through his ears, the "ineluctable modality of the audible". And MacDiarmid's first book was called *Annals of the Five Senses*.

Yet for MacDiarmid sensation exists in order to be transcended. In some of his early poetry — in "A Moment in Eternity" for example — he seeks the transcendence directly, and the language is abstract and visionary. But he soon learned to anchor his vision in the individual sensation. What Duns Scotus called the *haecceitas*, the "thisness" of the individual natural object, was the sign both of its individuality and its capacity to serve as a microcosm, a complete world in itself. Gerard Manley Hopkins was fascinated by this aspect of Duns Scotus' thought, but it is equally relevant to MacDiarmid, for whom the concept of the microcosm is all-important. Let me quote again from *In Memoriam James Joyce*:

> We must look at a harebell as if
> We had never seen it before . . .
> The parsley fern — a lovelier plant
> Than even the proud Osmunda Regalis—
> Flourishes in abundance
> Showing off oddly contrasted fronds
> From the cracks of the lichened stones.
> It is pleasant to find the books
> Describing it as 'very local'.
> Here is a change indeed!
> The universal *is* the particular.

This explains MacDiarmid's fondness for *naming* things. And here again there is a paradox. For in his later poetry MacDiarmid often uses long catalogues, sometimes lists of technical terms — he is especially fond of geological terms — which some readers have found disturbingly unpoetic. But naming has always been a source of magical power to poets, as it is in the primitive folk mind. Adam acquired power over the animals in Eden by giving them names.

He demonstrated what MacDiarmid has called:

> The unity of thing and word,
> Of feeling and its articulation,
> Which is the essence of poetry.

For the poet, a word is not simply a sound which by convention has a specific denotation. It is in a way a means of physical entry into whatever it denotes. An author of a book on language reminds us that Bernard Shaw thought *love* too small a word for so big a thing, and proceeds to point out that the relationship between the length of a word and its meaning can be significantly paradoxical: "a large fish in Hawaii is called *ô* and a very small fish is known by the lingual leviathan *homomomonukunukuaguk*". This is the kind of information that would have been grist to MacDiarmid's mill.

MacDiarmid's catalogues, then, are naming devices which serve the same function as his picking out of a suggestively expressive single Scots word from Jamieson's Dictionary and placing it in a lyric where it will sing most loudly — as he did with the Orkney word "peerie-weerie" which he found in Jamieson defined as "very small" but which he re-defined as "diminished to a mere thread of sound" and made mean precisely that:

> An' the roarin' o' oceans noo
> Is peerieweerie to me:
> Thunner's a tinklin' bell: and Time
> Whuds like a flee.

You can, up to a point, re-define a word like "peerieweerie" by stretching or limiting, but you can't do this with scientific and technical terms. In dealing with such terms the poet has to submit himself to the facts, and tries to reach his vision by sheer concentration on them. There is a discipline here, the discipline of impersonality, which is something central in MacDiarmid's mature work. I have elsewhere called this aspect of his thought his "trans-humanism": it relates to a state of vision which gets beyond the limited and limiting personality of the observer, who becomes merely a prism through which the light of reality is refracted:

> So I am delivered from the microcosmic human chaos
> And given the perspective of a writer who can draw

> The wild disorder of a ship in a gale
> Against the vaster natural order of sea and sky.
> If a man does not bulk too big in his rendering
> He does not lose the larger half of dignity either.

Facts provide the road to vision. He seeks, he tells us

> A poetry of facts. Even as
> The profound kinship of all living substance
> Is made clear by the chemical route . . .
> The beautiful relations
> Shown only by biochemistry
> Replace a stupefied sense of wonder
> With something more wonderful
> Because natural and understandable.
> Such an understanding dawns
> On the lay reader when he becomes
> Acquainted with the biochemistry of the glands
> In relation to diseases such as goitre
> And their effects on growth, sex, and reproduction.
> He will begin to comprehend a little
> The subtlety and beauty of the action
> Of enzymes, viruses, and bacteriophages.

This is not the old "argument from design" that Robert Burns read about in William Derham's *Physico-Theology* and John Ray's *Wisdom of God Manifested in the Works of Creation*. It is an alternative route to a vision of reality — alternative to the microcosmic route that at other times he also used and which Blake had defined:

> To see a World in a grain of sand,
> And a Heaven in a wild flower,
> Hold Infinity in the palm of your hand
> And Eternity in an hour.

In moods when he sought a catalogue of facts, MacDiarmid sought to be "delivered from the microcosmic human chaos", the burden of too many sensed particulars in experience, but in other moods those sensed particulars, each with its own quiddity and *haecceitas*, are named, and in being named yield not only their own reality, but reality itself. The difference here is not simply that between his early Scots lyrics which evoke moods and situations with a remarkable association of precise sensation and more general human awareness, and his later discursive poems, for even in those later discursive poems — in *The Kind of Poetry I want*, for example — he can move from catalogue of scientific fact to the most individualised evocation of a particular scene or situation or activity — a salmon pool, a fishing fly, a breed of sheep, the movement of a dancer, the grace-notes of pipe-music. Intensity and discursiveness complement each other in MacDiarmid as they do in Joyce. Indeed in a sense they modulate into each other, for the catalogue is a catalogue of quiddities, and the whole is not the sum of parts but something greater, that the poet glimpses by naming the parts. It has been objected that the later MacDiarmid has written poems *about* the kind of poetry he wants rather than writing the kind of poetry he wants. But if poetry is, in a sense, the art of naming, then a proper naming of the kind of poetry one wants *is* the kind of poetry one wants. The real question is whether the names are always sounded properly, so as to produce the required power and insight. There is an *order* of naming that is not mere accumulation or exhaustiveness that enables the list of quiddities to fuse into a mystical harmony, and a sense of structure is not MacDiarmid's greatest quality as a poet. So his longer works do not fuse, as Joyce's do. But they do something else: they circle round, point to, illustrate, evoke and discuss the ineffable reality that lies at the centre. I am reminded of Robert Frost's little poem:

> We dance round in a ring and suppose,
> But the Secret sits in the middle and knows.

The point is that MacDiarmid knows that the Secret is there, and that it will not yield to the mere rush of human feeling or the solipsistic expression of personal emotion. It is worth noting that even in the most personal of his best Scots lyrics, there is what I call this trans-humanist quality, a distillation of something that goes beyond the poet's emotion.

Loquacity and silence; the catalogue and the distilled lyric — these are two sides of the same medal and an awareness of this helps us to understand the nature of MacDiarmid's poetic ambitions and poetic achievement. But there is something else in MacDiarmid's poetry which gives pause to any systematiser who tries to define it as an attempt to achieve and present through language some unified truth that lies behind the particulars of experience, that attempt "to circumjack Cencrastus", to contain and define that symbolic serpent whose contradictions represent reality. On the one hand there is the desperate discipline of art, the total commitment to the right kind of naming —

> Unremittin', relentless,
> Organized to the last degree,
> Ah, Lenin, politics is bairns' play
> To what this maun be!

And on the other there is the current of polemical journalism — exuberant, spontaneous, lively, topical — that runs right through his work and emerges at intervals to the surface. "My conception of poetry," he tells us in *Lucky Poet*, "is one that allows at once for the functions of education, historical guardianship, discussion of all manner of issues with all manner of people at all manner of levels, reportage of all sorts, exercises in the art of conversation, sheer entertainment, the fitting commemoration of great occasions, due summoning to high tasks, and, in short, all the forms of appeal and commentary compatible with intercourse with people who are . . . fully developed personalities possessing high-grade critical intelligences." Well: "reportage of all sorts" is hardly "unremittin', relentless, organized to the last degree". Journalism has its own qualities and its own demands, but it does not demand the relentless discipline of art; it is an altogether slacker kind of writing. By its very nature it is topical, and therefore hastily written. So weaving in and out of the work of MacDiarmid the poet is the work of MacDiarmid the verse journalist, sometimes popping up in the midst of a long poem, sometimes presented as a separate work. It can be very effective:

> Have we fewer starving, fewer in want
> In Scotland during the period in review?
> Have we fewer slums despite all the cant,
> Or thousands of homes yet that would make swine spew?
> Is there less land under cultivation or more?
> Aren't we worse off on every score?
> Then what the Hell are they famous for?

I am not saying that the comic and the satiric have no place in true poetry: there are both comic and satiric elements in many of

MacDiarmid's finest poems. But the casual slanging involved in rhyming "the period in review" with "homes that would make swine spew" belongs to another order of writing. Yet the poem from which I have quoted, "Scotland's Pride", appears in *Stony Limits* which contains some of MacDiarmid's finest poetry both in Scots and in English, including the "Shetland Lyrics" and one of the earliest and I should say the most brilliantly successful of his poems which use a highly technical English scientific vocabulary, "On a Raised Beach". It is in this poem, incidentally, that he expresses most concisely an important aspect of his trans-humanism:

> What happens to us
> Is irrelevant to the world's geology
> But what happens to the world's geology
> Is not irrelevant to us.
> We must reconcile ourselves to the stones,
> Not the stones to us.

This is worlds apart from "Then what the Hell are they famous for?". The disciplined coldness of "On a Raised Beach" takes us far from what Joyce called "kinetic" art to a realm of pure objectivity:

> We must be humble. We are so easily baffled by appearances
> And do not realise that these stones are one with the stars.
> It makes no difference to them whether they are high or low,
> Mountain peak or ocean floor, palace, or pigsty.
> There are plenty of ruined buildings in the world but no
>   ruined stones.

This is the poetry of a man who will not draw comforting conclusions from the uncanniness of reality. Oddly enough, Edwin Muir, with whom MacDiarmid was for so long at loggerheads, could write of the natural world with a similar kind of eerie intensity. But Muir drew a positive and comforting religious belief from his insights. MacDiarmid, who is in his own way a religious poet, steeled himself to be content with his awareness of the total neutrality of the universe. This does not *contradict* his social and political views — an existentialist Communist would take an identical position about the neutrality of reality — but it represents a different side of MacDiarmid's activities as a writer.

Sometimes, however, the poet who sees the necessity of reconciling himself to stone appears in the spokesman for Communism and Scottish Nationalism, as when he repudiates all the normal humanitarian reasons for social and political reform and sees politics simply as a way of getting rid once and for all of the "bread and butter questions" to enable men of high sensitivity and intelligence to engage freely in the ultimate task of defining their relationship with the neutral world of external reality.

> To hell wi' happiness!
> I sing the terrifying discipline
> O' the free mind that gars a man
> Mak' his joys kill his joys,
> The weakest by the strongest,
> The temporal by the fundamental
> (Or hope o' the fundamental)
> And prolong wi'in himself
> Threids o' thocht sae fragile
> It needs the help and contrivance
> O' a' his vital poo'er
> To haud them frae brakin'
> As he pu's them owre the gulfs.

As he wrote in *Lucky Poet*, "As a Socialist . . . I am . . . interested only in a very subordinate way in the politics of Socialism as a political theory; my real concern with Socialism is as an artist's organized approach to the interdependencies of life." Oscar Wilde, in *The Soul of Man under Socialism*, also believed that the objective of socialism was to release men from the necessity to perform daily labour to earn his bread and cultivate his potentiality as artist. But Wilde's view of the artist was a dilettante's view compared with MacDiarmid's sense of the "terrifying discipline" of impersonal thought.

One more contradiction in MacDiarmid, and then I shall try and relate the characteristics I have been trying to define both to the Scottish literary tradition and to MacDiarmid's sense of that tradition. Everybody knows "The Little White Rose":

> The Rose of all the world is not for me.
> I want for my part
> Only the little white rose of Scotland
> That smells sharp and sweet — and breaks the heart.

The Rose of the world was of course Yeats's phrase. "The quality symbolized as The Rose," Yeats wrote in a later note to the 1892 volume which included his Rose poems, "differs from the Intellectual Beauty of Shelley and of Spenser in that I have imagined it as suffering with man and not as something pursued and seen from afar." It may seem odd to some that MacDiarmid is on Shelley's and Spenser's side here, seeking the impersonal and the trans-human rather than an ideal that suffers with man. (There is incidentally another paradox in that the later and greater Yeats, the Yeats of "Byzantium" and "The Gyres" and "Lapis Lazuli", is on MacDiarmid's side, and would have accepted "the terrifying discipline o' the free mind that gars a man Mak' his joys kill his joys".) But I don't want to be side-tracked into comparing Yeats and MacDiarmid, tempting though that theme is. I quote "The Little White Rose" because of its simple lyrical cry about Scotland, its proclamation of a deep personal commitment to Scotland and only Scotland. It's a striking little poem, with its grandly dismissive first line: "The Rose of all the world is not for me". But of course the Rose of all the world was very much for MacDiarmid, and not only in those later discursive poems in which he ranged over all human language and over all geography, history and science. One of his earliest poems is called "A Moment in Eternity", and "eternity" and "infinity" are common words in his early poetry. The resolution of this apparent contradiction can be found in many places in MacDiarmid's work, perhaps most clearly in these lines from *A Drunk Man Looks at the Thistle*:

> And as at sicna times am I,
> I wad ha'e Scotland to my eye
> Until I saw a timeless flame
> Tak' Auchtermuchty for a name
> And kent that Ecclefechan stood
> As pairt o' an eternal mood.

This is not so much the microcosm, which I have already touched on, but that sudden shift in scale that shows eternity and the single individual thing as somehow illuminating each other. What I mean is perhaps more simply put in the little poem "The Bonnie Broukit Bairn" that first appeared in *Sangschaw*:

> Mars is braw in crammasy,
> Venus in a green silk goun,

> The auld mune shak's her gowden feathers,
> Their starry talk's a wheen o' blethers,
> Nane for thee a thochtie sparin',
> Earth, thou bonnie broukit bairn!
> *But greet, an' in your tears ye'll droun*
> *The haill clanjamfrie!*

The reduction of the planets to a group of stair-head gossips and the subsuming of "the haill clanjamfrie" in one fit of tears is a characteristic MacDiarmid ploy, linking the moment with eternity, all history with a single moss-covered tombstone, God's ultimate purpose with a group of shifty Scots villagers—

> *Fegs, God's no blate gin he stirs up*
> *The men o' Crowdieknowe!*

Now this, of course, is in a very Scottish tradition. It recalls the story of the Montrose minister who referred to Bethlehem as being on the Stonehaven side of Jerusalem. The juxtaposition of the divine and the familiarly matter-of-fact is popularly thought to be connected with the Scottish Presbyterian sense of intimacy with God and with divine matters. There may be something in this. When Robert Fergusson describes Adam's cultivating the Garden of Eden—

> When father Adie first pat spade in
> The bonny yeard of antient Eden—

and Burns, following him, talks of "Eden's bonie yard" and discusses familiarly Satan's part in the Fall of Man—

> Then you, ye auld, snick-drawing dog!
> Ye came to Paradise incog,
> An' played on man a cursed brogue,
> (Black be your fa'!)
> An' gied the infant warld a shog,
> 'Maist ruin'd a'—

these poets are doing something already well established in the Scottish literary tradition. I think, though, that there is more to it than Presbyterian finger-wagging. The sense of trying on for size, as it were, both the formal and the familar way of putting something has both an epistemological dimension and a dimension of comedy: I mean that it represents both a way of knowing and a

70

way of laughing. When Burns, in his fine poem "To a Louse", suddenly addresses the affected lady sitting in church with her fine Lunardi bonnet by her simple country name "Jenny", he restores her to common humanity, as it were, by his way of *naming* her. This is comic, but it also adds to knowledge, to understanding. It has a moral dimension, too. By suddenly transposing the key of your naming you can force a new vision on the reader. It has always seemed to me that such changes of key are a deliberate part of Robert Henryson's art in his *Fables*. Listen to the sententious opening of *The Taill of Schir Chantecleir and the Foxe*:

Thocht brutall beistis be Irrationall,
That is to say, wantand discretioun,
Yit ilk ane in thair kynd naturall
Hes mony divers inclinatioun.
The Bair busteous, the Wolff, the wylde Lyoun,
The Fox fenyeit, craftie and cawtelous,
The Dog to bark on nicht and keip the hows.

In that last line we leave the generalised description of the qualities of beasts and see and hear the dog barking at night to frighten away marauders. "The Dog to bark on nicht and keip the hows" is a line consisting entirely of monosyllabic words, as opposed to the polysyllables of the earlier lines in the stanza — "discretioun", "inclinatioun", "cawtelous". The difference is not only one of key, to use the musical analogy, but, to use an analogy from another art, one of camera angle. There is also a difference in degree of stylization. The other animals mentioned are either exemplary or heraldic: the dog is just a dog, barking, right there before us. The shift is from a catalogue to a realised individual, and it will not take much searching to find *that* kind of shift in MacDiarmid.

Henryson is continually moving from the more abstract to the more concrete.

This fenyeit Foxe, ffals and dissimilate,
Maid to this Cok ane cavillatioun:
'Ye ar, me think, changit and degenerate,
Fra your ffather off his conditioun;
Off craftie crawing he micht beir the Croun,
For he wald on his tais stand and craw.
This was na le; I stude beside and saw.'

"Dissimulate", "cavillatioun", "degenerate", "conditioun" — and then again that vivid line of monosyllables: "This was na le; I stude beside and saw". And I need hardly remind the reader of the three lines in *Troilus and Cresseid* which Troilus had carved on Cresseid's tomb:

> 'Lo, fair Ladyis, Crisseid, of Troyis toun,
> Sumtyme countit the flour of Womanheid,
> Under this stane lait Lipper lyis deid.'

The Middle Scots poets had their own special kind of love affair with Latin, and their so-called "aureate" language in which they intermittently indulged reveal a sheer joy in polysyllabic sonority of a kind that reminds us strongly of MacDiarmid's use of technical geological, botanical and other scientific names.

> All is Lithogenesis—or lochia,
> Carpolite fruit of the forbidden tree,
> Stones blacker than any in the Caaba,
> Cream-coloured caen-stone, chatoyant pieces,
> Celadon and corbeau, bistre and beige,
> Glaucous, hoar, enfouldered, cyathifrom . . .
> Hatched foraminous cavo-rilieva of the world,
> Deitic, fiducial stones. Chiliad by Chiliad
> What bricole piled you here, stupendous cairn?

This reminds me of Dunbar:

> Hale, sterne superne! Hale, in eterne,
>   In Godis sicht to schyne!
> Lucerne in derne for to discerne
>   Be glory and grace devyne;
> Hodiern, modern, sempitern,
>   Angellical regyne!
> Our tern inferne for to dispern
>   Helpe, rialest rosyne. . . .

It is true that Dunbar is here being deliberately more musical than MacDiarmid seeks to be in the lines I quoted from him, but in both poets we find the same relish of elaborate language.

There are of course many other aspects of Dunbar that reminds us of MacDiarmid, and this is not simply because MacDiarmid, with his cry "Back to Dunbar", deliberately turned to Dunbar, but because there seem to be some similarities of temperament between the two poets. The gaiety and verbal exuberance of such a poem as "Of a Dance in the Quenis Chalmer" shows language creating a scene in a way suggestive of one of MacDiarmid's moods and modes:

> Then cam in the Maister Almaser,
> Ane hommiltye jommeltye juffler,
> Lyk a stirk stackarand in the ry;
> His hippis gaff mony hoddous cry.

Dunbar introduces himself into the poem: he came into the room where the dance was and "He hoppet lyk a pillie wanton". I don't know what a "pillie wanton" is, and I haven't found anybody who does, but it is a MacDiarmid-like word, and it carries its own kind of suggestiveness. Dunbar and MacDiarmid share a linguistic exuberance which Henryson lacks. This exuberance is not an unmixed blessing to a poet: it can encourage a baroque proliferation of language that may utter more than it says. But it can also be an enormous source of poetic strength and excitement.

Like MacDiarmid, Dunbar could write poetry of deep religious feeling as well as comic, ironic, grotesque, obscene and abusive poetry. There was also a streak of the poetic journalist in Dunbar that is another link with MacDiarmid: he could quarrel in verse, beg in verse, sneer in verse, and even (something I don't think MacDiarmid has ever done) apologise in verse — though it is true that the apology is in every case ironic.

In an article on MacDiarmid, Anthony Ross linked him with Henryson rather than with Dunbar, and considers Henryson a greater poet than Dunbar. He considers that "with Dunbar, as with Burns, too much is occasional writing — triviality thrown off to entertain the court" and that this "illustrates the weakness of nearly all Scottish poetry in being so much confined to lyrics and satire". Ross finds lacking in Scottish poetry, apart from Henryson and MacDiarmid, "the poetic stamina necessary for long narrative poems or for sustained intellectual poetry of facts and ideas". This is an interesting point, but it seems to me to derive from too theoretical an approach to poetry rather than from a response to how it actually operates. The poetry of Henryson, however much we may describe him, as Ross does, as "the one great example before modern times of a Scottish poet with a comprehensive vision of the world in which he lived and able to project that vision in his writing", is not memorable, it seems to me, for its superior command "of facts and ideas", but for its beautifully articulated modulation of attitudes; and MacDiarmid's most successful long poems are achieved by the sequence of lyrics and shorter pieces, as in *A Drunk Man*, or by a cumulative reformulation, illustration and quotation which is not structurally unified in that it can effectively begin and end almost anywhere. (I am not saying that this is necessarily a fault, but it is a characteristic.) Ross seems in his article to value the intention more than the realisation: "MacDiarmid," he says, "like all great poets, will suddenly produce a line of startling force in a prosaic waste" — this hardly constitutes the "sustained intellectual poetry of facts and ideas" that Ross calls for. But I do not wish to quarrel with any assertion of Henryson's greatness nor with any comparison of Henryson and MacDiarmid, though I would compare rather different aspects from those that Ross compares, and I believe that the parallel with Dunbar is closer.

My aim, however, is not to pick out isolated points of similarity between some characteristics of MacDiarmid and some characteristics of early Scottish poets, but to see if MacDiarmid's characteristics can be related to anything that can be considered a Scottish literary tradition. The easy shifting from formal to colloquial modes that I have discussed does seem to run through a great deal of Scottish literature, Gaelic as well as Scots. I speak with some hesitation here, as my knowledge of Gaelic is very limited, but it does seem to me that in the poetry of Mary MacLeod, for example, there is a remarkable mixture of the formal and the spontaneous, the stylised and the familiar, while in the 18th century Scottish Gaelic poets, who were further removed from the formal traditions of the old bardic schools, the startlingly immediate appears side by side with the elegantly contrived poetic phrase. In William Ross's poem on the death of Prince Charlie, "An Suaithness Ban" ("The White Cockade"), the poet begins with a formal farewell to the white cockade and then immediately goes on to tell how he was walking across a hill on a Sunday with a friend when together they read a letter which brought the sad news. I am reminded of that line in MacDiarmid's "Lament for the

Great Music" where he suddenly adds "And, besides, as *The Scotsman* says, . . .". The element almost of journalism comes in — in the *tone* as much as the content — and I seem to see this occasionally in the midst of the well-wrought language of the Scottish Gaelic poets as in much literature in Scots. It was an English minister who is alleged to have said, in the course of an eloquent prayer, "And as thou hast doubtless seen, O Lord, in the *Manchester Guardian* . . ." but the story is more in the Scottish tradition.

The verbal exuberance of Dunbar and MacDiarmid is again clearly a Scottish literary tradition. This can work in two ways. In MacDiarmid's translation of Duncan Ban McIntyre's "Praise of Ben Dorain" we get the constant searching for language that matches the enormous variety of detail in nature; the verbal exuberance here matches a sense of inexhaustible individuality of nature's component parts, as it were, and this is in the original as well as in MacDiarmid's version. Other kinds of verbal exuberance manifest themselves in "aureation", in the exhibitionist use of technical terms, in verbal playfulness, in invented words, even in a sort of "mouth music" where language becomes essentially varied rhythmic sound with suggestions rather than denotations. All this is in MacDiarmid as it is in Dunbar, and it seems to be in some degree built into the Scottish approach to language. (I will not speculate on possible historical and psychological causes of this phenomenon, but it may have something to do with the fact that Scotland was for centuries a multi-lingual country.) Only a Scottish poet, it seems to me, could have produced MacDiarmid's "Water Music" or the relish of geological terms in "On a Raised Beach" or the varied catalogues found in his long later poems. The Scots like lists of words and names. That extraordinary mid-16th century Scots prose work known as *The Complaynt of Scotlande* not only employs in one section a Latinised and Frenchified Scots of remarkable virtuosity but also includes what is probably the most famous list in the whole of Scottish literature. The author insists that he has not "lardit this tracteit vitht exquisite termis, quilkis ar nocht daly vsit, bot rather i hef vsit domestic scottis language, maist intelligibil for the vlgare pepil" but at the same time admits "yit

75

nochtheles ther is mony vordis of antiquite that i hef rehersit in this tracteit, the quhilkis culd nocht be translatit in oure scottis langage, as auguris, auspices, ides, questeours, senaturus, censours, pretours, tribuns, ande mony vthir romane dictions: ther for gyf sic vordis suld be disusit or detekkit, than the phrasis of the antiquite vald be confundit ande adnullit: ther for it is necessair at sum tyme til myxt oure langage vitht part of termis dreuyn fra lateen, be rason that oure scottis tong is nocht sa copeus as is the lateen tong, . . .". MacDiarmid too sometimes deplored the limitations of Scots and the results of seeking to enrich it into a general mish-mash:

> God gied man speech and speech created thocht,
> He gied man speech but to the Scots gied nocht
> Barrin' this clytach that they've never brocht
> To onything but sic a Blottie O
> As some bairn's copybook micht show.

But more usually he enjoyed enriching it, as the author of *The Complaynt of Scotland* did, through the adoption of technical and learned terms.

The famous list that I mentioned is a catalogue of stories, songs and dances told and sung and danced by a company of shepherds: it is one of our main sources of knowledge of the lost literature of Scotland. It includes ". . . the tayl of the volfe of the varldis end, Ferrand erl of Flandris that mareit the devyl, the taiyl of the reyde eyttyn vitht the three heydis, the tail quhou perseus sauit andromada fra the cruel monstir, the prophysie of merlyne, the tayl of the giantis that eit quyk men, on fut by fortht as i culd found, vallace, the bruce, ypomedon, the tail of the three futtit dog of norrouay, the tayl quhou Hercules slei the serpent hidra that had vij heydis, the tail qhuou the kyng of est mure land mareit the kyngis dochtir of vest mure land, Skail gellenderson the kyngis sone of skellye, the tayl of the four sonnis of aymon, the tail of the brig of matribil, the tail of syr euan, arthours knycht, rauf coilyear, the seige of millan, gauen and gallogras, lancelot du lac, Arthour knycht he raid on nycht vith gyltin spur and candil lycht, the tail of floremond of albanye that sleu the dragon be the see, the tail of syr valtil the bald leslye, the tail of the pure tynt, claryades and maliades, Arthour of litil bertangye, robene hude and litil ihone, the merveillis of mandiueil" and many, many more, to conclude with "Orpheus kyng of portingal, the tayl of the goldin appil, the tail of the thre veird systirs, the tayl quhou that dedalus maid the laborynth to keip the monstir minotaurus, the taul quhou kyng midas gat tua asses' luggis on his hede be cause of his auereis". After that, we seem to be on fairly familiar ground when we read in *In Memoriam James Joyce*:

> We have of course studied thoroughly
> Allspach, English, and the others who have written
> On 'Psychological Response to Unknown Proper Names',
> Downey on 'Individual Differences in Reaction to the
>   Word-in-Itself',
> Bullough on 'The Perceptive Problem
> In the Aesthetic Appreciation of Single Colours',
> Myers on 'Individual Differences in Listening to Music',
> And Eleanor Rowland on 'The Psychological Experiences
> Connected with Different Parts of Speech'.
> Know Plato in 'Cratylus' on the rhetorical value
> Of different classes of consonants, and Rossigneus's
> 'Essai sur l'audition colorée et sa valeur aestétique',
> Jones on the 'Effect of Letters and Syllables in Publicity',
> Roblee and Washburn on 'The Affective Value of Articulate
>   Sounds',
> And Givler on 'The Psycho-physiological Effect
> Of the Elements of Speech in Relation to Poetry',

—and so on for a further two pages. There is a joy here in merely rolling out the titles as well as a response to the sheer amount of learning contained in the books.* This respect for learning, this love of the polymath, this exhibitionist glorying in the naming of sources of knowledge, is a very Scottish characteristic. It is recorded in the folklore of the Scots dominie and even in the language of Scottish student debaters — at least at the time when I was a student. It was Professor Nichol Smith who pointed out that only in a Scottish university, at an undergraduate debating

---

*
>   "So beyond all that is heteroeptic, holophrastic
>   Macaronic, philomathic, psychopetal
>   Jerqueing every idioticon
>   Comes this supreme paraleipsis."
The macaronic is also a Scottish tradition.

society, would a student rise and begin his remarks by saying: "I rise to homologate the sentiments of the previous speaker". Perhaps this tradition is dead now, but the tradition of learned language and polymathic ambitions was certainly still very much alive in the Scottish universities in the 1930s. (I hope the Philomathic Society is still flourishing at Edinburgh: I myself was a member of its sister society, the Diagnostic.)

And then of course there is Sir Thomas Urquhart, the 17th century master of verbal bravura, who wrote a book called *Pantochronochanon* tracing his father's descent from Adam and his mother's from Eve, and another called *Logopandecteision* which put forth a scheme for a universl language. But Urquhart's greatest claim to fame is his masterly translation of Rabelais, in which he made marvellous use of his characteristically Scottish polymathic verbal virtuosity. The fact that he is said to have died of a fit of uncontrollable laughter on hearing of the Restoration of Charles II to the throne emphasises the comic element in this tradition of polysyllabification, cataloguing, and general verbal exuberance. MacDiarmid is thoroughly recognisable in this context.

MacDiarmid is himself aware of all this, and sees himself in a Scottish tradition, though on different occasions he has concentrated on different aspects of the tradition. The aspect which he has most consistently emphasised, and which he feels illustrated most clearly in his own work and character, is that incorrigible dualism, that yoking together of opposites, that Gregory Smith called the "Caledonian antisyzigy". The term itself in the Urquhart tradition, a piece of playful pedantry, but the diagnosis was offered seriously by Gregory Smith and accepted seriously by MacDiarmid. "There is more in the Scottish antithesis of the real and the fantastic," he has written, "than is to be explained by the familiar rules of rhetoric. The sudden jostling of contraries seems to preclude any relationship by literary suggestion. The one invades the other without warning. They are the 'polar twins' of the Scottish Muse." MacDiarmid is haunted by the Caledonian antisyzygy, and use the term again and again. He wants to pack the whole world into his poetry, he tells us in *Lucky Poet*, and this comprehensive aim, he argued, "has been the conscious or unconscious aim of my people throughout the ages; it is what lies behind their world-ranging propensities, the endless capacity for simultaneously entertaining the most diverse interests, the encyclopaedic character (elsewhere dismissed as 'the Scotsman's pedantry — there is always a dominie at his elbow') of their intellectual curiosity, the polymathic powers that manifest themselves so markedly in the field of Scottish biography, from the wandering scholars downwards to our own day, and, too — lest anything should escape them! — behind that Caledonian Antisyzygy with which I deal in a later chapter." In a later chapter he relates the Caledonian antisyzygy to what he calls "the Chinese Tin-Tang dichotomy". He goes on: "It is not an easy relationship. It entails unceasing conflict, a conflict not of extermination, but rather akin to that state in biology known as hostile symbiosis, and a counterpart also of the fact that in higher animals we usually find a well-developed symmetry and muscles, of which the activities oppose the results of the activity of other muscles. Such muscles are called *antagonists*. If two *antagonists* of equal strength are stimulated equally, no macroscopic effects of the stimulation of both muscles results. If one of the antagonists is stronger than the other, the macroscopic effects of the stimulation of both muscles results not in some general convulsion, but in one-sided action of the stronger muscle. Obviously these results are the necessary consequence of *structure on ·different levels*. Professor Henrick's terms, *differential dynamogenic cortical influence* and *differential activation*, cover all known facts, a selection of which, in their particular Scottish form, I call the Caledonian Antisyzygy." (Notice that by now he has wholly appropriated Gregory Smith's term.)

I began by noting some of the contradictions in MacDiarmid's work and in his attitude to himself as a poet. The point I am now making is twofold: firstly, that these contradictions are bound up with something identifiably Scottish, and secondly that MacDiarmid not only recognises this but has spent a great deal of time and energy trying to explore its meaning both for himself and for the Scottish character. In his later work MacDiarmid has carried into his poetry combined impulses which operated separately in his earlier poetry. And he has carried into poetry qualities which, though they emerged earlier in many aspects of Scottish life and letters, did not represent a continuous tradition in

Scottish poetry. As Kenneth Buthlay has pointed out in his admirable study of MacDiarmid, "the traditional short lyric is the only unbroken tradition in Scots verse" and he has shown how in his early Scots lyrics MacDiarmid could use these simple, traditional stanza forms to achieve powerful cosmic effects. It is largely by the juxtaposing of short lyrics that he achieves the comprehensively reverberating meaning of *A Drunk Man*. Later, when he works not through the microcosm but the macrocosm, he abandons the traditional lyric measures to employ immense verse paragraphs which can contain without strain not only exhaustive catalogues but massive prose quotations. It is interesting that MacDiarmid has shown little interest, so far as I am aware, in the heavier, more complex stanza forms which Scottish poetry has sometimes used — the stanza of "The Cherry and the Slae", for example, or of "The Solsequium". Some of the poems in *Stony Limits* are in stanzas of considerable richness and weight, but for the most part MacDiarmid seems to have preferred to move straight from the simple lyric form to the large unstructured verse-paragraph.

Let me conclude by concentrating for a moment on MacDiarmid's later poetry, if only because in what I have written about him in the past I have mostly concentrated on his earlier work and because I think the later poetry is frequently misread. The Scots share with the Americans a feeling for a kind of rhetoric that hovers between verse and prose and easily accommodates both. This feeling emerges splendidly in Walt Whitman, who is in many ways more similar to MacDiarmid than any other poet of the English language. It is Whitman who once wrote, and MacDiarmid who quoted from him: "The true use for the imaginative faculty of modern times is to give ultimate vivification to facts, to science, and to common lives." Whitman, like MacDiarmid, sought the poetry of facts. And both poets could communicate their sense of the individuality of creatures and things by *naming* them, and sought to arrive at the ultimate vision of reality through the intensity of detailed individual perceptions.

I too and many a time cross'd the river of old,
Watched the Twelfth-month sea-gulls, saw them high in the
air floating with motionless wings, oscillating their
bodies,

Saw how the glistening yellow lit up parts of their bodies and
 left the rest in strong shadow,
Saw the slow-wheeling circles and the gradual edging
 toward the south,
Saw the reflection of the summer sky in the water,
Had my eyes dazzled by the shimmering track of beams,
Look'd at the fine centrifugal spokes of light round the shape
 of my head in the sunlit water,
Look'd on the haze on the hills southward and south-
 westward,
Look'd on the vapour as it flew in fleeces tinged with violet,
Look'd toward the lower bay to notice the vessels arriving,
Saw their approach, saw aboard those that were near me,
Saw the white sails of schooners and sloops, saw the ships at
 anchor,
The sailors at work in the rigging or out astride the spars,
The round masts, the swinging motion of the hulls,
 the slender, serpentine pennants, . . .

That is Whitman. And this is MacDiarmid:

As I walk this Autumn and observe
The birch tremulously pendulous in jewels of cairngorm,
The sauch, the osier, and the crack-willow
Of the beaten gold of Australia;
The sycamore in rich straw-gold;
The elm bowered in saffron;
The oak in flecks of salmon gold;
The beeches huge torches of living orange.

Billow upon billow of autumnal foliage
From the sheer high bank glass themselves
Past the ebon and silver front that floods freely
Past the single shelves.
I linger where a crack-willow slants across the stream,
Its olive leaves slashed with fine gold.
Beyond the willow a young beech
Blazes almost blood-red,
Vying in intensity with the glowing cloud of crimson
That hangs about the purple bole of a gean
Higher up the brae face.

And yonder, the lithe green-gray bole of ash, with its boughs
Draped in the cinnamon-brown lace of samara.

81

(And I remember how in April upon its bare twigs
The flowers came in ruffs like the unshorn ridges
Upon a French poodle—like a dull mulberry at first,
Before the first feathery fronds
Of the long-stalked, finely-poised, seven-fingered leaves)—
Even the robin hushes his song
In these gold pavilions.

The two voices are surely very similar. In both examples the poet is using his senses in order to read facts. The sensing, reading and recording of facts is something quite different from the mere turning of a camera eye on one's environment. In the precision of the recording lies the wonder of the individual reality; in the accumulation of individual recordings lies the sense of the mystery of all that is outside oneself. Whitman wanted to embrace the universe, while MacDiarmid wants to *relate* to neutral otherness. Yet though their aims are different, their means are almost identical. Neither of them can get rid of the observer and the rememberer. ("And I remember how in April upon its bare twigs. . . .") Yet both have a tremendous sense of the otherness of all that the observer observes. Both poets use an intensely personal idiom, even though one of them seeks the impersonality of the poetry of facts. Both remained outside and beyond their poems in the stance that Whitman described:

. . . before all my arrogant poems the real Me stands yet
    untouch'd, untold, altogether unreach'd,
Withdrawn far, mocking me with mock-congratulatory signs
    and bows,
With peals of distant ironical laughter at every word I have
    written
Pointing in silence to these songs, and then to the sand beneath.

"Yet hae I Silence left, the croon o' a'."

I set out to reflect on MacDiarmid's relation to the Scottish literary tradition. I find myself ending with an American poet. That is the measure of MacDiarmid's comprehensiveness. The Rose of all the world is indeed for him; but always he stands in Scotland to contemplate it and sense its meaning. "Give me a place to stand and I will move the world," said Archimedes. MacDiarmid *has* his place to stand, and he *has* moved the world. The place where he stands is Scotland.

The Language Problem in Hugh MacDiarmid's Work ,

DAVID MURISON

Poetry is essentially creative artistry with language. When the poet has added another dimension to a word, linked it with others in unusual juxtapositions to produce new images, or often simply used it for its sound or literary associations to suggest sensuous impressions or new aspects of its meaning, he achieves not a little of his success. Great poets like Spenser or Shakespeare in English have had an inborn interest in words, and this is no less true of Scots poets like Dunbar or Douglas or Burns. Furthermore, since the 17th century Scots have been more or less bilingual and bilingualism in itself sharpens one's sensitivity to language and broadens one's linguistic base considerably. Add to this the fact that the Scots have an acute historical sense which may derive partly from their mixed linguistic background, and are by educational tradition bookish. They find fascination in dictionaries, encyclopaedias, textbooks and the like. William Soutar for instance tells how he went through Chambers's *Twentieth Century Dictionary* from end to end and there is good evidence that he consulted those parts of the *Scottish National Dictionary* published in his lifetime.

About MacDiarmid's bookishness there can be no doubt at all. We know the story of the Langholm library and its 12,000 volumes read by the young Grieve, and we see the first fruits of this and his further reading in *Northern Numbers* and his pre-1922 writings, as in:

> And now Aldebaran in the keen dawn dies,
> Vega and Althair from the kindling zenith pass,

which smells somewhat of Shelley, and "A Moment in Eternity", which incidentally in theme faintly fore-

83

shadows *A Drunk Man*. Already he is exploiting the abstruser vocabulary of English, scientific and psychological terminology, some of it no doubt from the popular writings of the time, articles and reviews in periodicals, and also by browsing in the dictionary, which Dr Ruth McQuillan has identified as being again Chambers's. In *Northern Numbers* he was still obviously under the influence of the imagists, the symbolists, and all the rest of them, Yeats, Pound, Eliot and Joyce, and though in the three series he gives progressively more space to younger poets, most of the newcomers, including himself, were writing in English.

The story of his sudden volte-face on Scots, which he had previously dismissed as effete, has often been told, most fully by Duncan Glen in *Hugh MacDiarmid and the Scottish Renaissance*. But when a poet tells us in one breath that the Scots dialect is no longer adequate for poetry, and in the next is claiming it against allcomers as a *sine qua non* of a spiritual renaissance in Scotland, we naturally seek an explanation. The question is easier to ask than to answer. Glen suggests the influence of Lewis Spence, who tried out a kind of what he called "gentlemen's" Middle Scots in his poems, rather more successfully than he gave himself credit for, pastiche though it was, and Grieve praised it highly in *Contemporary Scottish Studies*. Spence later gave the attempt up and recanted. About this time too, as Glen points out, Grieve was beginning to take up Scottish Nationalism, as in his manifesto in *Scottish Chapbook* in August 1922, but whatever other influences were at work, the chief one seems undoubtedly to be from books. He tells us himself how he came across Sir James Wilson's study, *Lowland Scotch*, one of the first twentieth-century works on Scots and one especially devoted to the treatment of idiom; and while Soutar says again, "Poetry makes the words, not the words the poetry", MacDiarmid in *Lucky Poet* says the exact opposite: "The act of poetry is not an idea gradually shaping itself in words, but deriving entirely from words — and it was in fact in this way that I wrote all the best of my Scots poems." It was out of the transition from the previous prissy attitude to "the Doric" to the theorisings about the Scots language that Hugh MacDiarmid was born, the prosateur Grieve pushing the poet MacDiarmid ahead of him, presumably to draw the fire of the critics. But he was obviously getting down to his rationale in the deductive way common to France and Scotland of producing an idea and then hunting around for arguments to back it up. In this case he found one to hand in Gregory Smith's characterisation of the tension of opposites common in Scottish literature as the "Caledonian antisyzygy". But even more important was his close study of Jamieson's Scottish Dictionary which resulted in *Sangschaw*. Of the many reviews of this book probably the most perceptive and sympathetic, if puristic from the language point of view, was that in the *Times Literary Supplement*. The writer opined that to reform Scots poetry involved creating a new poetic diction based on Lothian Scots but admitting words from any quarter, and pointed to the methods used by Aasen in the Landsmaal movement in Norway. This line of talk was completely up MacDiarmid's street; he quotes liberally from it in his *Scottish Studies* and it must have sent him straight to a study of the Norwegian situation which surfaced later in his poem "Gairmscoile" in *Penny Wheep*.

Fortified by this suggestive review and with the fine scientific-looking polysyllable "antisyzygy" in his armour, Grieve goes on to call it "a distinguishing faculty . . . potentially expressible in the vernacular to which it belongs", and speaks of "the possibility of a great Scottish Literary Renaissance . . . from the resources that lie latent in the vernacular", "the unexplored possibilities of vernacular expression", "a *vis comica* in the Doric and its potential uprising". Readers may note "possibility" and "potential", two words much favoured by Grieve throughout his long literary career, expressing essentially the faith that is the substance of things hoped for and the evidence of things not seen, the faith that kept him going through a hard and difficult life, and that survived his failure to turn it into a science. Indeed we may say that had he succeeded in this, he would have ceased to be a poet.

An idealist seeks fortification from analogies and there were plenty of these in the many post-war language revivals going on in Europe and elsewhere in the 1920s. MacDiarmid took comfort from a paper given in 1924 to the Scottish Vernacular Circle of London by Sir William Craigie, a patriotic Scot, editor of the *Oxford English Dictionary*, who dealt with this very "potential" of revival of Scots, drawing comparisons with Norway, Iceland, the

Faeroes, Friesland, and so on, and possibly having his subject suggested to him by the appearance of *Sangschaw* the year before. This notion of Scotland participating in an international movement was also grist to the poet's mill, as he had already revolted vehemently from the provincial rut which Scottish literature and language had got into, and in this language restoral he saw another justification for his theory.

We must now look at MacDiarmid in practice. A chance remark in the *Chapbook* early in 1923 shows that he had been delving in Jamieson and had been struck "by the moral resemblance of the Dictionary to Joyce's *Ulysses*", whatever "moral" may mean in that context. Some day some bronze-bowelled scholar will undertake the indispensable task of producing an annotated supplement to the Grieve-Aitken text, tracing the myriad-headed vocabulary, quotations and allusions to their sources. But we may already get some idea by dipping here and there into *Sangschaw* and *Penny Wheep*. The task is not altogether straightforward, as we cannot be entirely certain how much he kept of his own native tongue of Langholm. In conversation his normal speech was almost entirely in English, and to questions about where he got this or that word he most frequently referred one to a book. In the "Watergaw" the first line "Ae weet forenicht i' the yow-trummle" seems to be his own but he may have heard it from a local shepherd; "antrin" is a rare word in the Borders, though common in the North-east and he may have picked it up in Montrose, but it may have come from Jamieson's "of a kind met with singly and occasionally or seldom". He seems to extend its sense to "eerie, unearthly", for which he was taken to task by the *TLS* reviewer. "There was nae reek i' the laverock's hoose" is a Perthshire saying recorded in Wilson's book. In the next poem "There's teuch sauchs growin' i' the Reuch Heuch Hauch" is a Hawick tongue-twister quoted by Sir James Murray in his *Dialect of the Southern Counties of Scotland*, which MacDiarmid certainly knew. But the full quotation is not there but, supplied by Murray, in Vol. V of Ellis's massive work *On the Pronunciation of English*, a rather inaccessible book for MacDiarmid, one would have thought. So he may again have picked it up on the streets of Hawick as a local byword.

Handlawhile in the same poem is in Jamieson, Murray and Watson's *Roxburghshire Word-book*, and is still known in Border dialect, but *amplefeyst* died out long ago and could have come only from Jamieson. In "I heard Christ sing" *quhile* is spelt medieval fashion but not used in its medieval sense of "until", and *wersh* has its modern sense, deriving from a misunderstanding, of "bitter". "Overinzievar" on the other hand, though its title is the name of a farm near Dunfermline, has the current vocabulary of the Border area. In "Ex Vermibus" the poet has had recourse to Watson's *Word-book*, where many of the words, *whuram, spatril, airel*, are marked as obsolete in his area, and he has lifted Watson's definitions verbatim into his glossary; *back-lill* in "Au Clair de la Lune" is from "Wandering Willie's Tale" in Scott's *Redgauntlet*, either direct or via Jamieson; *keethin-sicht* is an Aberdeenshire salmon-fishing term from Jamieson; *luchts* is from the Ettrick Shepherd via Jamieson; *reid e'en* is a North-East form of *ruid e'en*, again from Jamieson; "Crowdieknowe", possibly because it is Langholm born and bred, is in straight Border speech; "The Eemis Stane" on the other hand is quite synthetic Scots; the striking first line "I' the how-dumb-deid o' the cauld hairst nicht" is from a story in *Blackwood's Magazine* for November 1820, quoted by Jamieson; *eemis* is an Angus and North-east word, long obsolete; so also are the evocative *yowdendrift*, driven snow, and *hazelraw*, lichen; and much the same applies to "The Frightened Bride". "Country Life", being more domestic altogether, passes for Border dialect, except for *goloch* which may have been picked up in Montrose, *fochin*, which is from Wilson's *Dialect*, and English *fly* for *flee* for the sake of the rhyme.

The same cursory analysis of *Penny Wheep* gives us very similar results. Here also is the same close study of Jamieson. The first verse of "Blind Man's Luck" is devised from two consecutive pages of O in the dictionary: the first line of the next poem, "The Currant Bush", "There's no a ressim to the fore", is again from the same source, quoting a Northern Scots usage; *daberlack* in "Hungry Waters" is another Moray Firth word; "white as a loan soup" in "Sabine" is from Kelly's *Scottish Proverbs* of 1721 via Jamieson; the first verse of "In Mysie's Bed" is from Galt's novel *Ringan Gilhaize*, possibly mediated through Wright's *English Dialect*

87

Dictionary; and in "Morning", "like a paddle-doo i' the raim-pig" is adapted from Gregor's *Folk-Lore of North-East Scotland*, but again through Jamieson as the altered spelling shows. The fine lyric "Empty Vessel" — some think it's his best — owes its first line to a song by Allan Ramsay about 1730; the last verse of "Supper to God" is adapted from Sempill's "Blythesome Wedding" of the 17th century, while in "Gairmscoile" the frequent alliterative passages are achieved by dipping into Jamieson at the appropriate letters, as *dorbel, drob, drochlin, drutling, drings, drotes*, etc. He did the same thing later on in "Water Music". One notices incidentally that some words reappear several times, e.g. *skinkle, datchie, nesh, eelie, keethin, eisen, undeemis*, as if we were seeing the rudimentary beginnings of a new and rather heterogeneous poetic diction, and some of these were in fact taken up by MacDiarmid's imitators. But what is conspicuously rare is word-invention. I have noted *wan-shogin* in "Sea-Serpent" and there may be one or two more, but whatever the theory about the need to develop Scots on the model of Landsmaal from Old Norse "with words and idioms from all the dialects and all the periods", in practice MacDiarmid sticks cautiously to Jamieson and rejects usages earlier than the 18th century. *Skrymmorie* from Gavin Douglas's *Palice of Honour* in "Gairmscoile" is exceptional. Though Grieve, as we have seen, at first applauded Spence's experiments in imitation of Middle Scots, by 1928 he had started to refine his theory somewhat, perhaps in the light of his practice. He now speaks of the dangers of pastiche and we get an early note of politicising in the argument that Middle Scots literature has upper-class associations and "ignored a great mass of popular words and idioms", an idea stemming from an erroneous assertion in Gregory Smith's *Specimens of Middle Scots*, which he wisely abandoned in his later *Scottish Literature*.

Space prevents a close analysis of *A Drunk Man* but it can be said briefly that as the style itself is attuned to the colloquial incoherent speech of a drunk man talking to himself, with a few lyrical passages interspersed, of which one or two may have been written earlier, so the Scots has been considerably modified too. For about the first quarter of the poem the language is with few exceptions a kind of common vernacular such as any Scots speaker might use today. Towards the middle of the poem Jamieson has been pressed into service again with *coutribat, ganien, corbaudie, gaadies, corneigh, munkie, knool,* and so on, even to following Jamieson's slips, as in *cree legs* for *creel eggs*. Again medieval Scots is rare, *belth* and *swelth, ramel* and *fullyery* are from Douglas out of Jamieson, *foudrie* seems to be his own adaptation of French *foudre,* unless of course he got it all mixed up with the Orkney legal term *foudrie* for a stewartry; but this procedure peters out and the last third and a bit more of the poem, with more argument and metaphysical speculation, reverts to the everday Scots of the beginning. There is such a variety and intermingling of the modes in the poem that it is hard to categorise his procedure precisely, but in a rough and ready way one might say that the more lyrical the passage the more chance of synthetic Scots being found in it.

With *To Circumjack Cencrastus* (1930) the lyrical impulse, often as satire, is still strong and stanzaic and rhyme forms prevail. As in *A Drunk Man,* the poet speaks more *in propria persona,* arguing a great deal with himself, and so likewise the language is all the more conversational and pedestrian, the memorable phrase is scarcer as the words themselves become more copious and at times even garrulous; in other words the verbal discipline imposed in the earlier work begins to break up and sometimes, one fears, the thought with it. Among his "curses" incidentally is a malediction "on my double life and double tongue — guid Scots wi' English a' hamstrung" and welcoming the evening "when I wha needs use English a' the day, win back to the true language o' my thochts". For all that, quite a proportion of the poems in *Cencrastus* are in English and there are still more in *Scots Unbound* (1932). But it contains the well-known "Water Music", located in Langholm, and a linguistic tour de force out of Jamieson, where pleasure in words and their sounds and their onomatopoeic force *per se* takes precedence of their meaning, and "Tarras" is expanded imagery after the same mould. As a broad generalisation we might say that his stanzaic verse is in Scots, as for instance in the "First Hymn to Lenin" published in 1931. But in *Stony Limits* (1934) the longer discursive and expository pieces , "On a Raised Beach", "The Progress of Poetry" and "Lament for the Great Music", are in polysyllabic English, with scraps of Gaelic in the last. Not unnaturally, "The Ballad of the Holy Grail", with its curious

89

echoes of the Edda poem Hymiskvija, being a "ballad", is in Scots; so too are the "Shetland Lyrics", when contact with a richly dialect-speaking area no doubt fostered his linguistic interests, and he had obviously, from his representation of Shetland words in "On a Raised Beach", been studying Jakobsen's *Lectures on Dialect in Shetland*. "Balefire Loch" he himself calls an exercise of delight in the Scots sense of colour, and adds a glossary partly from Jamieson and partly from Chambers's *Dictionary*, one of the first Scots poems incidentally to incorporate scientific terminology.

With the "Second Hymn to Lenin" (1935) English takes over and there is the significant fact, pointed out by Glen, that the more innocuous parts of the suppressed "Ode to all Rebels", written originally in Scots, appear here in an Anglicised version. English from then on prevails in almost all the rest of his work, though the rather chaotic relationship between composition date and publication date leaves room for error. We know for instance that "Off the Coast of Feideland" was written in June 1936 (from *A Kist of Whistles* (1943), otherwise an English collection), and here the influence of Shetland speech has produced one of his most vivid and sincerely human poems. There is yet more Shetlandic in the sequence "Let us arise", but in a purely lexical context, in a poem which is itself a virtuoso piece of linguistics, source untraced, with allusions to Sanskrit, Greek, Welsh, Navaho, Hebrew, and a lot more, all of it a measure of the new stance taken up by our poet and of the aim he set himself of trying to universalise the particular, to see all things *sub specie aeternitatis*, and this meant in practice trying to comprehend modern science in all its multifarious complexity and to find a language to express it.

The theory was that some kind of universal scientific language would have to evolve to fill the bill, not a kind of esperanto, but rather an illimitable extension and mélange of national vocabularies to encompass the exploding bounds of human knowledge. One wonders what place Scots would have in this galère, and we find that in MacDiarmid's practice, as opposed to his theory, it has almost no place at all. The rest of his work, a few personal and lyrical interpolations apart, is in English, and of a kind often more abstruse than his Jamiesonian Scots, with great slabs of psychology, physiology, geology, linguistics, etc., etc.

from textbooks, reviews and the like, sometimes from untranslated foreign sources. This may indeed be science, of a kind, but is it poetry? The purpose of this essay is fortunately not to answer that question, but one is inclined to agree with Iain Crichton Smith that if we want systematic information or even argument on any particular science, we would be as well to read the textbooks for them rather than have them mediated in this second- or even third-hand hit-or-miss fashion. MacDiarmid poses yet another problem for himself in "Let us arise" when he says:

> "I am troubled by the tendency in science today
> For the law to be derived from limited groups of observations
> Rather than from the wide generalisations of understanding."

And I suppose so are many of us, but this is harking back to the great days of the 17th and 18th centuries when philosophy reigned supreme and subsumed such natural sciences as then existed, a state of affairs exemplified by the Scottish university term "natural philosophy" for physics. And this is essentially a metaphysical or epistemological problem, not a linguistic one.

There can be little doubt that the transition from Scots to English corresponds to some kind of upheaval in his own thinking, though not a sudden one, as we have certain intimations of scientific didacticism as early as *Northern Numbers*, but one which came to a head about 1933 — another symptom may be the fact that he joined the Communist Party in 1934 — as if he were now polarising his attitudes. It seems he had come to a full conviction of his mission, possibly on a hint from his oft-quoted dictum of Lenin that the true Communist has to assimilate "all that is of value in the more than two thousand years of development of human thought". But I suspect that there was some psychological trauma behind it, if we are to judge by the unusual bitterness of the introduction to *Lucky Poet*.

MacDiarmid never really clearly or satisfactorily explained his changeover from Scots to English. We have the statement in his preface to *A Lap of Honour* in 1967: "It is believed in some quarters that in recent years I have ceased to write in the aggrandised Scots in which I wrote my early lyrics in the Twenties. The fact is that after the success of these, I found, like Heine, I could no longer go on with that sort of thing but required to break up the unity of the lyric and introduce new material on different levels of significance." For MacDiarmid this is a remarkably laconic observation and does not tell us very much not already obvious; what is more, it deals with the form and content of his new work rather than with its language. Why not in Scots, after all that he had said about its potential and indeed had achieved with it in his lyrics? Away back in the palmy days of 1925, when he was still speaking well of some of his later bêtes noires, he says of Edwin Muir that "he would have done better work still if he had not contented himself with ballad Scots but had employed a full braid Scots canon of his own devising based upon a *de novo* consideration of the entire resources of the language on the one hand, and its tractability to the most significant processes and purposes of ultra-modern literature on the other"; and he then quotes Muir as saying that "since English became the literary language of Scotland there has been no Scots imaginative writer who has attained greatness in the first or even the second rank through the medium of English. Scott achieves classical prose only when he wrote in the Scottish dialect, as in 'Wandering Willie's Tale'," adding himself: "That is the choice — either go back to Scots, or to be content to be indefinitely no more than third-rate in an English tradition which is declining."

But Muir backtracked on Scots in his famous chapter in *Scott and Scotland* in 1936 in saying that the predicament of the Scottish writer in a Scotland that has lost its cultural identity and tradition will not be solved by writing poems in Scots, because for the modern Scot, Scots is the language of emotion and English of the intellect and only when emotion and intellect can be integrated in one language can a whole literature arise. Though in a sense MacDiarmid had been saying the same thing with a different emphasis on the need to extend Scots, Muir, like Spence before him, seemed to be publicly throwing up the sponge. His were discouraging words and to MacDiarmid an unforgivable stab in the back. But the stark and uncomfortable fact is that in practice MacDiarmid's own poetic career would seem to corroborate them; which no doubt made Muir's dictum even more unpalatable, though by his own work in the period 1922-34 MacDiarmid had done more to improve it than any of his contemporaries.

The linguistic task which he set himself was indeed a formidable one of trying to convey the salient facts about modern science and its relevance to the human condition and to the poet's own complex metaphysical speculations about the universe, all in a language that had suffered arrested development four centuries before and had never gone through the process, as English, French, German, etc., had, of acquiring a scientific vocabulary, for science as we know it begins in the 17th century, when Scots had practically ceased to be a national language and was disintegrating into a series of rural dialects. Early Scottish men of science, like Napier, Sibbald and the Gregories, used Latin; by the 18th century the problem had been solved for them by the breakdown of Scots and the adoption in Scotland for all formal and official and academic purposes of contemporary English prose. To revive Scots for this would mean condensing into a human lifetime the work that had taken at least twelve generations for English.

Given his postulates about the unexplored riches and potential of Scots at least as a language for intellectual poetry, MacDiarmid had to set about extending its range and vocabulary, resuscitating its decayed idiom and systematising its grammar which was becoming more and more confused with English. For the first two he naturally turned to the dictionary, though as we have seen he used them in a pretty conservative and selective manner; for the grammar his idea was apparently to leave it to Sir William Craigie, though I am sure Craigie was never consulted in the matter; and MacDiarmid himself was no Aasen in grammar.

This is not a new problem for poetry. Lucretius, who is often mentioned in critiques on MacDiarmid, had the same trouble in his poetic version of atomic philosophy with *patrii sermonis egestas*, and Dante had to expound scholaticism in the dialect of his native Tuscany, which indeed his genius helped to make the classical language of Italy. MacDiarmid of course was not so constrained, in being free-ranging in his themes and bilingual in his speech. But he deliberately chose the impoverished and more difficult language for his vision of man and the cosmos. And it must be

93

remembered that although he must have been brought up to speak Langholm, it is not in his native Langholm that he writes, despite much loose talk as if it were. He had to puzzle his language out from the dictionaries and his own reading. It is an artificial construct and there must have been a good deal of midnight oil spent on it—he speaks somewhere of having to think out such problems as what the Scots word for "motor-car" would have been if Scots had survived, as a full language—a rather odd task for a poet, one might think, though it *does*, I suppose, give some exercise in the use of imagery. Later on, when Norman MacCaig had appeared on the scene as MacDiarmid's familiar and criticised the dangers of rummaging in dictionaries for forceful words, incidentally quoting a rather bad example from Maurice Lindsay, we have the impressive spectacle of MacDiarmid making excuses for Lindsay to MacCaig, which is certainly the bard in an unusual light. But there is at least this small advantage in consulting a dictionary in that you learn what words really and not apocalyptically mean and the limits of their associations and connotations; you are rid of superfluous ornament and fuzzy semantics; what imagery there is, is spare, relevant and precise, and the whole exercise is astringent, intellectual and anti-romantic.

MacCaig's second criticism,* that Scots is deficient in imagery, MacDiarmid dismisses as a mere passing fashion. "Poetry must be direct and stripped of ornament; the direct method is in keeping with our whole national republican and radical traditions, and it is this vein of 'unfigured' Scots that must be strenuously cultivated" — this is in tribute to Fergusson for his excellence in this style. So the argument here is put on a national, almost nationalist, footing, and not unconnected is the further argument, carried into the enemy's camp, that English has grown bloated and effete and useless for creative purposes or for embodying the poetry of the new age. For the modern English poet it needs injections of obsolete words, dialect, and specialised vocabulary; the Scots poet has his own solution to hand in Scots, "a great untapped repository of the pre-Renaissance or anti-Renaissance potentialities which

* Norman McCaig (sic): "Image and Makar", *The Scots Review*, vol. 9. no. 4, July 1948.

94

English has progressively forgone"; but if that implies Middle Scots, as one might be led to think, there is, as we have seen, surprisingly little of it in his work. And of course when it really came to the poetry of the new age, we find Scots being abandoned in favour of English, synthetic as the English itself may have been.

But in 1925 theory and practice were still going hand in hand and he was giving advance notice of *A Drunk Man* where "the intention has been to show that Braid Scots is adaptable to all kinds of poetry . . . the distinctive elements in Scottish psychology which depend for their effective expression upon the hitherto unrevealed potentialities of Braid Scots." Certainly *A Drunk Man* is a most remarkable attempt to prove it, and here two points are worth making. The burden of the thought and the symbolism, which is very complex and intricately developed, is lightened for the reader in two ways, first by employing the "direct unfigured utterance" (with exceptions of course); difficult ideas have to be condensed and reduced and the abstractions made as concrete as possible since the language is now the language of matters of fact. All this imposes the same discipline of clarity and verbal economy (which of course is by no means the same as semantic simplicity) and dramatic intensity at which Burns was a master ("Scots since has tint his maikless vir") and which are the outstanding characteristics of MacDiarmid's earlier lyrics so that the very limitations of Scots are in many ways a source of their strength. The other point is the device of the drunken Scots farmer, an extremely well-read farmer of course, as the poet's mouthpiece. Here the drunkenness makes the sudden antisyzygies plausible; the Eskdale (or is it Angus?) farmer, being none of your Lothian latifundian gentry, would naturally speak Scots and so the conventional reader's reaction of surprise and possibly irritation at finding abstruse metaphysical and psychological speculation in conversational Scots is deftly sidetracked. Linguistically this is the same device used by Galt and Gibbon in introducing an good deal of Scots in their narrative through the mouths of a veteran minister or a small-town baillie or a superannuated laird or the communal voice of a rural village.

A Drunk Man is the high-water mark of the use of Scots by MacDiarmid just as some would say it marks also the summit of his poetic achievement. One has to fight against the penchant, innate in a Scot and undoubtedly tied up with our literary and linguistic traditions of the last three hundred years, for the short simple lyrical and balladic mode, which was certainly getting into a rut and which MacDiarmid fought tooth and nail to change. His methods were basically sound in trying to recover the fuller canon of Scots, to which the dictionary was not an entirely satisfactory short-cut, and it is a pity he made so little use of Middle Scots vocabulary and idiom, though this would have involved a closer study of texts than he could give. But within the limits imposed by himself his touch is remarkably sure. No doubt he had his native knowledge of Scots to help him but there is an uncanny skill in his manipulation of his dictionary words which are fitted into their contexts with great felicity. Artificial as the process is bound to be, it is amply vindicated by its results; there is a new creative force at work and the Scots tongue has again as under Burns, who had the same flair for language, been given a new lease of life and has been successfully extended from the local and personal and trivial to the universal by another humanist.

But if there was in truth a kind of psychological bouleverse-ment after this period, which he hints at in the 1953 edition of *A Drunk Man*, the humanity of his earlier work is replaced by a polymathic pedagogical propagandist obsession; his passion for intellectualising poetry, which in effect turns out to be a rather hotch-potch exposition of popular contemporary science, orthodox and heterodox alike, arises from a confusion of knowledge with understanding, a mistake to which Scots with their bookishness are particularly prone, and about which MacDiarmid, as we have seen, had already expressed fears; and the language of science is a universal mechanised sort of jargon based chiefly on Latin and Greek structure, in which indeed native English has little place, let alone Scots. So long as the common human predicament, in which he himself shared, interested him, he can speak out of the language of his subconscious, his childhood, his imagination, his experience and sympathy, and Scots comes naturally to his hand. When he thinks he has found the answer in informed speculation, which is solitary, austere, and the business of the philosopher, he turns to English, which was basically an alien speech to him (and he was always stressing the degree of alienation); and it is common knowledge how appalling his English could at times be, whether in prose or poetry, so that in some of his work it is not possible to tell the difference. To put it in another way he became so much the less a poet. Edwin Muir perhaps saw the danger better than he did. But there can be no doubt about his achievement with Scots.

Sangschaw begins in fine style with medieval symbolic colours and ballad echoes: "Mars is braw in cramasie, Venus in a green silk goun"; and ends appropriately on a homely note: "Earth, thou bonnie broukit bairn", which came via Jamieson and an editorial note by Burns from an 18th century folk-song. There is the historical phrase of Scotland's War of Independence brilliantly incorporated into the allusion to Judas: "I wot he did God's will wha made Siccar o' Calvary". The intensity of vision could not be better brought out in words than in lines like: "A watergaw wi' its chitterin licht ayont the onding", or "Owre't the forkit lichtnin' flees like a cleisher o' a whup", or "That licht-lookin' craw o' a body, the moon, Sits on the fower cross-win's peerin' a' roon", with its added touch of humour; or in the vividness of "The Diseased Salmon". Bright too is the ring of words in "My eerie memories fa' Like a yowdendrift. Lie a yowdendrift so's I couldna read The words cut oot i' the stane"; and in *Penny Wheep* the onomatopoeia of breathless energy in "I lo'e the stishie O' Earth in space Breengin' by At a haliket pace"; even the music of the spheres in "Wunds wi' warlds to swing Dinna sing sae sweet, The licht that bends owre a'thing Is less ta'en up wi't". He can get the full value out of plain colloquial speech, as Burns could: "Wi' a scoogie o' silk An' a bucket o' siller She's shown' the haill Coort The smeddum intil her", "The Lassie looked at her an' leuch, 'Och, plaise yersel!' said she, 'Ye'd better gie me what I seek Than learn what I've to gie' "; and "Crowdieknowe" is a prime example. And he can create the memorable line: "The fug o' fame an' history's hazelraw", "A' the starnies an' he are sib", "Dern the dreams that glint a wee through Time's shawls", "Wae for the hoose whaur a buirdly man Crines in a windin' sheet", "I lo'e Love wi' a scunner in't". *A Drunk Man* also has a splendid conversational opening and the drunk's haverings are excellently done. He says what he has to say in a kind of basic Scots, as in the passage beginning "I doot I'm geylies mixed, like Life itsel' "; one of his most ambitious sequences in Scots is "Nerves in stounds o' delight . . .". The whole poem is an astonishing piece of linguistic as well as conceptual versatility. If only he had kept to his assignment and applied himself more slowly and methodically to the line he successfully pioneered from *Sangschaw* to *A Drunk Man*, he might have done more for the language. In fairness it must be said, and indeed he said it himself, that to rebuild Scots was beyond the power of one man; and in similar attempts abroad the task is in hands of government commissions and academies and conclaves of pundits, though frequently it was the poets who inspired it.

But the problems seem to have worried him intermittently and he came back to it again in his later days as in 1967 in his preface to *A Lap of Honour* already quoted. And he goes on to say that the "poems 'By Wachopeside' and 'Whuchulls'" realise the sort of poem I wanted when I ceased to write the kind of short lyric". It is indeed a pity that he did not persevere in this vein. 'Whuchulls" is still basically lyrical and has affinities in theme with the much earlier "A Ballad of the Five Senses", and yet it looks forward to the later period of existentialism and spiritual isolationism of, say, "On a Raised Beach". David Craig has perceptively compared Wordsworth's "Tintern Abbey" in this connection. Some years before his death, MacDiarmid told me he was working out a solution to the problem of using Scots to expound science. Unfortunately he did not elaborate the point and I do not know how far he got in the process, alluded to in the second preface to *A Drunk Man*.

So there we have it. In the last analysis, I suppose the majority view that his fame rests securely on his earlier work is fundamentally sound and will prevail. Probably he attempted too much and came unstuck in the end by trying to extend the art of poetry beyond its natural limits. It meant too abandoning his invaluable and successful experiment with Scots, but at least not before he had not merely asserted but demonstrated some of its potentialities. Dr Johnson speaks ruefully of his career as the dreams of a poet doomed at last to wake a lexicographer. With

MacDiarmid it seems to have been the other way round — lucky
poet indeed!

1936–The Borderer and the Orcadian

GEORGE BRUCE

"For a' that's Scottish is in me"

A Drunk Man Looks at the Thistle

In the summer of 1936 I went to St Andrews to visit Francis George Scott, who was staying with his family on holiday in a house owned by James Whyte, the editor and proprietor of *The Modern Scot*. I cannot recollect the preliminaries to the question the composer threw at me, or whether there were any, but the question shouted rhetorically, rather than asked, "What will Chris say to this!" still remains in my ears. Scott had in his hands a copy, I think an advance copy, of Edwin Muir's *Scott and Scotland*, from which he proceeded to quote: ". . . a Scottish writer who wishes to achieve some approximation to completeness has no choice but to absorb the English tradition, and that if he does so his work belongs not merely to Scottish literature but to English literature as well. On the other hand if he wishes to add to an indigenous Scottish literature and roots himself deliberately in Scotland, he will find there, no matter how long he may search, neither an organic community to round off his conceptions, nor a major literary tradition to support him, nor even a faith among the people themselves that a Scottish literature is possible or desirable, nor any opportunity, finally, of making a livelihood by his work. All these things are part of a single problem which can only be understood by considering Scottish literature historically, and the qualities in the Scottish people which have made them what they are: it cannot be solved by writing poems in Scots, or by looking forward to some hypothetical Scotland in the future."

Scott may not have quoted the entire passage from the *Introduction*, as I have done, in which Muir's main thesis is set out, though it is taken further in the chapters which follow. In Chapter 1 Muir wrote:

> Scots has survived to our time as a language for simple poetry and the simpler kind of short story, such as *Thrawn Janet*: all its other uses have lapsed, and it expresses therefore only a fragment of the Scottish mind. One can go further than this, however, and assert that its very use is a proof that the Scottish consciousness is divided. For reduced to its simplest terms, the linguistic division means that Scotsmen feel in one language and think in another.

I went on to see Edwin Muir, who lived at Castlelea — the matter of a few hundred yards away — leaving Scott mulling over the book and breaking out in astonished, indignant exclamations, and told him of the disturbance his book had caused in Scott and its probable effect on MacDiarmid. He was quite unperturbed, explaining that Borderers would be expected to react in this way, since they had experienced the threat of destruction from the English over a long period of history as those, such as himself, from the islands, and especially the northern islands, had not done. At the time, possibly under the influence of the poet from Orkney, and not yet in possession of the full implication of the book, and having mainly in my mind the idea that "Scotsmen felt in one language and thought in another", I considered there was a good deal to be said for the point of view, and that it offered matter for academic discussion.

To MacDiarmid the book was a "betrayal" — so he called it to me. He carried his rage into polemics and to the exclusion of Muir's poetry from his anthology, *The Golden Treasury of Scottish Poetry*, which was first published in 1940, though he found room in the *Introduction* for comment on "a well-known Scottish (or rather Orcadian) critic" who "recommended his countrymen to cast aside Scots altogether as a 'trash of nonsense'". There was further comment in the *Notes* at the end of the book, though here Muir is cited alongside other "enemies" of the revived Scottish tradition. Surprisingly MacDiarmid finds an ally in Virginia Woolf, whom he quotes from her essay, *Gas at Abbotsford*, in which she depicts a

101

scene at Abbotsford in which "There is Lady Scott gossiping with kind Mrs. Hughes; there is Scott himself, prosing and pompous, grumbling about his son Charles and his passion for sport. To complete the horror, the Baron D'Este strums on the guitar. Miss Scott — or is she Miss Wardour or another of the vapid and vacant Waverley novel heroines? — hangs over him entranced. Then suddenly the whole scene changed. Scott began in a low mournful voice to recite the ballad of Sir Patrick Spens:

> O lang, lang may the ladies sit
> With their fans into their hands
> Or e'er they see Sir Patrick Spens
> Come sailing to the land.

The guitar stopped; Sir Walter's lips trembled as he came to an end. So it happens, too, in the novels . . . the lifeless English turns to living Scots."

MacDiarmid comments: "This was the first objective of the new Scottish Movement — to break into real life again, and to get rid of the false values of the pro-English 'courtier school', represented in our time by the late Lord Tweedsmuir, Professor Sir Herbert Grierson, Mr Edwin Muir and Dr Agnes Muir Mackenzie. The way in which critics who contend there is no basis in speech today for literary work in Scots disregard the testimony in this connection of the poets themselves . . . is highly significant. 'There cannot be a Scottish poetry in the fullest sense unless there is in the fullest sense a Scottish speech', says Mr Speirs in his *The Scots Literary Tradition*; 'what survives of such a speech among what survives of the peasantry is in its last stages and is something its speakers have learned to be half-ashamed of.' This is not the case."

The purpose of this essay is not to go over ground which was most extensively covered in the pros and cons for the new poetry in Lallans especially before and after the 1939–45 war. Its purpose is to examine certain of the assumptions on which the lines of battle were drawn up, assumptions which were made about an opposition between Scots and English, and even an assumption that the two protagonists were inevitably conditioned by their childhood environments. Certainly the sense of tranquillity and the sense of each individual building in the Orkney scene having a special meaning was provided by Edwin Muir's childhood environment, and more strikingly the proximity of the English border and the tales and history of Border warfare was a conditioning element in the psychology of MacDiarmid but, I suggest, these conditions became uses for the differing vocations of both poets. One can be confident too that in so far as they were poets, at the point of creation their theories were forgotten. Certainly this was the case of the greater poet, MacDiarmid, whose first achievement of the lyrics in Scots surprised himself as well as everyone else, and who continued thereafter to proliferate and diversify at first sight as if there was no controlling ethos. Yet, properly I believe, Norman MacCaig entitled a broadcast programme on MacDiarmid, *The Invisible Man*.

But first I return to Edwin Muir of whom MacDiarmid wrote in *Contemporary Scottish Studies*: "—a critic incontestably in the first flight of contemporary critics of welt-literatur. . . . I am not sure that the extent to which the present organisation of British literary journalism compels him to be an English critic rather than a Scottish critic in international appreciation is not inhibiting him to some extent creatively as well as critically. . . . It is significant, at all events, that he 'found himself' most convincingly as a poet not in his work in English, but in his Braid Scots ballads: and in my opinion he would have done better work still if he had not contented himself with conventional ballad Scots, but had employed a full Braid Scots canon of his own devising based upon a de novo consideration of the entire resources of the language on the one hand, its tractability to the most significant processes and purposes of ultra-modern literature on the other."

Here one sees MacDiarmid in 1926, ten years before the publication of *Scott and Scotland* rejoicing in the discovery of a critic in Scotland of the first water, and one who had already in his essay, *The Scottish Ballads*, supplied, according to MacDiarmid, "a sufficient *raison d'être* for the Scottish Renaissance movement in general, and the attempt to revive the Scots vernacular in particular". In the article, which MacDiarmid quotes, are these passages: "Since English became the literary language of Scotland there has been no Scots imaginative writer who has attained greatness in the first or even the second rank through the medium of English." Of Carlyle, Muir wrote: ". . . his style expressed, in spite of its overstrain, and even through it, something real, the struggle of a Scots peasant born to other habits of speech and of thought, with the English language. Stevenson — and it was a sign of his inferiority, his lack of fundamental merit — never had this struggle, nor realised that it was necessary that he should have it." Muir summed up his views: "No writer can write great English who is not born an English writer and in England: and born moreover in some class in which the tradition of English is pure. . . ." But for the simplicity, and clarity of style, and a certain detachment in the tone, this might be the voice of MacDiarmid. And MacDiarmid recognised the Renaissance movement required just such a critic to help it survive. MacDiarmid knew that this new thing, but some three years old, disliked in some quarters, and ridiculed in others, going against the tide of English letters, yet nervously and breathingly alive through his own poetry, could readily be snuffed out. To keep it going was required not only individual genius and new appreciations of the cultural situation, but smeddum, which MacDiarmid had in large measure. And now he had recruited Muir.

I use the word deliberately, though I do not mean any unfair influence was brought to bear on Muir. At the time of the new confidence in the renewal of Scottish letters, he responded to the occasion in his ballads in Scots and in his unqualified assertions on the required qualifications of birth and class in order to write English prose of a high order. He had conveniently forgotten Conrad, Melville and Henry James, to name but three outsiders. If such qualifications were required then there must be doubt as to how organic the "organic culture" of England could be, to which Muir refers with confidence ten years later in *Scott and Scotland*. By the thirties the problem of finding forms to comprehend our "much divided civilisation" — as Yeats called it — in which Eliot had attempted in *The Waste Land* to shore "fragments against my ruins" and Joyce had used a comprehensive stream of consciousness technique in his *Ulysses*, was accepted. And, of course, Edwin Muir in writings other than those to which I have referred showed a true response and an awareness of what those writers, particularly European writers, who were in the van of achievement in the thirties, were about. That he may have been off-beam in the writings referred to did not mean there was not an underlying consistent writing persona.

In her book, *Belonging*, a memoir, published in 1968 ten years after Edwin Muir's death, Willa Muir wrote:

> Prodded by F. G. Scott, whose enthusiasms were ebullient, Edwin had sent three Scottish Ballads to the first number of *The Scottish Chapbook* in 1923,* and later, for another number an early fragmentary version of his *Chorus of the Newly Dead*: but although the two Borderers had generated a heat of enthusiasm for Scotland and what they called the 'Scottish Renaissance', Edwin's interest in it was tepid, except that he was fond of F. G. Scott. The Lowland Scottish vernacular was not his vernacular. It was Orkney he spoke, not Lowland Scots or Lallans.

In these circumstances, however sympathetic Muir may have been to the cause, he was an outsider who first lent his imagination to the universe inhabited by Scott and MacDiarmid, and then when new conditions affected him decided there was no justification for supporting it. In both these circumstances his literary perceptions were less to be trusted than when he was working the field out of which his own visionary poetry came. Muir's recognition of the ordered world of Henryson, of the allegory that runs through Kafka's novels, and the light of eternity in which he saw his childhood world — the animals, parents, and the buildings in Orkney — conditioned the visionary character of his poetry. He seemed to wait for his poetry to happen. Sometimes it grew out of his dream, not that the dream did not take account of the terrible happenings of the modern world, of which the Muirs knew only too well, when twice they had to leave Prague and their friends on account of its occupation by the Nazis and the Communists, but the resolution was in an English poetry refined of locality. It was detached from the actual world as was the spirit of this poet. Orkney may have been his original dialect, but it left no trace in his poetry. Consequently when he wrote off the prospect of a future for Scots and for a distinctive culture for Scotland he did not perceive that he was aiming a death blow at all that his friend

* 1922—Mrs Muir was wrong.

Christopher Grieve had worked for, was working for and stood for. Inevitably MacDiarmid held to his vision passionately, more passionately than Muir. His poetry did not operate within the categories in which Muir made his statements in *Scott and Scotland*, but Muir had made his statement in public and MacDiarmid took him up in his own terms, attacking the theory and the man. Professor T. C. Smout in his *Introduction* to the reissue of *Scottish Journey* has referred to the breach with Grieve thus: ". . . with whom, however, he came to quarrel most bitterly in 1936 after Muir's attack in *Scott and Scotland* on the futility of Scottish writers attempting to communicate through a made-up Lallans".

It is a little sad that even now it is necessary to assert that the Lallans, which MacDiarmid used was not "made up", nor was this what Muir attacked, nor for that matter was there a quarrel. It takes two to make a quarrel and Muir never entered into debate with MacDiarmid. Had Muir merely attacked "a made-up Lallans" which was the currency of a deal of disputation in the newspapers, the matter would have been less serious. In any case some twenty years later, after the publication of Sydney Goodsir Smith's masterpiece, *Under the Eildon Tree*, Edwin Muir changed his mind about the prospect of the contribution which Lallans still might make. Even then I doubt if he understood the depth of the offence he had given to MacDiarmid in 1936.

The polarities on which Muir and MacDiarmid stood, and which made an intimate understanding between them impossible, were more than geographical and historical, though these aspects played their part in supporting their insulation from the literary effects of each other. Ultimately they were psychological, and because they were poets their differing psychologies led them to different conceptions of their poetic vocations. Both created distinctive poetic universes and both looked out on the modern world from these. Keats makes a distinction between two kinds of genius, the one "the Wordsworthian, or egotistical sublime; which is a thing per se and stands alone", the other "which Shakespeare possessed so enormously — I mean *negative capability*, that is, when a man is capable of being in uncertainties, mysteries, doubts, without any irritable reaching after fact and reason". If one

106

withdraws the name Shakespeare from consideration, the second appellation will be seen to apply to Muir, and the first to MacDiarmid. Muir was first of all a listening man. He did not seek to impose his opinions — Eliot described him as "a reserved, reticent man, not fluent in conversation. Yet his personality made a deep impression on me, . . .". This reticent, sensitive man of "unmistakable integrity" and "utter honesty" — I quote again from Eliot's *Preface* to the *Selected Poems of Edwin Muir* — was subjected to the traumatic experience of moving from the personal, organic, traditional, farming community of Orkney to the conurbation of Glasgow. There by his connections with a meaningful past were severed. In this event the characteristic experience of disjunction of "aware" modern man was telescoped. His concern was not with the survival of a Scottish identity, but with a personal identity. The distress of the way of life sanctioned by generations was increased by the death of two brothers, his father and mother. When his memory went across the gap to his childhood in Orkney, the life there presented itself as "a stationary indivisible pattern". From that life his memory and imagination extracted unchanging and unfading pictures disinfected of the mortal properties of smell or the sensation of touch, while all about him life fell way or buildings crowded in on him.

It is significant that the most useful poet to Edwin Muir, psychologically at least, from the Scottish Middle Ages, was Robert Henryson, who lived in an age when "an agreement had been reached regarding the nature and meaning of human life, and the imagination could attain harmony and tranquillity" (*Robert Henryson–Essays on Literature and Society*). That continuity which came to mean most to him as a person and poet were Christian symbols, especially as they were expressed in medieval paintings — he carried about in his pocket a postcard of an *Anunciation* by Fra Angelico — and medieval poetry. This was the base, allied to his vision of Orkney, for Muir's clear-eyed visionary poetry.

The case of MacDiarmid was markedly different. There was no rupture between his childhood and his maturity. Out of the past he carried the whole inheritance of a Border boyhood. He writes about it as if his experience may still be going on. Part of a sentence

THE AGE OF MACDIARMID

is enough to suggest the richness of this inheritance. In *My Native Place* he writes:

> The delights of sledging on Lamb Hill or Murtholm Brae; of gathering 'hines' in the Langfall; of going through the fields of Baggara hedged in honeysuckle and wild roses, through knee-deep meadowsweet to the 'Scrog-nit wood and gathering the nuts or crab-apples there; of blaeberrying on Warblaw or the Castle Hill; of 'dookin' and 'guddlin' or making islands in the Esk or Ewes or Wauchope and lighting stick fires on them and cooking potatoes in tin cans— these are only a few of the joys I knew, . . .

And on goes the sentence effortlessly, and apparently endlessly un-coiling itself, rejoicing in the naming of places for the sake of their sound and their reality, and encompassing with relish the vernacular. Now the charge that was levelled against MacDiarmid, especially against his lyrics in Scots, was that his "aggrandised Scots"—to use Alexander Scott's phrase—was unrealistic. It was "Dictionary grubbing". While MacDiarmid extended his vocabulary in Scots through Jamieson particularly (and for that matter in English by referring to books on several sciences) insufficient attention may have been paid to the heritage of his environment. A few years ago, while taking an Extra-Mural Class for Glasgow University in Dumfries, at which I had just referred to MacDiarmid's extension of his Scots vocabulary by means of the dictionary, and was glossing *The Watergaw*, and so to *the Eemis Stane*, I was interrupted by an elderly member of the class, saying: "He didn't need to go to a dictionary for any of these words. I know every one of them." On request he proceeded to give a detailed account of Scots in the poems. He told me he had been a shepherd on the hills behind Langholm, where several of the words were ordinarily used in the trade. So the reality was co-present with the word. The thing itself was in the word immediately. And these interests in MacDiarmid were indissoluble. The fact and the idea were relentlessly pursued through his poetry with a thoroughness which amounted to obsession, and in this pursuit a larger universe of Scottish poetry was created in one man than had existed before. Little wonder that the poet most sib with MacDiarmid in all Scottish poetry was Dunbar. "Back to Dunbar" he advocated;

Dunbar who relished, despite his avowed objections, the unsavoury, robust life in the High Street of Edinburgh, whose poetry ranged from personal complaints to the aureate allegory, and from the richly textured, bawdy *The Twa Merrit Women and the Wedow* to the sonorous *Lament for the Makars*, and who matched these varied interests with a verbal virtuosity and a variety of styles. Dunbar had one great advantage over MacDiarmid. His variety was within the compass of an integrated society and one which, apparently, did not assume poetry had a single lyrical function, but could roam at large, whereas every move into an area other than that cultivated by Burns or by MacDiarmid's predecessors, met with critical asperities. To this day critics will place one part of MacDiarmid's achievement against another, some regretting that he moved on from the lyrics to satire in Scots and the majority that he conducted debates at length in a kind of English. But necessity drove him on. He was *The Indivisible Man* in a deeply divided society.

Widely different as are (say) *The Eemis Stane* and *On a Raised Beach*, one may detect the same mind at work in each, and curiously as Edwin Muir went about Scotland in 1934, in order to write his book, *Scottish Journey*, seeking unsuccessfully to discover a single Scottish identity, he put his finger on a characteristic of many Scots, which he regarded as a national characteristic, and which applies strikingly to MacDiarmid. "For," he writes, "the Scottish character has a thoroughness, or in other words an inability to know where to stop, which is rarely found in Englishmen, who make a virtue of compromise." Once MacDiarmid found his direction, the pursuit through word to fact to theory, through particular knowledge to the ontological, was relentless, and never would he allow what he had done to stand in the way of what he might do. The first astonishment was how Scots words worked for him in the Scots lyrics, how they not only made a new, strange music that had not been heard before in Scottish poetry, but how they took him to a vision of the earth as a stone, seen under the moon — a stone — and from the moon, and so the tradition which had abandoned intellect in poetry, now by the leap of imagination and intelligence gave vast new perspectives encapsulated in a few lines. So at once we had the sensations that arose from touch and sight of the commonest objects and at the same time a symbolic awareness of a cosmogany. Within this perspective in *A Drunk Man Looks at the Thistle*, social and political responsibilities are observed. Then necessity takes MacDiarmid to Shetland and he is in the presence of a world of stone and water, and the stones speak to him.

> We must be humble. We are so easily baffled by appearances.
> And do not realise that these stones are one with the stars.
>
> . . . . .
>
> What happens to us
> Is irrelevant to the world's geology
> But what happens to the world's geology
> Is not irrelevant to us.

Set alongside these lines this:

> The warld like an eemis stane
> Wags i' the lift.

In both cases intellect and antennae are reaching out. In the latter a few lines give off the most subtle sensation of unfathomable mystery: in the former in MacDiarmid's English in line after line as the stones and the naming of stones pile up and as an imperious voice places moral man within the geological context the mind of the reader is stretched, his curiosity stimulated, and his sense of the strange marvel of mere being invoked. To the poet language is a resource, not a recourse, and for MacDiarmid the movement of his interest is towards an enlargement which will encompass and bring into play whatsoever words are to his purpose — Scots, English or Gaelic. In Joyce's *Finnegan's Wake* words and the sensation of words take over, and in the Anna Livia Plurabelle passage objects disappear into a flood of words, but in MacDiarmid's English poems at least, the words point to the object, which has its strong independent existence. The poem *Direadh* (Part 1), first published in *The Voice of Scotland*, begins with a device which poises the poem between Gaelic and English, the glosses becoming part of the poem, as in:

> Cut, cleft, sheer edge, precipice,
> *Bearradh* (from *bearr*, clip or shear)
> With here a *beithe* (a birch of wood)
> And there a *bad* (a clump of trees)
> *Basdalach* (cheery) with birds. . . .

There are quotations from other languages, and I am not sure what right the poet has to project so many bewilderments on the reader, but the poem runs through to:

> Scotland small? Our multiform, our infinite Scotland *small*?
> Only as a patch of hillside may be a cliché corner
> To a fool who cries 'Nothing but heather!' where in
>   September another
> Sitting there and resting and gazing around
> Sees not only heather but blaeberries
> With bright green leaves and leaves already turned scarlet
> Hiding ripe blue berries; and amongst the sage-green leaves
> Of the bog-myrtle the golden flowers of the tormentil
>   shining.

Thereafter MacDiarmid goes on to name and describe exactly milkworts, sphagnum moss, sundew, butterwort, harebells and "stunted rowans with harsh dry leaves of glorious colour". No sooner are these observed facts recorded (and we know they were observed because he told me that F. G. Scott took him to the hillside and pointed out the varying vegetation so as to teach him botany) than the thorough nature of his mind compels him to explore possibilities of certainty, and in a kind of despair because he cannot find a rationale, he writes:

> Was it only yesterday I was struggling still
> With frames of reference, patterns of culture, cyclical phases
>   of causation. . . .

And then he states:

> And in the twinkling of an eye arrived
> At knowledge of the whole and absolute truth.

I take it he is referring back to the apprehension of the nature of things that may arrive through exact observation, which returns us to the "thing".

Three quotations preface *Scottish Scene* or *The Intelligent Man's Guide to Albyn*, the guide consisting of comment, poems and short stories by Hugh MacDiarmid and Lewis Grassic Gibbon, being published in 1934 — the year of Edwin Muir's journey through Scotland. Significantly the first of these is:

"To an Englishman something is what it is called: to a Scotsman something is what it is."

Compton Mackenzie

In a review of *Horizons of Death* by the American poet, Norman Macleod, published in *The Modern Scot*, Summer 1935, MacDiarmid comments: "He has the advantage of a great wealth of first-hand observation, a very keen selectivity, and the racy strongly differentiated American English, which stands him in similar stead to Mr Soutar's Scots Vernacular." The comment continues to observe that his best work is similar to the best work in "documentary films" (one cannot quote the phrase without recollecting the name of the Scot, John Grierson), placing it as "'literature of fact' that sheer description, which not only tells what a thing is but goes a long way to tell why it is".

By now the reader will be aware that I have made the foregoing quotations because they all apply with peculiar force to the work under consideration of MacDiarmid, and they allow me to make the point, that while Scots is no longer used in measure, an English is used, a deal of which may relate more pertinently to American prose writers than to English poets, and it allows the assertion that the cast of mind comes close at some points to Edwin Muir's description of Carlyle: ". . . his style expressed, in spite of its overstrain, and even through it, something real". "Overstrain" — yes, MacDiarmid's unwieldy, portmanteau poems are burdened with a plethora of ill-assorted, verbal specimens, in *his* hands struggling for life, and expected to form a total unity. The expectation was inordinate, as surely was the idea that a new poetry of consequence could be made in Scots, for, according to MacDiarmid, "The Scots Vernacular is a vast storehouse of just the very peculiar and subtle effects which modern European literature is assiduously seeking . . .". And yet on the page previous to this quotation from the *Causerie* in *The Scottish Chapbook*, Vol. 1 No. 8 (March 1923), where *The Eemis Stane* is printed, he had gone some way to proving his point. That achievement is not in doubt: the assessment of the long poems is another matter. My concern here is to establish the presence of the same character of mind in both projects, and here Muir's statement about Carlyle is again useful, as in the remark that Carlyle's style expressed "the struggle of a Scots peasant, born to other habits of speech and of thought, with the English language". But for the word "peasant" there goes MacDiarmid, a Scot incapable of feeling and thinking in other than Scots.

Despite MacDiarmid's return — a temporary one — to a dense Scots, that density is not the factor that determines the character of the mind. In the four lines from *Sir Patrick Spens* which Virginia Woolf quoted in her article on Scott, the only word which does not belong to the shared language of English and Scots is "lang" though the ballad is undeniably Scottish. Muir's assertion about the failure to produce a literature in Scots, or — to broaden the reference — to produce new Scottish literature even by 1936 was out of date.

The short story, *Smeddum*, by Lewis Grassic Gibbon, first published in *Scottish Scene* (1934), begins:

> She'd nine of a family in her time, Mistress Menzies, and brought the nine of them up, forbye — some near by the scruff of the neck, you would say. They were sniftering and weakly, two-three of the bairns, sniftering in their cradles to get into their coffins; but she'd shake them to life, and dose them with salts and feed them up till they couldn't but live. And she'd plonk one down — finishing the wiping of the creature's neb or the unco dosing of an ill bit stomach or the binding of a broken head — with a look on her face as much as to say *Die on me now and see what you'll get.*

Without losing one jot or tittle of the original racy, familiar, ironic Aberdeenshire dialect, which on previous occasions had been transliterated on to the printed page to the delight of the natives only, Gibbon has developed an idiom, through which characters spring vividly to life, landscapes have a new being, and in which there is room for a flow of witty commentary, all of which is acceptable to an English reading public. This writing is more secure in its style than the narrative in *A Scots Quair*, and it is on this base that more recent writers, such as Fred Urqhart, have made their contributions to the affirmation of a continuing confident, energetic, independent, sometimes eccentric life. Further north on the different basis of a Gaelic culture, though writing in English — an English that differed in tone and temper from that of the English tradition — Neil Gunn in *Morning Tide* (1931) had begun to reflect his traditional society.

One writer who might have been expected to appreciate MacDiarmid's point of view in the dispute about the use of Scots was William Soutar (1898-1943). Born and brought up in Perth, the son of Scots-speaking parents, his boyhood companions also Scots speaking, he had all the necessary equipment for becoming a Scottish "makar", yet when he promised himself as a young man that he would be a poet, the idea of the achievement being in Scots never crossed his mind. This was understandable for by the early twenties no one, not even MacDiarmid, contemplated the idea of the vocation of poet in terms of a medium largely taken over by at best conservationists and at worst sentimental imitators of Burns. Still Soutar was early in touch with MacDiarmid, who published Soutar's poem, *The Quest*, in the first number of *The Scottish Chapbook* in August 1922. It was a very English, even Georgian poem, but for that matter MacDiarmid's admittedly more adventurous poem, *A Moment in Eternity*, also romantic English, gave no hint of the transformation in MacDiarmid's writing which was to astonish his readers within two months by the publication of *The Watergaw* in the third number of the magazine in October. But by this date the perfervid imagination of MacDiarmid had got a hold on the whole literary and social necessity. In the same issue of *The Scottish Chapbook*, the editor, C. M. Grieve, in *Causerie*—the editorial—comments on his alter ego, Hugh M'Diarmid: ". . . he is, I think, the first Scottish writer who has addressed himself to the extendability (without psychological violence) of the Vernacular to embrace the whole range of modern culture. . . ."

This, the first shot in the promotion of his *Theory of Scots Letters*, was characteristically vintage MacDiarmid. On the one hand the objective "to embrace the whole range of modern culture" is so large as to be absurd, and on the other hand he is entirely on the beam in the word "extendability". Scots in the fields, factories and in literature had been doing the reverse — its use had been contracting. MacDiarmid's clarion calls in the *Causeries* — from No. 7 of the *Chapbook*, February 1923, they were to be devoted to *The Theory* — had not apparently the slightest influence on Soutar's idea of his poetic vocation. Seventeen years later, and after the publication of five collections of poems in English, the staple idiom in Soutar's collection, *In the Time of the Tyrants* (1939), is on the lines, "Men who go forth to feud" (The Iron Tree).

There was, of course, another Soutar. As early as 1923, the year in which he published anonymously *Gleanings* by an Undergraduate, he would get off his high horse and ride off on his cuddy. In that year he wrote three charming triolets in Scots, and then independently of MacDiarmid, his rhyming for fun increasingly took the form of what he called Bairn Rhymes. He was encouraged in the production of these by the arrival in 1927 of Evelyn, aged five, the orphaned niece of a cousin of Soutar's mother. By that date the illness, which was to confine Soutar to bed from 1930 to the end of his life, was restricting his activity. The conditions in which he was to make his rare contribution to the revival of poetry in Scots were then operating within the confines of a family community. Whatever his physical condition, however, he would have written a poetry far more restricted by traditional conventions than did MacDiarmid. This limitation inhibited his relating his English poetry to his Scots, and so there could be no cross-fertilising. It was to be expected, in these circumstances, that he would give a cautious welcome to MacDiarmid's new poems.

In *The Scots Observer* (October 24, 1929) Soutar wrote:

> ". . . *Sangschaw* appears to have been but a momentary, though happy, articulation, which faltered through *Pennywheep* into the logorrhea of *The Drunk Man*. . . ."

In a short time Soutar had altered his opinion of *A Drunk Man Looks at the Thistle*. In the same article he also wrote, referring to "Moonstruck":

> "What strikes us about these verses in comparison with Burns is not the linguistic difference but the quality of thought. It is the different intellectual approach which is the new thing."

115

He also wrote:

> "His canon is the dictionary. This is barren enough ground
> for art yet *Sangschaw* grew out of it."

And again:

> ". . . Scotland can never be true to itself until it is
> autonomous and until it has a centre of culture within it. This
> will further a deeper interest in Scots — but does not
> warrant the adoption of synthetic Scots as our literary
> language. Such experiences as can find adequate expression
> in dialect, and there are some experiences which can find
> their fullest expression only in dialect, will continue to be
> expressed, but if any great artists arise among us they will
> write in English."

If a poet in Soutar's situation found himself equivocating over
MacDiarmid's solution to the literary problems of the Scottish
writer, Soutar, whose Diaries witness to his endlessly seeking for a
unity which would integrate varieties of experience, and whose
home itself was an entity, with a language spoken based on Scots,
it is little wonder that Edwin Muir had stronger doubts than
Soutar about MacDiarmid's way forward. But one can see Soutar
modifying his position and taking account of the views and
practices of MacDiarmid. In 1931 Soutar wrote to MacDiarmid:
"If the Doric is to come back alive, it will come first on a cock-
horse. How are you going to get it into the schools otherwise?
. . . I fancy the best beginning would be in bairn-rhymes. . . ." This
is a light-toned comment, but Soutar is increasingly aware of the
possibility of his making a serious contribution to the movement
which MacDiarmid had set going. His doubting comment about
the use of a dictionary as a resource for poetry in Scots, was
quickly forgotten. In his *Journal* on 28th January 1934 he wrote
about Jamieson's Dictionary:

> Jamieson is not a museum wherein we peer for "stunning"
> words — but a racial memory to which we bring our own
> for corroboration.

Increasingly Soutar is seeing the Scots tongue as a repository of
national, or at least communal, experience, and this is in line with
MacDiarmid's views expressed in his *Theory of Scots Letters*, though

MacDiarmid takes the idea of the community of speech into the dimension of mysticism, as in his first paragraph of the *Causerie* in Vol. 1 No. 8 (March 1923) which begins:

> The Scottish Vernacular is the only language in Western Europe instinct with those uncanny spiritual and pathological perceptions alike which constitutes the uniqueness of Dostoevski's work, and word after word of Doric establishes a blood-bond in a fashion at once infinitely more thrilling and vital and less explicable than those deliberately sought after by writers such as D. H. Lawrence in the medium of English which is inferior for such purposes. . . .

One may be more persuaded of the validity of this case for Scots if one has approached it, after reading the poem on the opposite side of the page. It is *The Eemis Stane*. I suspect at least part of the theory may have been generalised from the realisation of mysteries, the sense of which is immediately created by the opening line itself, "I' the how-dumb-deid o' the cauld hairst nicht". Gradually Soutar's poems in Scots increasingly reverberate and carry undertones of what cannot be exactly specified. Though these poems did not proceed on MacDiarmid's lines one at least suggests a susceptibility to his influence. In *The Voice of Scotland* Vol. 1 No. 2 Sept.-Nov. 1938, these lines from Soutar's poem, "Scotland", are quoted:

> Atween the world o' licht
> And the world that is to be
> A man wi' unco sicht
> Sees whaur he canna see:
>
> Gangs whaur he canna walk:
> Recks whaur he canna read.

This is not Soutar's best, but the lines suggest a pervasive MacDiarmid influence. The true usefulness of MacDiarmid in the development of a new literature in Scots was in widening the field of reference, making available a richer vocabulary, and most important in creating a confidence in the possibility of a significant Scottish literary identity under which there would be room for much variety of enterprise. Edwin Muir's verdict in *Scott and Scotland*, in MacDiarmid's view, amounted to total surrender. In Vol. 1 No. 1 of *The Voice of Scotland*, June-August 1938,

MacDiarmid's own paper which was virtually replacing *The Scottish Chapbook*, he gave Soutar the first opportunity to respond to Muir's views. He did so under the heading, *Faith in the Vernacular*. The article began:

> The revival of Scots as a literary potential is a very debatable affair; but its significance as an act of faith is beyond equivocation; it is our temporary necessity. . . . If, however, we are conscious of the relative nature of this effort towards vernacular rehabilitation we are also made aware of its paradoxy; namely to be the symbol of a process, which in fulfilment, offers no promise of its own; but to appreciate we must look beyond Scotland.
>
> We live in a period of transition and disintegration and are given two pathways towards stability — Fascism and Socialism: nationalism is integral to both but in the former it is an end in itself; in the latter a means or subsumption. This world-wide struggle is peculiarly complicated in Scotland which is but a pseudo-entity and therefore confronted by a choice which demands an epicyclic response. Symptomatic of this dilemma is the movement to rehabilitate the vernacular which not only testifies to the need for the rediscovery of our national roots but also for an alignment with the worker, nor is it fanciful to see the dilemma embodied in synthetic Scots itself; which by its virtue, namely, the increasing comprehension of its vocabulary, tends to alienate the ordinary reader. One can sympathise with the critics who maintain that the Scottish poet must accept the ready-made vehicle of English as his only solution to a linguistic impasse; but these have failed to recognise the symptomatic nature of the renaissance of Scots which has been indicated above. In a transitional period there are temporary loyalties which are necessities for faith: such a loyalty at this moment in Scotland is the effort to re-establish the vernacular, and ought to be accepted even with the self-consciousness that it is but temporary.
>
> . . . It follows, therefore, that although the preoccupation with Scots is recognised to be a necessary declaration of faith now; it is not pursued in the assumption that Scots must be established in a corporate Scotland. Let us be fulfilled as an integrated people and we shall find our true speech whatever

it may be. At the moment the revival of Scots is indicative of the desire for nationhood and by reciprocality, would increase that desire. It is therefore imperative that faith in the vernacular be maintained.

In view of the prophetic stance of MacDiarmid on the subject of Scots it is to his credit that he allowed Soutar's qualified views expression in his official organ. Soutar's statement comprehends both MacDiarmid's and Muir's points of view. It is a little ironic that the man in bed should produce the most realistic treatment of the subject. This in some respects was an advantageous position. At the centre of Scotland, geographically, he was at the receipt of custom, a listening post, at which the opinions of the Scottish literati were given a hearing, adjudicated, and formulations made with care. As I have indicated, Soutar's approach to MacDiarmid's innovations was critical. He moved step by step to a new position, and once there held it. Some three years after the publication of *Faith in the Vernacular* in a letter to me (13/8/41) Soutar wrote:

> Purely as a linguistic movement I see no promise of a growing revival, merely a temporary outcropping; and Muir's analysis in *Scott and Scotland* is in the main correct within its orbit.

Muir was later to modify his view so as to come closer to Soutar's position. One must never forget that all three men were poets, and that ultimately the determining factor is personal experience. They go their ways digesting what comes at them according to their psychologies. On the one hand we must take account of the inordinate, obsessive energies of MacDiarmid and on the other Muir's sensitive mental plate.

As Edwin Muir made his Scottish journey, sensitively and honestly assembling the impressions of the state of the nation which were to appear in his book in 1935, little or nothing of the vitality, which found expression in the novels of Lewis Grassic Gibbon and in the poetry of MacDiarmid, came to his notice. It was a bleak time socially, the unemployed to be seen everywhere, and his residence in St Andrews, with its acute class consciousness, its hierarchies and university, on which Professor Lorimer of that university once made the comment "There are three Scottish

Universities and St Andrews", seemed to confirm the idea that
Scotland was emptying itself of life. Willa was aware that the
book, *Scott and Scotland*, was written under constricting
circumstances. In *Belonging* she refers to "an undertone of personal
exasperation in it, to be found in no other book of Edwin's". She
goes on to comment: "The emptiness of Scottish life which he had
been aware of during his Journey and was now aware of in St
Andrews, a hiatus caused, he felt, by the lack of an organic society
with an alive centre. . . ."

The surprising aspect of the diagnosis of the Scottish condition
by Muir to me was his assumption that Scotland was in the
condition of being less organic than England. To the contrary the
structure of English society, with its separate schools for the rich
and the poor, its polite English which prejudiced communication
between those earning the weekly wage and the salaried,
aristocratic or wealthy, made it well nigh impossible for the
writer to energise his writing by communications from those who
worked in fields or factories, or fished the seas, yet we in Scotland,
in my day at least, were still in contact with the active language of
doing. So far from Scots being a language of feeling, it was the
reverse — a language of naming things and of doing. From all this
Edwin Muir was excluded. He was an outsider, pushed further
outside by residence in St Andrews. Because of his abilities,
modesty and understanding, in addition to the poetry of great
purity of vision he was yet to write after the 1939–45 war, he came
to make perceptive comment on certain Scottish achievement, but
in 1936, at the point when some justifiable confidence in the new
Scottish literature might be shown, when instead of exporting the
feeble curiosities of Barrie or Scotch comics, we could take a stand
on the evidence of the intelligence in the new literary product, he
reneged. But then, as I said, he was an outsider.

Muir's is the typical position, MacDiarmid's the atypical. The
developments of mass civilisation have told one thing to all true
artists. There is nothing inside the society which gets by from day
to day on an endless lust for goods and money and on narcotics —
physical and mental. Eliot came to London, knowingly or
unknowingly, to project from the heart of the dessication, the
fragmentation and sterile ending of a culture, yet in the very

season of the publication of *The Waste Land*, of the poem of "desert and stony rock", MacDiarmid is singing in a foreign tongue, of the mysterious, endlessly productive universe, in a traditional, communal speech, enlarged and ornamented by his imagination; and following this with increasing directness and range of application, with a less unusual vocabulary, but with the same character of mind, his productions multiply. Because he worked from the inside of this language, that is to say perceived by means of it, he would not perceive how peculiar and unlikely were his developments, and those of other writers, born to the Scots tradition of speech and mental habit, and now accepting the inheritance of MacDiarmid's perception.

"The Genius of Poetry," wrote Keats in a letter to Hessey (9/10/1818), "must work out its own salvation in a man. It cannot be matured by law and precept, but by sensation and watchfulness. That which is creative must create itself." In Keats's case, the new direction having been given by Wordsworth, the conditions were generally propitious, in MacDiarmid's, his avid pursuit, even "by sensation and watchfulness" in unpropitious conditions, brought great success, and much that was flawed.

The Scotched Snake

KENNETH BUTHLAY

In a review of MacDiarmid's *Complete Poems*, David Daiches has made a forthright statement of the reader's needs beyond the bare text: "We want information about the relation of the poems to each other, about the sources of quotations, about the meaning of the more esoteric allusions, and so on, so that as we read we can fully enter into MacDiarmid's poetic world and appreciate what is going on in each poem."[1] If we look at the poet's work chronologically, *To Circumjack Cencrastus* (1930) seems to mark the point at which most readers begin to feel this need acutely, and it may therefore be useful to say something about *Cencrastus* along the lines suggested by Daiches' remark.

Information about allusions and quotations is very obviously pertinent in this case, and there is also some rather hazy overlapping with the major work that preceded it, *A Drunk Man Looks at the Thistle* (1926). For example, take some of the obscure but related themes in the later sections of *A Drunk Man* which commentators on the poem have tended to pass over: the idea, which came to MacDiarmid via Tyutchev and Shestov, of trying his luck, as a metaphysical gambler, with Chaos rather than Cosmos; the concept of the Unknown God, hidden in the darkness of Chaos, as distinct from the lesser deity which, under various names, mankind has made accountable for the Creation; and the eternal silence of Thought which endures unbroken by the Word which allegedly commanded, "Let there be light".

The mysterious silence which is the "croon o' a'"[2] at the end of *A Drunk Man* has behind it, among other things, Tyutchev's line in "Silentium", "an uttered thought is a lie"; and this becomes clearer to the reader through the reference to that same poem in *Cencrastus*:

> Silence is the only way. . . .
> Tyutchev was richt and men maun gang
> Awa' frae life to find
> Haill worlds o' magic thochts
> Day's licht can only blind.   (70-71; 218-9.)[3]

The relevant passage in "Silentium" is this:

> Know how to live within—
> Your soul contains a world
> Of mysterious, magical thoughts;
> The outer tumult stifles,
> The beams of daylight blind;
> Hear their song and be silent.[4]

Some familiarity with Tyutchev's work will also cast light on the immediately preceding passage in *Cencrastus*:

> Silence—like Chaos ere the Word
> That gar'd the Play enact
> That sune to conscious thocht
> Maun seem a foolish dream.
> Nae Word has yet been said,
> Nae Licht's begun to gleam.

Compare with that (and with the extended treatment of the themes of darkness and chaos in *A Drunk Man*) the following account of the Russian poet:

Tyutchev views the universe as the stage of an enormous drama, a tragic conflict between the opposing forces of order and disorder, between the consoling illusion of life and the awful mystery of creation. The poet symbolizes this drama or conflict in a series of polarities or antitheses such as Chaos and Cosmos, . . . Night and Day. The conflict is, however, more apparent than real: the drama is perhaps a mere play. Yet the struggle, if any, ends with the inexorable victory of what man deems to be the negative and destructive element, although it may well be the positive and constructive one. Creation is also annihilation: this is why Night is always bound to triumph over Day.[5]

In *Cencrastus*, as in *A Drunk Man*, there is contempt for "God the Creator", "the common God" as conceived by men, in contrast to the "unkent God",

> . . . Him that lifts unkennable ayont
> Creation and Creator baith! (116; 244.)

Although getting only a passing mention, I think, in the Bible,[6] the Unknown God is central to the conception of supreme deity in the Cabbala, which MacDiarmid cites, via his friend Denis Saurat, as a main source of ideas for poets. (187; 283.) To the Unknown God he gives the emblem of the Golden Eagle, and then, with some difficulty, aligns the world-serpent,

> The immortal serpent wa'd up in life
> As God in the thochts o' men, (117; 244.)

with Cencrastus, of whom he had said at the opening of the poem,

> There is nae movement in the warld like yours.

There are also in *A Drunk Man* hints of MacDiarmid's interest in Solovyov, and these become more pronounced in *Cencrastus*, to the extent of an explicit reference to that rare man, a mystic with a sense of humour, and his love affair with a Finnish lake. (52; 208.) Typically, examples may occur sixty pages apart:

> The consciousness that maitter has entrapped
> In minerals, plants and beasts is strugglin' yet
> In men's minds only, seekin' to win free. . . .   (12; 187.)

> The day is comin' when ilka stane
> 'll hae as guid as a human brain
> And frae what they are noo men
> Develop in proportion then
>   (At least it's hoped they will
>   And no' be owretaen still)
> While sex and ither hauf way stages
> Perish wi' the barbarous Ages. . . .   (75; 221.)

A succinct statement of the belief that lies behind this is made in one of MacDiarmid's letters: "In Russian religious thought (e.g. Soloviev) man's destiny is through his consciousness to reconcile the lower orders of creation — animals, plants, minerals — to St. Sophia, the Wisdom of God, who is the female hypostasis of the

Deity."[7] Mankind is to raise the material world to consciousness, and so to reunion with God. And as to "sex and ither hauf way stages" in human development — in Solovyov's somewhat theurgical conception of love, "to create the true human being as a free unity of the masculine and feminine elements, which preserve their formal separateness but overcome their essential disparity and disruption, is the direct task of love".[8] This is in order to restore the divine image in mankind, and:

> Since God created man, in his own likeness, and as male and female, it follows that the image and likeness of God (that which is capable of restoration) does not refer to the moiety, not to the half of man, but to man complete, i.e., to the positive union of the male and female principles — a true androgyny — without external fusion of forms, which would be a monstrosity, and without an inner separation of personality and life, which would be an imperfection and a principle of death.[9]

How one is to reconcile this with the Unknown God, who "gin e'er He saw a man, 'ud be/E'en mair dumfooner'd at the sicht than he", I leave to the reader to decide. But it is at least of some practical use to recognise where some of the stranger ideas in *Cencrastus* have come from.

This modest utility might be thought particularly welcome to readers of this poem because *Cencrastus* really is a gallimaufry — very much more so than *A Drunk Man*, to which MacDiarmid applied that term. And since it is such a Scotch broth, Irish stew, and ultimately international *olla podrida* of bits and pieces, the obscurity encountered in the poem tends to be obscurity of an undesirable kind, not the kind that may be imaginatively stimulating. Merely identifying some of the ingredients may therefore be reassuring, and help one to savour the good bits, of which there are not a few.

One of the main reasons why this work strikes one as a gallimaufry is the poet's failure to sustain an imaginative response to his solitary key-symbol of the serpent in the course of his very long poem-sequence. He had made effective use of this symbol in the poem "Sea-Serpent" in *Penny Wheep* and also, as one of a cluster of important supporting images around the thistle, in *A*

Drunk Man. He then evidently thought of it as potentially of such power that it could stand by itself as the imaginative core of a work which is about a third as long again as the book-length *Drunk Man.*

The verbal impulse his imagination seems to have so often required was forthcoming in Jamieson's *Dictionary: Cencrastus*, the name of a greenish serpent with a belly speckled with spots like millet-seeds; and *To Circumjack Cencrastus*, to agree to, or correspond with (from *circumjacere*, to lie round or about). Lascelles Abercrombie had told him in a letter that "you have a serpent in you which will eat up everything else", and MacDiarmid associated this with a winding path near Langholm called the Curly Snake, of which he said that "it has always haunted my imagination and has probably constituted itself the ground-plan and pattern of my mind".[10] So he was all set: he would show that "it's a big beast there's no room for outside", by circumjacking Cencrastus in a poem which from the start he envisaged as "a much bigger thing than the *Drunk Man* in every way" (even before the latter was published). His own account of what he then had in mind, in 1926, was as follows:

> Cencrastus is the fundamental serpent, the underlying unifying principle of the cosmos. To circumjack is to encircle. To circumjack Cencrastus — to square the circle, to box the compass etc. But where the *Drunk Man* is in one sense a reaction to the 'Kailyard', *Cencrastus* transcends that altogether — the Scotsman gets rid of the thistle, 'the bur o' the world' — and his spirit at last inherits its proper sphere. Psychologically it represents the resolution of the sadism and masochism, the synthesis of the various sets of antitheses I was posing in the *Drunk Man*. It will not depend on the contrasts of realism and metaphysics, bestiality and beauty, humour and madness — but move on a plane of pure beauty and pure music. It will be an attempt to move really mighty numbers . . . ideally complementary to the *Drunk Man* — positive where it is negative, optimistic where it is pessimistic, and constructive where it is destructive.[11]

At that time, he allowed that it would be "about a year at least" before Cencrastus would be duly circumjacked. It was in fact four years before he finished the poem, after much agonising, and he then told the same correspondent:

> I did not do in it what I intended — I deliberately deserted my big plan, because I realised I had lots of elements in me, standing between me and really great work, I'd to get rid of — and I think I've done it. My next book will be a very different matter — with none of the little local and temporary references, personalities, political propaganda, literary allusiveness etc.[12]

And he was off again, "working very hard", he said, on a project based on Goethe's *Faust* as Joyce's *Ulysses* had been on Homer.

Now, whatever he thought the elements were in himself which had frustrated the great poem he had envisaged, it is known that he had personal problems concerning his job, his finances, his wife, and not a few of his associates in literature and politics, before he left Montrose in August 1929.* And there followed on that move from Scotland to London a series of acute crises, involving a serious accident which he described as "a miraculous escape from death", a grim struggle with unemployment, and the breaking up of his marriage, all in the period when he was trying to put *Cencrastus* together for his waiting publishers. Compton Mackenzie, whose offer of a job on the new and under-financed radio magazine *Vox* had brought MacDiarmid to London in the first place, has said all that is needed about the conditions in which the poet was then working. Soon after its publication, he wrote of

---

*Since this essay was written, a letter from F. G. Scott to Maurice Lindsay has been exhibited at the National Library of Scotland. In this letter, dated 20 May 1945, Scott emphasises the importance of his advice and guidance to MacDiarmid, who, he says, "never had any sense of form". Having described his famous visit to Montrose to create order from the chaos of MacDiarmid's material for *A Drunk Man*, Scott says that the poet's "next call for a visit was before the 'Cencrastus' MS was sent off to Blackwoods. Again I went through to Montrose but he was very disappointed that I couldn't give him my approval of the poem and he was still more disappointed when the MS was returned to him. I know that for some time after this he was very unsettled and gladly went off to London. . . . He pottered on with the 'Cencrastus' MS for a few months and it finally appeared in 1930, but Blackwoods dropped him I fancy after completing their contract and when he wrote me from London enclosing the book he asked me never to discuss it with him."

the author of *Cencrastus*: "the fact of his being able to produce a book at all under the conditions in which he has had to be working during the last two years makes me judge it too much as a miracle, too little as a work of art".[13]

But what sort of a work was it that he had spent so long not only writing but "arranging and re-arranging"?[14] Although he said he deliberately abandoned his "big plan", traces of *Cencrastus* as conceived on a highly metaphysical level of "Godheid and Scottishness" show through the poem as published like a palimpsest. It also contains a lot of inferior verse, dashed off in irritable frustration, or sometimes forced humour, because of his failure to rise to his original theme, as indeed he himself acknowledges:

> (Hell tak this improvisin'
> That leads a' airts and nane;
> A kind o' anti-poetry
> That is true poetry's bane!)   (105; 238.)

Much of this is encumbered with the "little local and temporary references, personalities", etc., mentioned in the letter already quoted. But there is also a major theme of a very different order which MacDiarmid never mentions in any of his references to the writing of the poem that I have read, though one can see it growing strongly in influence on his thinking in other respects from at least as early as 1927. By then he felt he could see a trend in the "many-sided and widespread national movement" he had pioneered finding its proper basis in the Gaelic heritage, to which "a return must be made before a foundation can be secured for the creation of major forms either in arts or affairs".[15] His growing conviction of the radical significance of this Gaelic heritage was reinforced by various contacts, including his meetings with prominent literary and political figures in Ireland in 1928. His "Scottish Idea" was becoming "the Gaelic Idea" — his vision of a revival of the ethos not of Lowland Scotland but of Gaeldom, which he already believed to have much more momentous ramifications — and it is my belief that what he tried to do about the problem of a pining *Cencrastus* was to orientate the poem towards his conception of a Celtic renaissance, in which Scotland would be internationally aligned with the other Celtic countries.

However, he failed to carry this out effectively, and the Celtic polarity of the poem remains relatively weak. When the reader encounters "the Gaelic Idea", more than a third of the way through the poem, he is very unlikely to perceive its bearing on the scattered mass of Celtic material and allusions with which the poet confronts him. Rather, he will be inclined to see it as a more or less isolated and eccentric political puzzle:

> If we turn to Europe and see
> Hoo the emergence o' the Russian Idea's
> Broken the balance o' the North and Sooth
> And needs a coonter that can only be
> The Gaelic Idea
> To mak' a parallelogram o' forces,
> Complete the Defence o' the West,
> And end the English betrayal o' Europe. (77; 222-3.)

Even such readers as have come across in MacDiarmid's occasional prose his application of the Gaelic Idea to the Defence of the West will have some difficulty in pinning it down to its context in the poem, though they may at least recognise it as a shorthand version of what emerges from the following passages:

> As to . . . 'The Defence of the West', or the Conservation of European Civilisation — the old balance or conflict between the North and the South has been violently disrupted by the emergence of Russia and the Soviet conception of things. That constitutes a third side; where is the fourth to come from — not from England; but whence else if not from Gaelic culture — the fourth side upon which European civilization can re-establish itself. . . .?[16]
>
> How is a quadrilateral of forces to be established? England partakes too much of Teutonic and Mediterranean influences; it is a composite — not a 'thing-in-itself'. Only in Gaeldom can there be the necessary counter-idea to the Russian idea — one that does not run wholly counter to it, but supplements, corrects, challenges, and qualifies it. Soviet economics are confronted with the Gaelic system with its repudiation of usury which finds its modern expression in Douglas economics. The dictatorship of the proletariat is confronted by the Gaelic commonwealth with its aristocratic culture — the high place it gave to its poets and scholars. And so on.[17]

129

Now in the poem, there are some indications of the aristocratic aspect of Gaelic culture, but there is little enough to lead the reader to suspect the significance of this for the Gaelic Idea so described. The Gaelic economic system is not suggested in any form that we could oppose to Soviet economics, should it occur to us to do so, and we only become aware of Douglas economics because the poet supplies a note to tell us that this is what he had in mind when he said (on p. 88; 229) that everyone could easily be millionaires tomorrow.

It will hardly be helpful if we happen to recall MacDiarmid's alternative version of the "Defence of the West" in anti-*American* guise: "the reconcilation of Europe and opposition to American conceptions in particular".[18] But that apart, how many readers will have picked up the primary reference to Henri Massis's book, *The Defence of the West* (serialised portentously in the *Criterion* in 1926 before publication the following year), in which the West is represented by Catholic Latin civilisation, threatened by the "dark barbarism" of "Bolshevism and Asiaticism" abetted by developments in post-war Germany?

A further difficulty may present itself to readers familiar with MacDiarmid's enthusiasm for "The Russian Idea" as originally conceived by Dostoievsky: how to reconcile that ultimately religious idea of Russia's historic national destiny with what we are now told is "the Soviet concept of things"? The answer is given in "The Caledonian Antisyzygy and the Gaelic Idea" as follows:

> The point is that Dostoevski's was a great creative idea—a dynamic myth — and in no way devalued by the difference of the actual happenings in Russia from any Dostoevski dreamed or desired. So we in Scotland (in association with the other Gaelic elements with whose aid we may reduce England to a subordinate role in the economy of these islands) need not care how future events belie our anticipations so long as we polarize Russia effectively — proclaim that relationship between freedom and genius, between freedom and thought, which Russia is denying — help to rebalance Europe in accordance with our distinctive genius — rediscover and manifest anew our dynamic spirit as a nation.

If we put aside the economic theory, since it is hardly present in the poem, the essential point for MacDiarmid thus appears to be that a great historical opportunity exists for Scotland and the other Celtic countries to contribute to the survival of Western European culture in a way impossible to England. This involves the rediscovery of the Celtic ethos and its expression in a dynamic myth, the Gaelic Idea, to counter-balance the emergence of the Russian Idea in its Soviet form.

Now, linked with the Gaelic Idea in the poet's mind, and intended to be linked with it in the poem, is the theme of "The Unconscious Goal of History" — the title he gave to a section of *Cencrastus* when he included it in *More Collected Poems* (1970). This section is placed very near the end of the poem (pp. 194-9; 287-9), which is one reason why readers may not be apt to connect it with the announcement of the Gaelic Idea (back on pp. 77; 222-3). And the poet's failure to supply anything in the interim that would substantially strengthen the connection is due, I think, to his lack of confidence in himself, a failure of nerve.

Again there is some explanatory material available in his prose: "[Nations] move towards the unconscious goal of history and as long as they have failed to realise any fraction of their distinctive function in that great process, they will and must continue to strive for it, however they may seem at any particular period to forget or neglect it. . . ."[19] But the aspect of this theme which is given most emphasis in *Cencrastus* is the capacity of men of genius to embody the aims of history, and ultimately even to achieve full consciousness of its "unconscious goal". When it comes to the point of affirming the Gaelic Idea as this particular man of genius's contribution to the process, however, the poet becomes uncharacteristically tentative, even diffident. Not so much, I think, because he is unwilling to stake his claim to genius, but rather because he is aware that the real basis for any such claim in his case — a level of poetry worthy of the vision — is not forthcoming in this poem. The best he can rise to is really a covert apology for not having found the poetry for his vision of the Gaelic Idea:

> Unconscious goal of history, dimly seen
> In Genius whiles that kens the problem o' its age

131

And works at it. . . .
Sae History mak's the ambitions o' great men
Means to ends greater than themsels could ken,
—Greater and ither—and mass ignorance yields,
Like corruption o' vegetation in fallow fields,
The conditions o' richer increase; — at last
The confusion's owre, the time comes fast
When men wauk to the possibility
O' workin' oot and makin' their destiny
In fu' consciousness and cease to muddle through
Wi' nae idea o' their goal—and nae mair grue!

Let nane cry that the right men arena here
—That urgent tasks await that nane can dae.
Times oft mistak' their problems in that way.
At the richt time the richt men aye appear.
If Scotland fills us wi' despair we may
Be proposin' a goal that disna lie
Onywhaur in history's plan the noo. . . .
But a'e thing's certain—nae genius'll come,
Nae maitter hoo he's shouted for, to recreate
The life and fabric o' a decadent State
That's dune its work, gien its Idea to the world,
The problem is to find in Scotland some
Bricht coil o' you that hasna yet uncurled,
And, hoosoever petty I may be, the fact
That I think Scotland isna dune yet proves
There's something in it that fulfilment's lacked
And my vague hope through a' creation moves.
(194-6; 287-8.)

We are given this "vague hope" instead of the "dynamic myth",
the "great creative idea", because of MacDiarmid's lack of
confidence in himself, not in the myth or idea itself, of which he
said: "it does not matter a rap whether the whole conception of
this Gaelic Idea is as far-fetched as Dostoevski's Russian Idea".
Hence the reader's attention is turned to the more general line of
thought which in fact carries the drift of the poem at this point: the
relation of the unconscious goal of history to the man of genius.
And this is one of the points at which he may feel the need for some
sign-posting.

One might point in the direction of Hegel and his "world historical individuals", but that would only take us where many speculations about the historical role of the hero or man of genius began. The most useful reference here would be to Eduard von Hartmann, whose *Philosophy of the Unconscious*, having enjoyed a great popular success in his own day, was attracting attention again when MacDiarmid was writing *Cencrastus*: a new edition of the English translation by W. C. Coupland in fact came out in 1931. Hartmann's relevance to the passage just quoted from *Cencrastus* may be seen in what follows, from the beginning of the second volume of the *Philosophy of the Unconscious*:

> Undoubtedly since the close of the last century we have been making approaches to that ideal state where the human race *consciously* accomplishes its destiny. . . . Centuries of retrogression seem to contradict it; this contradiction, however, is only apparent, for they serve the purpose of . . . allowing a vegetation to grow corrupt, in order that it may manure the ground for something fresh and fairer. . . . History attains, by the initiative of eminent individuals, results which were quite beside the conscious purposes of such men. . . . Other ends are attained by the Unconscious . . . when it calls forth the right genius at the right time, who is enabled just to solve that problem, whose solution his age urgently needs. . . . The right man has never been wanting at the right time; and the cry sometimes heard, that men are lacking for certain urgent tasks, only proves that the problems have been wrongly proposed by human consciousness, that they do not at all (or at least not now) lie in the plan of history. . . . (Such an *absolutely* insoluble problem, *e.g.*, is the regeneration and strengthening of States doomed to decay and dissolution. A *temporarily* insoluble problem, on the other hand, is the revival of original production in some special field of mental work, which, in the hands of the Epigoni, must lie fallow for a season, before a new phase of development commences under the influence of a new and fertile idea.)

There can be little doubt that MacDiarmid believed the "new and fertile idea" in this case was the Gaelic Idea, and, to put it bluntly, the ultimate truth of such a belief could happily be left for God to judge, if there is one, just so long as it issued in a great poem that would reawaken the Celtic world. But the Gaelic idea is left all too nebulous here to be a source of the vitality he seeks:

> Sae that my people frae their living graves
> May loup and play a pairt in History yet.   (197; 288.)

Faced with this impasse, the poet attempts an instant switch back to *Cencrastus* on the religious level by means of an allusion to T. E. Hulme's "religious attitude", the basis for this piece of sleight-of-mind being the coincidence that Hulme also used the image of a snake:

> A' roads are closed;
> North, South, East, West nae mair opposed.

(Here the reader is expected to recall the "parallelogram o' forces" 122 pages earlier on, and presumably to regard the compass as having been boxed.)

> Withoot a leg to stand on, like a snake
> Wi' impossible lustres I shake.
> Earth contracts to a single point of licht
> As men, deceived by their een, see stars at nicht,
> And the religious attitude has found
> In Scotland yet a balancin' ground.   (289.)

The reader, feeling perhaps that he too has been left without a leg to stand on, may welcome a little light on the allusion. MacDiarmid quotes it from Hulme ("Humanism and the Religious Attitude") in the course of an essay on Gertrude Stein:

> . . . to force the mind back on the centre by the closing of all roads on the plane. . . . The result is what follows the snake eating its own tail, an infinite straight line perpendicular to the plane. In other words, you get the religious attitude. . . . It is the closing of all roads, this realization of the tragic significance of life, which makes it legitimate to call all other attitudes shallow.[20]

But, having performed the trick of balancing Hulme's religious attitude on such shifting Scottish ground, the poet abruptly takes off in pursuit of images of Sea and Snake in quite different territory, discovered in an article in the *New Age* by someone calling himself "Filioque".[21] It is of course much too late, in terms

of the structure of his poem, to make anything of this new symbol
of the sea in relation to this snake, which in any case turns out to be
no legitimate relative of Cencrastus but an emblem of belligerent
imperialism (contrasted in the original with socialism and
freedom). And thus MacDiarmid appears to end up by
circumjacking the wrong snake.

Not that the other snake in Hulme's little joke will have been
observed by the reader to have had much more relevance to
Cencrastus, whose movements, according to the author, were
supposed to be forming the patterns of world history at that point.
Although he gave that account of Cencrastus's function in a
letter[22] written for purposes of explanation long after the
publication of the work, a letter which must therefore be handled
with care, there is no reason why the movements of the great
snake should not have been effectively associated with the
patterns of history, as is indeed suggested fitfully in parts of the
poem. But the fact is that the poet does not make the relevant
association when it is most needed, and in the event, any such
association is bound to be weakened by the emphasis he has given
to the reiterated invocation of Cencrastus: "There is nae
movement in the warld like yours". If there is nothing like it in the
world, it is hard to see it as the movement of world history.

One has to conclude, I think, that for MacDiarmid at the end of
his epic voyage, any refuge will do in a storm, and, as he himself
says, he has been

> Oot in ilka brainstorm
> Withoot an umbrella.   (131; 252.)

His difficulties were such that he did not contrive to end the work
with even a forced application of the great serpent symbol with
which he began it, but felt compelled to interrupt his sea-and-snake
passage with a fine but awkwardly placed poem, "My Love is to
the Light of Lights", based on the image of a golden fawn, which is
perhaps more likely than the snake, as handled by him, to evoke
the Celtic ethos for the reader. Indeed, as already suggested, one
of the crucial weaknesses in *Cencrastus* is the poet's failure to put
his master-image of the serpent to effective structural use, as he
had done with the thistle in *A Drunk Man*. Most conspicuoulsy
perhaps, the snake-motif in its more familiar Celtic forms cries

out to be exploited as an imaginative link between his metaphysical speculations about Cencrastus and his exploration of the Gaelic heritage, but MacDiarmid's rather sad gesture in that direction goes little beyond a reference to himself as a poet

> Wha aince o' verses like the serpent work
> On Innis Draomich's crosses dreamt. (29; 196.)

With so little real coalescence of imagery to support the poem's allusiveness, readers become all the more aware of, and sometimes frustrated or irritated by, "the more esoteric allusions" and quotations in what they encounter mainly as a succession of separate items, some fragmentary, some apparently complete in themselves, some embedded in others. There are two broad literary contexts within which the poet manipulates these materials, Celtic and European, in heavy contrast to the provincial Scots kailyard, and although they are indeed all too broad, a few notes on one reader's findings in these two areas may be of interest to others.

A small beginning has already been made on the Celtic side by Douglas Sealy, with his passing reference to the Gaelic background of *Cencrastus*.[23] This indicated that MacDiarmid's main source for Irish material was Aodh De Blácam, and was rather disappointing for anyone who had taken up MacDiarmid's recommendations of De Blácam's *Gaelic Literature Surveyed* and read the book for himself. Sealy considers that MacDiarmid was led to overestimate certain Irish Gaelic poets by De Blácam's propaganda, but his own estimation of them varies between the two versions of his essay, and does not materially affect the main issue. Propaganda, whether his own or others, was very much to MacDiarmid's purpose in trying to redress centuries of neglect and condescension where Gaelic literature was concerned; and in any case, Sealy does not tell us what he should have read instead of De Blácam.

Not Douglas Hyde's classic *Literary History of Ireland*, or Magnus Maclean's *Literature of the Celts*, it would seem, since they were responsible for MacDiarmid's belief in the astonishing originality of the Scots Gaelic poet, Màiri Nighean Alasdair Ruaidh:

Mary Macleod
Wi' a wheen sangs frae her careless hert owreturned
The traditions o' thoosands o' years
And altered twa literatures—aye gied her mode
Sae strang a haud that a' that gaed afore
Was blotted oot as it had never been,
Folks' natures and notions changed until
It seemed impossible they'd been ocht else
Ev'n in the deepest things—the way they loved
And saw the coloured warld wi' their ain een. . . .
It alters the haill complexion o' life
And mak's a deid language o' a' we've kent.
The music the bards for thoosands o' years
Missed is hers by an accident. (139-141; 256-7.)

That is based on the view of Mary as a revolutionary pioneer put forward by Hyde and accepted by Maclean and others, according to which, although she was evidently not literate, she ushered in developments in technique which were amongst

> the most far-reaching changes that could overtake the poetry of any country. . . . Almost in the twinkling of an eye, Irish poetry completely changed its form and complexion, and from being, as it were, so bound up and swathed with rules that none who had not spent years over its technicalities could move about in it with vigour, its spirit suddenly burst forth in all the freedom of the elements, and clothed itself, so to speak, in the colours of the rainbow. . . . The remnant of the bards . . . threw behind them the intricate metres of the schools, and dropped too, at a stroke, several thousand words. . . . The Gaelic poetry of the last two centuries both in Ireland and in the Highlands is probably the most sensuous attempt to convey music in words, ever made by man.[24]

Sealy objects to MacDiarmid's celebration of the part played by Mary Macleod in bringing this great change about, on the grounds that W. J. Watson had discredited the view that the new Gaelic poetry originated in her poems. And it is true that Watson adduced evidence against that view in the introduction to his *Bardachd Ghaidlig*, which, being published in 1918, was available to MacDiarmid. It seems rather hard on the latter, however, to

137

condemn him on that account without mentioning the fact that, if he was wrong about Mary Macleod, he shared his error with scholars of repute, including the great Douglas Hyde himself.

Sealy concludes his note on the Mary Macleod passage in *Cencrastus* by remarking that "the situation is hardly redeemed at the end of the passage with the following verse:

> Auld Mary Macleod in her tartan tonnag
> Has finished her bottle and toomed her mull
> And the sang the Lord put new in her mooth
> Has turned unspeakably dull.

This seems to be offered for our ridicule as fortuitous bathos, which indeed may be its effect if one is unaware of what MacDiarmid had in mind when he wrote it. Clarification of the details is available via Magnus Maclean: "It needs some of Mary's own imagination to picture her going about in after days wearing a tartan *tonnag*, fastened in front with a large silver brooch, and carrying a silver-headed cane. Hardy to a degree in mind and constitution, the venerable nurse and poetess, when long past the natural span of years, was much given, we are told, to gossip, snuff, and whisky."[25] But the main point of MacDiarmid's lines is that, although he celebrated what he believed to be the astonishing originality and influence of the venerable Mary, he by no means accepted the assumption, made by Hyde and others after him, that the poetic revolution associated with her name was an unmitigated good. In his view, the ultimate product of that radical change in technique and sensibility had proved to be the prolonged "Celtic Twilight", which he found not only "unspeakably dull" but thoroughly deplorable, and he believed that a swing back in the direction of the old bardic disciplines, with an accompanying re-intellectualisation of the Gaelic ethos, was long overdue.

One can assert with the more confidence that this was the point of MacDiarmid's concluding lines about Mary Macleod if one has read what he wrote about her elsewhere at the time, but the point is far from being clear in the context of the poem itself. And there are other allusions which stand in need of clarification if one is to follow what is going on in this very long work, some of weighty importance, other much less so but liable to become accumulatively irritating to the reader.

Sealy doesn't mention the fact that MacDiarmid drew on De Blácam not only for Irish quotations and allusions but also for the notes to *Cencrastus* which he supplied, none too generously, for his readers' assistance. As an authority on Irish poetry, however, Sealy might have noticed — as I see the editors of the *Complete Poems* have — that one of these notes stood in much need of correction: a poem by Hugh MacCurtin which De Blácam says, "exhibits the same spirit as 'The Parliament of Clan Thomas'", was said by MacDiarmid to *be* "The Parliament of Clan Thomas". Also, amongst MacDiarmid's sins of omission, there is at least one heinous example:

> . . . Blessings on the honey mouth
> That loved the forests of Alba,
> Cut down now, that may grow again
> Thanks to the branch of Ireland
> Growing among us with might and main. (52; 208-9.)

The "honey mouth" belonged to a Scot into whose possession had come a treasured Irish harp which the bard Gilbride Albanach MacNamee went to Scotland to redeem, if need be at the price of a shipload of Irish sheep. However, the Scotsman would not part with it, saying (in Gilbride's poem, *Tabhroidh chugam cruit mo ríogh,* "Bring to me the harp of my kind"): "Dear to me (my due by birth), the fair forest of Alba; strange it is, yet more I love this tree from Eire's woodlands." And the absence of that piece of information obscures MacDiarmid's intention, which was to have the unknown Scotsman's feelings for the Irish harp suggest his own attitude to what was a very live and controversial issue at that time: the question of "The Irish in Scotland" — the title he had in fact given these verses when he published them in the *Irish Statesman* prior to their inclusion in *Cencrastus*. This lacuna is particularly important because it occurs at a point in the poem where the author wants to emphasise that his exploration of the Celtic past is not something remote from contemporary reality but has a profound bearing on such urgent questions of the day as the massive influx of the Irish in Scotland's population. MacDiarmid, in the light of his Gaelic Idea, which is here all too faint for the reader, of course takes a highly optimistic view of the outcome.

139

The possibility of anyone forging singlehanded a living link between contemporary poetry in Scots and the Gaelic poetic tradition is, however, a rather different matter. Even MacDiarmid's inveterate optimism barely stretches so far; and the implications of this will be heightened for the reader if he is aware of the irony in the image the poet chooses for his purpose here: the Mavis of Pabal (Paible, in North Uist). There is a strong contrast between the message MacDiarmid puts into the mouth of the mavis and that of the original, in a poem by John MacCodrum, "Smeorach Chlann-Domhnuill" ("The Mavis of Clan Donald"). Though he echoes the opening lines of John Stuart Blackie's translation of MacCodrum, that is just MacDiarmid's starting point. The sadness of MacCodrum's bird is in fact only a memory of the past, and he goes on joyfully to celebrate the good that comes to him from his native land:

> The Mavis of Pabal am I; in my nest
> I lay long time with my head on my breast,
> Dozing away the dreary hour,
> In the day that was dark, and the time that was sour.
>
> But now I soar to the mountain's crest,
> For the chief is returned whom I love best;
> In the face of the sun, on the fringe of the wood,
> Feeding myself with wealth of good.[26]

In marked contrast to this, MacDiarmid's mavis can only revive his song "if singin' depends on will", which, despite his Nietzschean exercises, he knows it doesn't — and "there's nae sign o' a mate to be seen". He has come back to the hilltop in Paible, but he says,

> I should ha'e stayed wi' the rest
> Doon in Coille Ghrumach still
> And no' ettled to be on the crest
> O' this bricht impossible hill,
>   For poetry's no' made in a lifetime
>   And I lack a livin' past;
>   I stand on the tap o' the hill
>   —But the miracle canna last! (21; 192.)

MacDiarmid has already left MacCodrum's poem behind him. The reference of Coille Ghruamach (so it should be spelled, I believe, and it means "gloomy forest") is to a Highland emigrant's poem, *Am Bàrd an Canada*, written by John Maclean after his arrival in Nova Scotia in 1819. It opens with the poet suffering in the Coille Ghruamach, "in a wilderness by Barney's River" which is "at strife with the laws of nature". The strength is leaving his heart and brain, he can no longer sing "the old songs of Albyn", the Gaelic is dying. And clearly it is only when the reader can pick up this reference that he is able to savour the full bitterness of MacDiarmid's last stanza, beginning:

> Maun I flee the Atlantic tae
> Whaur ten thoosand o' the clan
> Host whaur the first ane landit
> —I'd leifer ha'e seen nae dawn.

It should now be rather easier to relate "The Mavis of Pabal" to the piece that precedes it in *Cencrastus*:

> Yet wae for the poet wi' nocht but his bluid
> For a bardic goon.
> Like the last dark reid crawberries under the firs
> His life'll be sune.
> Bodach cleòcain deirg.

> For he that's aince lain in the Yellow Stag's Couch
> —Leabaidh an Daimh Bhuidhe—
> 'll never sing frae the Ruigh Bristidh Cridhe
> The sangs he s'ud to ye.
> Bodach cleòcain deirg.

Here the reader without Gaelic gets the explicit idea from the first two lines; and since, for any category of reader, the Gaelic placenames have to act by suggestion, I doubt if even tracing them back to the source where MacDiarmid found them supplies much that is needful beyond their literal meaning. However, this procedure has the added interest of showing how the little poem was put together, which will be evident from these fragments, noted in Seton Gordon's book on the Cairngorms:

> Beneath the firs the dark red crawberries lingered. . . .
> Coylum, the former haunt of Bodach Cleocain Deirg, or the

141

Spectre of the Red Cloak. . . . The old name for the hill-top
[the summit of Ben A'an] is Leabaidh an Daimh Bhuide—in
English, "the couch of the Yellow Stag".[27]

Seton Gordon also suggested the following verses:

> At dawn at the heid o' Clais Linneach
>   A mile frae Fuaran Dhé
> I saw a wee clood that awa doon
>   In Glen Guisachan lay.
> It grew as the sun's strength grew
> Till it filled ilka glen and corrie
> And covered a' but the heichmaist taps
> O' the Cairngorms billowin' hoary.
> The sun's licht on the clood reflected
>   As on the waves o' a sea,
> And as frae the Ark on Ararat
>   The warld then was to me;
> Syne fifty miles owre the mist-ocean
> Wha but Alasdair MacMhaighstir stude?
> Pricked oot in the blue and gowd there
> In his maist idiosyncratic mood!   (53-4; 209.)

The relevant passage in Gordon runs:

> One day of early June my wife and I pitched our small tent at
> the head of Clais Linneach, a mile from Fuaran Dhé, as the
> Springs of Dee are known in the Gaelic. . . . Far beneath us,
> in Glen Guisachan, a tiny cloud formed. Despite the
> increasing power of the sun it grew imperceptibly, until it
> overflowed into each glen and corrie, and covered all the
> Cairngorms except their highest tops. It was a memorable
> experience to look over that great expanse of low-lying
> cloud upon which the sun's light was reflected as though
> upon the waters of the sea. Fifty miles across the mist-ocean
> stood Ben Nevis, appearing several times its actual
> height. . . .[28]

The metamorphosis of Ben Nevis into Alasdair MacMhaighstir
(Alexander MacDonald) heralds MacDiarmid's tribute to the
great Scots Gaelic poet, in which there are perhaps two references
which require some acquaintance with the latter's poetry, in
addition to the author's note. When MacDiarmid complains of the
praise of Burns' and Tannahill's mice by people who have never

seen The Lion, it is helpful to know of MacDonald's bellicosely
patriotic poem, "The Praise of the Lion". And there is a special
treat for anyone who remembers the imagery of MacDonald's
"Sugar Brook", summarised thus by Nigel MacNeill:

> the cuckoo . . . the blythsome brown wren and the vieing
> linnet tune up their choicest pipes. The blackcock croaks,
> and the hen. . . . Then come the fishes, the bees, and the
> frisking calves. . . . The wailing swans. . . .[29]

Consider what MacDiarmid makes of that:

> The blythe broon wren and viein' linnet
> Tune up their pipes in you,
> The blackcock craws, the reid hen's in it,
> Swan and cuckoo;
> Fishes' and bees' and friskin' calves'
> Acutes and graves!   (57; 211.)

The Scottish bardic tradition as such is treated so obliquely in
Cencrastus that the general reader, in a country which has long
congratulated itself on a national educational system in which
such matters merit no attention whatsoever, may miss the point of
the passage where it is introduced:

> Wad that I held Staoiligary
> And the four pennies o' Drimisdale,
> And had never seen a news-sheet,
> No' even 'The Daily Mail',
> The fifteen generations afore me
> Could lippen me no' to fail
> Into the darkness o' alien time,
> To carry my sang and sgeul
> As the duck when she hears the thunder
> Dances to her ain Port a' Beul!   (53; 209.)

The *locus classicus* for the first part of this is the declaration by
Lachlann MacMhuirich in 1800: "According to the best of his
knowledge, he is the eighteenth in descent from Muireach, whose
posterity had officiated as bards to the family of Clanranald; and . .
. they had from that time, as the salary of their office, the farm of
Staoiligary and four pennies of Drimisdale during fifteen
generations."[30] MacDiarmid's immediate stimulus, however, was
probably a reference to the MacMhuirich bardic family by Seton
Gordon, from whom he would seem to have got that splendid image

of the duck: "when the duck hears the thunder she dances to her own Port a' Bial (mouth music)".[31] At any rate, Gordon will supply the necessary information about a number of other passing references that readers are likely to find puzzling. Thus, on page 165 (271) of *Cencrastus*, "Buachaille herds the waves", not with reference to any of the many possible place-names, but apparently because "in Gaelic the great northern diver is Bun a' Bhuachaille, which in English is the Herdsman of the Tide-race". "By the Feshie the sandpipers twitter/And the reid and white foxgloves wag in the wind" (192; 285) because Gordon saw and heard them there. And MacDiarmid's statement about the stags in the Forest of Gaich (Gaick?) which one has to strike on the flanks to waken, is an "enriched" version of a single such incident related by Gordon.[32]

Of course, the vast majority of MacDiarmid's readers need help with the Scots Gaelic just as much as with the Irish in the poem (as indeed *he* did), but he offers them only token assistance. Of the Gaelic expressions used on pp. 144-45 (259-60), he glosses only one: *tràigh adhairt*, we're told, is "used here in the literal sense, 'the coming forward of the beach' ". Which doesn't take the reader very far in his efforts to make sense of the passage. And the new gloss, "landfall", in *More Collected Poems* (1970), though it makes sense, does not I think indicate MacDiarmid's original meaning. Alasdair Alpin MacGregor is more helpful. One learns from him that the term is used to connote the spring tides; and he casts welcome light on the reference which follows, to the "deeper joke/Ahint the *gàir nan tonn*". This phrase is used of the sound of the waves, and "in the Hebrides the laughing of the waves is a term to which we frequently refer. In Gaelic we call it *gair nan tonn*, or *gair nan mara*, because of the close resemblance it bears to laughing. Very often this phrase is used in irony". And MacGregor also supplies the context for the use of *siantan dubha* to mean "tears": "black rains — the torrential rains that, according to Coinneach Odhar, the Brahan Seer, would one day leave Lewis desolate and unpopulated".[33]

Ignorance of our Gaelic inheritance is, of course, one of the principal targets for MacDiarmid's sarcastic assaults in *Cencrastus*, where he bitterly laments his own linguistic predicament:

> O wad at least my yokel words
> Some Gaelic strain had kept. (81; 225.)

Some of his other targets may now appear all too familiar: Harry
Lauderism, the Kailyard novel, and its equivalent in Scots verse,
Whistle Binkie. These are precisely the aspects of Scotland which
Cencrastus was planned to transcend altogether when the poem, it
may be recalled, was to be positive, optimistic, and constructive;
but in the upshot the Scotsman is very far from getting rid of "the
bur of the world". Even in these cases, however, the broad
sarcasm may be accompanied by formidable allusive agility which
might be expected to stretch most readers. For example, near the
beginning of the poem, a movement of Cencrastus transforms the
world into a sunny flood in which the poet sees humanity imaged
as a trout in the Esk or Ewes,

> Yet as I look its gantin' mou' becomes,
> Clearer than Whistle Binkie bards could draw,
> Tho' this was a' the ettle o' their clan,
> The waefu' gape o' a wee bairn's smile,
> *Semihiante labello* o' Catullus, there.
> > —O my wee troot! (9; 185.)

The reader, who is expected to have picked up the reference to
Catullus's infant "with half-opened lips" (*Carmina* lxi. 209), is
next given a stanza constructed from paraphrase and quotation of
T. E. Hulme, who to start with is himself paraphrasing Bergson:

> Freedom is *inconceivable*. The word
> Betrays the cause—a habit o' the mind,
> Thinkin' continually in a certain way,
> Generation after generation, till it seems
> This is Thocht's fixed unalterable mode;
> And here's the reason at aince why human Thocht
> Is few men's business and sae scant and shawl,
> And men hate poems dry and hard and needs
> Maun hae them fozy wi' infinity.
> 'The way a woman walkin' in the street
> Kicks oot her skirt ahint her is the thing,
> Mair than her sould, gin the exact word's found,
> > To gar the Heavens open.'

The material for all of that comes ultimately from Hulme's essays
on "The Philosophy of Intensive Manifolds" and "Romanticism

and Classicism",[34] though I think MacDiarmid did not take it directly from him but made use of an intermediary. Then, having injected that dose of Hulme's "classical" imagism as an antidote for Whistle Binkie sentimentalism, the poet returns to the Kailyard briefly before broadening out his theme:

> Then fix the babby in a guid Scots word,
> That language no' o' Pan but Peter Pan,
> (Christ leuch wi' toom gans aince, the Lord Buddha
> Was in a crawl o' bairns aboot the doors)
> The dowf and daft-like babby and the way
> Its murgeons munk oor manhood and gaup up
> Sillier than ever on the face o' Daith.
> Mankind ends as it sterted, mappiemou'd,
> And never bites aff mair than it can—sook.

One might think that Peter Pan is not the aptest available reference for the Scottish kailyard side of Barrie as an illustration of our sentimental infantilism, but there is perhaps a subtler allusion there also: to Babbie, the once adored heroine of Barrie's most ambitious attempt at a kailyard novel, *The Little Minister*. At any rate, it is Babbie one may recall much later in the poem, when MacDiarmid begins to doubt the genuineness of the Scottish Muse who seems to appear to him as the "Gile na gile" had appeared to the Irish poet Egan O'Rahilly in his *aisling* or vision-poem:

> . . . aiblins I am sair beginked
> Thro' sma' experience o' life,
> And favoured here wi' nae King's dochter,
> But juist . . . a minister's rinawa wife.   (84; 226.)

In somewhat similar fashion, in the humorously sarcastic piece on "Hokum", the reader may wonder what exactly the Rev. Dr Lauchlan Maclean Watt has in common with the more familiar Scottish exploiters of that profitable commodity:

> I wish I was Harry Lauder,
> Will Fyffe or J. J. Bell,
> —Or Lauchlan Maclean Watt
> For the maitter o' that!
> —Dae I Hell!   (134; 254.)

The clue when it comes is not easily spotted. There is first of all a reference to Gertrud von Petzold's study, in German, of the influence of Nietzsche on the atheist poet John Davidson, whose career ended in suicide. Then comes the allusion to the godly Dr Watt's patriotic tribute to sentimental imperialism, *The Grey Mother and other poems*,[35] violently juxtaposed against a list geological terms. These represent hard-cored science, a respect for which MacDiarmid would share with Davidson as a corrective for all such soft-centred hokum:

> The relation o' John Davidson's thocht
> To Nietzsche's is mair important
> Than a' the drivel aboot 'Hame, Sweet Hame'
>
> Fower million cretins mant.
> And gin we canna thraw aff the warld
> Let's hear o' nae 'Auld grey Mither' ava,
> But o' Middle Torridonian Arkose
>   Wi' local breccias,
> Or the pillow lavas at Loch Awe.   (148; 261.)

There are in *Cencrastus* a fair number of recondite allusions, the purposes of which I take to include the deliberate mystification of the reader — admittedly not always a bad thing in poetry. One example, "a seven-whistler in Kintyre", so intrigued me that I was almost sorry to have it explained when I came across it in a book by a Highland naturalist. The whimbrel is called the sevenwhistler from the seven notes of its song. Normally these birds go to the far north to breed, but one year a pair nested on the Laggan Moor of Kintyre.[36]

The seven-whistler, thus symbolising a very rare find, is itself to be found in one of the finest sections of *Cencrastus*, the well-known poem entitled "North of the Tweed", and some readers may welcome a little light on a pair of curious literary allusions there:

> Leid in nae mere Longinian hypsos come
> But in inhuman splendours, triumphin' wi'
> 'A dazzlin disregard o' the soul.'
>   Nocht else'll dae.   (163; 270)

This passage is made clear in H. P. Collins' *Modern Poetry*, where Collins refers to Milton's "sheer sublimity — not the Longinian hypsos", and quotes T. S. Eliot to the effect that "Milton and Dryden triumphed with a dazzling disregard of the soul".[37]

147

MacDiarmid's attitude that "nocht else'll dae" but "inhuman splendours", harking back to his original conception of *Cencrastus*, accounts for his paradoxical procedure at this point in admonishing himself to abandon the very imagery in which much of the value of the poem he is writing resides:

> Water nor licht nor yet the barley field
> That shak's in silken sheets at ilka braith,
> Its lang nap thrawin' the quick licht aboot
> In sic a maze that tak's and gies at aince
> As fair oot-tops the coontless ripplin' sea.

And it is a significant fact that, in all the passages I have been discussing, the imagery, however attractive it may sometimes be in itself, is not effectively connected up with the master-symbol for the work as a whole. The consequences of this for the structure of the work are all too obvious.

Even what one might think of as ready-made connections, asking only to be exploited in the poem, are neglected. For example, one feels that one of the reasons why MacDiarmid thinks so often of Paul Valéry in the course of *Cencrastus* must surely be that, along with an intellectual concentration on "inhuman splendours", he was likewise fascinated by the archetypal image of the snake. It seems extraordinary in the circumstances that, except for a passing reference to the smoothness of the snake that "mak's cacophony o' Valéry's esses" (64; 215), he makes no use of the many serpent-links available in his favourite French poet's work.

Instead, he takes from Valéry the mysterious figure of Athikte. But this is liable to be a source of frustration to the reader, who is unlikely to make much sense of MacDiarmid's erratic use of her, much less perceive her function as a subsidiary symbol to Cencrastus, as I think he originally intended.

Never having heard of Athikte myself, I once asked MacDiarmid who she was. He told me she was the goddess of measurement, which is how she is identified in *More Collected Poems*, and added that he had come across her in Valéry's *Eupalinos*. But his memory must surely have been at fault, as I have found no trace of her in the pantheon and, although I suppose it is possible to conceive of her figuratively as a symbol of *measure*, in the sense of "rhythm", there is nothing in Valéry's account of her to suggest that *measurement* comes into it.

She appears as the leader of the dancers, not in *Eupalinos*, but in another of Valéry's prose dialogues, *L'Ame et la Danse* (1921). And the particular aspect of her that seems to have attracted MacDiarmid is suggested by H. A. L. Fisher's remark (in a published lecture on the French poet which MacDiarmid reviewed for the *New Age* in 1927) that Valéry found "in the movements of Athikte, the consummate dancer, . . . the bare expression of that metamorphosis which runs through all nature".[38] Thus MacDiarmid could see her (and there is some evidence that he originally did so) as a feminine embodiment of the life-force for which Cencrastus in world-serpent form was his principal symbol, taking her place in the poem along with that other vision of the creative spirit, the "Brightness of Brightness" that had been Egan O'Rahilly's Muse.

But Athikte's first appearance in the poem is as follows:

Here at the heicht o' her dance
Athikte's off in a dwam
—Gane in a kink
And no' able to think
By what mischance
She's tint her 'I am'. . . . (95-6; 233.)

This presents formidable difficulties for the reader, who is unlikely to know who she *was* in the first place. In the relevant passage of *L'Ame et la Danse*, as Athikte approaches the climax of her dance, Socrates sees this as a liberation or sublimation of the body. She falls to the ground, totally exhausted, and as she begins to come round, he asks her, "D'où reviens-tu?" And she answers: "Asile, asile, o/mon asile, o/Tourbillon! — J'étais en toi, o/ mouvement, en dehors de toutes les choses." ("Refuge, refuge, O my refuge, O Whirlwind! — I was in thee, O movement, outwith all things.") This ends the work, on a note which is quite rarified enough in context. With no hint of a context at all from MacDiarmid, and no link with *Cencrastus*, what can the reader be expected to make of Athikte? If he eventually gives up, it is because the poet seems to have done likewise.

Her final appearance in the poems is as Athikitty, a lass the poet claims to have met in Maybole, the market-town in Ayr. She has come down in the world, as has the poet himself, increasingly uncertain of his power of vision and indeed of the poem he is trying to write. But why Maybole? Well, poets are sometimes hard up for a rhyme. And in *Cencrastus* there are all too many attempts at passing off as a low-level joke the painful frustration of the author's higher flights.

There are two other references to Valéry in the poem which MacDiarmid evidently found in Fisher's Taylorian lecture. One concerns the idea that we can detect "nationality in Algebra even". (15; 189.) Fisher quotes the relevant passage from a conversation with Valéry reported by Lefèvre: "True, the constructions of science are impersonal, but every act of a scientific constructor is the act of personality. The style of a mathematician is as recognisable as the style of an artist. Poincaré does not write like Hermite. There are even national styles in mathematics. In Algebra itself nationality reveals itself."

The other reference is to "Barefut Valéry, writin' *Pythia* . . . drunk wi' will'. (12; 187.) Fisher gives the poet's own account of this: "I tried to write *Pythia* and some other pieces in a park planted with the finest trees I have seen, near Avranches. There was a small tidal river meandering through the rich white soil. I would go down into the park before dawn barefooted in the cold grass. The first moment of dawn exercises a singular power over my nerves. There is a sadness in that moment and enchantment and emotion and a kind of lucidity which is almost painful. Hardly was the sky stained with colour when I would return to the house drunk with freshness and with will."

There is no hint in *Cencrastus*, however, of the debt it owes to Valéry for these lines:

> I sing the terrifying discipline
> O' the free mind that gars a man
> Mak' his joys kill his joys,
> The weakest by the strongest,
> The temporal by the fundamental
> (Or hope o' the fundamental)
> And prolong wi'in himself

> Threids o' thocht sae fragile
> It needs the help and contrivance
> O' a' his vital poo'er
> To haud them frae brakin'
> As he pu's them owre the gulfs.
> Oor humanity canna follow us
> To lichts sae faur removed.
> A man ceases to be himsel'
> Under sic constraint.
> Will he find life or daith
> At the end o' his will,
> At Thocht's deepest depth,
> Or some frichtfu' sensation o' seein'
> Nocht but the ghastly glimmer
> O' his ain puir maitter?   (185-6; 281-2.)

Compare with that splendid piece of verse, in which the tone of vomce seems so strongly characteristic of MacDiarmid, the following translations of Valéry's prose from *Une Soirée avec Monsieur Teste* and *Lettre d'Emilie Teste*:

> He was the being absorbed in his variation, he who becomes his system, he who gives himself entirely to the terrifying discipline of the free mind and who makes his joys kill his joys, the weakest by the strongest — the gentlest, the temporal, that of the moment and of the hour begun by that which is fundamental — by the hope of the fundamental.
>
> He prolongs within himself threads so fragile that they refrain from snapping only with the help and contrivance of all his vital power. He draws them across I know not what personal gulfs. . . . It is clear that one is no longer onself under such constraint. Our humanity cannot follow us toward lights so far removed. Will he find life or death at the end of his attentive will? Will it be God, or some frightful sensation of encountering, at the deepest depth of thought, only the pale glimmer of his own and miserable matter?

Valéry is not by any means the only European writer on whom MacDiarmid falls back in the concluding pages of *Cencrastus*. For example:

> Nature is
> A moment and a product o' the Mind,
> And no' a Mind that stands abune the warld

> Or yet rins through it like a knotless threid
> But coincides wi't, ane and diverse at aince;
> An eternal solution and eternal problem.   (187-8; 283.)

That turns out to be Croce, writing about his own philosophy, the "Filosofia dello Spirito". And this is from Georg Kaiser:

> Man's the reality that mak's
> A' things possible, even himsel'.
> Energy's his miracle. . . .
> Ilka change has Eternity's mandate.   (186; 282.)

Then there is a passing reference in *Cencrastus* (174; 275) to Franz Werfel's *Bocksgesang*. In this play, Juvan, a student tramp who leads an insurrection, says:

> All comes and passes lightly with the frivolous. But what can
> we do against our souls, those inexorable sisters?
> Unceasingly they strew darkness upon our days; and this is
> their pride, that they make life harsh in our hearts. . . .
> Because all that is eternal fears fulfilment.

MacDiarmid's version of the passage is as follows:

> To the foolish a' comes and gangs lichtly
> But what can we dae wha's spirits
> Unceasingly strew dark on oor days
> And pride themsel's on't, makin' life harsh
> In oor herts, since a' that's Eternal
>   Fears fulfilment.   (186; 282.)

The doctor who assisted at the birth of the monster in *Bocksgesang* remarks that "the ancients believed that, at high noon, a thing could spring from quivering Nature, formless but visible, horrible and full of majesty, blasting all that cross it, like the vision of the Whole compressed into a second". In *Cencrastus*, in the passage where MacDiarmid mentions Werfel's play, this becomes:

> The Thing that loups at noon frae nature whiles,
> Unshaped but visible, horrible and august,
> Blastin' the sicht like a'thing seen at aince.

And the next verse-paragraph is taken up with adaptations of some critical prose remarks about Werfel, Thiess, and the wave of mysticism that occurred in post-war Germany:

152

[Werfel] is not concerned, as are other poets, with the ultimate destination of his own spirit or its immediate place in the universe. He is not even concerned, tender as he is, for the individual fate of his neighbours. His urgent anxiety is for humanity. It is in the cause of this woefully imperfect humanity, in peril of destruction, that he searches the secret places of his spirit; that he cherishes the unfortunate; that like Dante, he inveighs against the indifferent and the laggard, and smites the sinful flesh with bitter rods.

Compare MacDiarmid:

> It's little I care for mysel' or my freens.
> My concern's wi' humanity, waefully imperfect
> And in peril o' destruction. *That* gars me seek
> In the secret pairts o' my spirit and like Dante
> Cry oot on the heedless and laggard.

Then, on Frank Thiess and others:

In the shock of despair, in the absolute hopelessness of renunciation in the orgasmos of liberated hatred or lust, a new element comes into being, higher and more strange than any that the mundane flesh surmises. This point of mysterious meeting, where the earthly joins for a moment with the divine and derives a new strength from the impact, . . . a small group of German writers seem to discern at the end of a different road. It is the confidence of this vague recompense which gives them the courage needful to face the present, for it promises that, out of the basest frenzies of the tormented flesh, the highest earthly beauty may yet be born.

Compare the rest of the passage in MacDiarmid:

> In the shock o' despair, the hopelessness,
> The orgasmos o' liberated hate and lust,
> A new element comes into bein' — wider
> And stranger than ocht that the clay can ken,
> The mysterious meetin' place, where for a flash
> Earthly touches divine and wins new strength,
> Courage to face past and present that promise
> That frae their base frenzies may come even yet
> Something worth while.

Readers who know their MacDiarmid will take these examples of his magpie habits as he says Apollinaire took the War, "wi' irony" — another reference which he lifted from the same source (which, by the way, he also found useful for *In Memoriam James Joyce*). In the B.B.C. television programme for his eightieth birthday, he was quite unrepentent of these habits. Indeed, as if to illustrate his dictum in *Cencrastus* that "the poet's hame is in the serpent's mooth", he appeared on that occasion to be claiming that "the greater the poet, the greater the plagiarist". "We're all full of quotations," he added, "only some of us are adroit enough to choose our quotations from sources that aren't so easily checked as others."

The source in this particular case is hardly an obscure one — William Drake's *Contemporary European Writers*, London (1929) — but there is no doubt that he delighted in seeing how much he could get away with. Where *Cencrastus* was concerned, he knew he was risking having to concede that his great ambitions had ended, after all, in a huge joke:

> It's eneuch to say
> 'Let's mak' a better joke in politics and art
> Than the English yet — and damn consistency!' (138; 255.)

But what an opportunity he missed in his source, by failing to use (without acknowledgement, of course) the following:

> Like Anatole France, whom he resembles in many ways, and like "those ineffable poets, Homer", Valle-Inclán commits his plagiarisms openly and unabashedly. His is the type of adaptive talent which requires a stimulus to creation outside of itself; and what he finds that he can utilize, he takes by the divine right of employment, without embarrassment and without attempting to dissemble what only pedants would consider as his shame.[39]

If applied to MacDiarmid, however, that would claim both too much and too little. His "adaptive talent" is not so innocent; nor is it anything like as limited as Valle-Inclán's. If it operates on a relatively undistinguished level in the later pages especially of *Cencrastus* — though there is some distinction in his ability to spot the nuggets amongst the dross in the first place — it is elsewhere employed with impressive skill in the service of extraordinary vision. His main weakness is to over-rely on it for the staple material of very long poems. I do not doubt that even *A Drunk Man* will be shown in time to have its share of that weakness, but neither do I doubt that *A Drunk Man* will stand as a great poem. *Cencrastus* is far from being that, though it contains much more of value than the approach I have taken to it reveals, and one can feel in it the desperation induced by the author's determination at any cost to follow *A Drunk Man* with "a much bigger thing". The snake is bigger, all right, but only scotched, not circumjacked.

References

1 "Sic Bonny Sangs", *New Edinburgh Review*, Spring 1979, p. 25.
2 Cf. Coventry Patmore, "The Child's Purchase":
   Silence that crowns, unnoted, like the voiceless blue,
   The loud world's varying view,
   And in its holy heart the sense of all things ponders!
3 References to *Cencrastus* will be given by page number, first of the original text (Edinburgh, 1930) and then of the *Complete Poems* (London, 1978), which contains corrections.
4 Trans. J. Zeldin, *Poems and Political Letters of F. I. Tyutchev*, Knoxville, 1973, p. 43.
5 R. Poggioli, *The Poets of Russia 1890-1930*, Cambridge, Mass., 1960, p. 36.
6 *Acts*, 17, 23.
7 Letter to Helen B. Cruickshank, February 1939.
8 "The Meaning of Love", *A Solovyov Anthology*, ed. S. L. Frank, London, 1950, p. 164.
9 V. Solovyev, *Plato*, London, 1935, p. 73.
10 *Francis George Scott*, Edinburgh, 1955, p. 42.
11 Letter to George Ogilvie, 6/8/26.
12 Undated letter to G. Ogilvie (December 1930?).
13 "The National Party", *Modern Scot*, Jan. 1931, p. 28.
14 Letter to G. Ogilvie, 6/1/30.
15 *The Present Condition of Scottish Arts and Affairs* (a pamphlet reprinting an article which appeared in various newspapers in November 1927), p. 7.
16 "English Ascendancy in British Literature", *Criterion*, July 1931. Reprinted in *At the Sign of the Thistle*, London, 1934, and *The Uncanny Scot*, ed. K. Buthlay, London 1968.
17 "The Caledonian Antisyzygy and the Gaelic Idea", *Modern Scot*, July 1931/Jan. 1932. Reprinted in *Selected Essays of Hugh MacDiarmid*, ed. D. Glen, London, 1969.
18 "The Purpose of the Free Man", in *At the Sign of the Thistle*.
19 "The Caledonian Antisyzygy and the Gaelic Idea".

20   *At the Sign of the Thistle*, p. 42.
21   "The Great Sea-Serpent", *New Age*, 11 March 1926, pp. 223-4. R. B. Watson has noted that MacDiarmid versified parts of this article for the concluding pages of *Cencrastus*. Watson assumed MacDiarmid was 'Filoque', but internal evidence suggests otherwise.
22   Letter to H. B. Cruickshank, February 1939.
23   "Hugh MacDiarmid and Gaelic Literature", in *Hugh MacDiarmid: A Festschrift*, ed. K. D. Duval and S. G. Smith, Edinburgh, 1962. And revised version in *Hugh MacDiarmid: A Critical Survey*, ed. D. Glen, Edinburgh, 1972.
24   Douglas Hyde, *A Literary History of Ireland*, London, 1899, pp. 541-42.
25   *The Literature of the Celts*, London, 1902, p. 270.
26   Quoted in Maclean, *Literature of the Celts*, p. 284.
27   Seton Gordon, *The Cairngorm Hills of Scotland*, London, 1925, pp. 67, 59, 122.
28   *Op. cit.*, p. 3.
29   *The Literature of the Highlands*, Inverness, 1892, p. 182.
30   From the Report on Ossian presented to the Highland Society of Scotland. Quoted in J. S. Blackie, *Language and Literature of the Highlands of Scotland*, Edinburgh, 1876, p. 220.
31   *The Immortal Isles*, London, 1926, p. 38. (The spelling of Gaelic is a notorious problem. In a holograph version of the lines that appear as part of *Cencrastus*, MacDiarmid has "Port a' Bail".)
32   *Ibid*, p. 42; *Cairngorm Hills*, pp. 122, 93.
33   *Behold the Hebrides!*, London, 1925, pp. 248, 114, 245.
34   See T. E. Hulme, *Speculations*, London, 1924. 1960 edn., pp. 193, 126, 136.
35   London, 1903.
36   D. MacIntyre, *Highland Naturalist Again*, London, n.d., pp. 186-7.
37   *Modern Poetry*, London, 1925, pp. 116-7.
38   *Paul Valéry*, Oxford, 1927, p. 16.
39   Drake, p. 134.

MacDiarmid and Ideas, with special reference to "On a Raised Beach"

IAIN CRICHTON SMITH

I must say that I've always had difficulty with MacDiarmid's longer poems, more so than with his lyrics, and it seems to me that his poetry of "fact" requires some new form of criticism that we haven't as yet got. These longer poems — such as *On a Raised Beach* — I find puzzling mainly because I think they require not my poetic sense but my intellectual assent. *On a Raised Beach* is about stones but so too is *The Eemis Stane*. However, when we read the latter poem we are not required to give intellectual assent, we are rather presented with an image which the poet leaves with us to make what we wish of it. A poem like *On a Raised Beach* is a more difficult structure to deal with. Here and there one finds flashes of imaginative power, of the same intensity as *The Eemis Stane*, but the content of the poem as a whole is statement and argument. The problem is that by limiting so much of the poem to statement the poet is allowing the reader to disagree with him at any point along the route. In *The Waste Land* Eliot uses stone imagery but not in this way. There the imagery is allowed to make its impact imaginatively, as simply a notation for barrenness. In *On a Raised Beach* MacDiarmid goes much further than this. The stone is seen both as itself and as notation and it is in the fluctuations between, that the trouble lies. Thus I can see the stones as MacDiarmid sees them as the ultimate inhuman audience, that which is obdurate and unchanging, a criterion of loneliness. On the other hand I am troubled by an animism in the poem which seems to me to be quite close to the poeticisms of someone like Teilhard de Chardin, as if MacDiarmid were investing the stones with thoughts and knowledge of their own. Thus he writes:

157

> It makes no difference to them whether they are high or low,
> Mountain peak or ocean floor, palace or pigsty.

where he is in fact talking in an animistic way about the democratic character of the stones. Again what sense does the following statement make:

> But it is as difficult to understand and have patience here
> As to know that the sublime
> Is theirs, no less than ours. . . .

"I lift a stone," writes MacDiarmid. "It is the meaning of life that I clasp."

I am not saying that any of these statements are untrue: all I am saying is that these statements allow the reader to think the opposite, if he wishes. It is possible for the reader to say MacDiarmid is making too much of this. Stones are, after all, nothing but stones, they have nothing to do with the sublime. There is a difference for example between this technique and the way we accept the verse in Yeats's poem "Easter 1916":

> Hearts with one purpose alone
> Through summer and winter seem
> Enchanted to a stone
> To trouble the living stream.

There is no question but that there is a sort of nobility about *On a Raised Beach* and that the visionary greatness of the mind that created the poem is of overwhelming brilliance and pathos. But in a strange sense one wonders whether this vision is truly and utterly poetic. It seems in fact to be trying to impose on us in an unpoetic way, as if the poem were an odd sort of propaganda. It is interesting to note how much the poem depends on direct unambiguous sayings almost like proverbs as for example:

> The widest open door is the least liable to intrusion

or

> The inward gates of a bird are always open

or

> Impatience is a poor qualification for immortality

or

> Hot blood is of no use in dealing with eternity.

158

These statements sound important but what in fact do they mean? What does it mean to say that

> Impatience is a poor qualification for immortality.

Other statements seem unambiguously correct and undebatable as for instance:

> What happens to us
> Is irrelevant to the world's geology
> But what happens to the world's geology
> Is not irrelevant to us.

On the other hand does such a statement lead necessarily to the following:

> We must reconcile ourselves to the stones,
> Not the stones to us,

and what meaning can we apply to such a statement? I am not saying that in places the quality of the poetry is not high but rather that the poet by concentrating so much on statement is allowing too much possibility of contradiction on the part of the reader. Great poetry cannot be contradicted since it doesn't proceed on the level of the idea.

The puzzle about this poem is that on the whole it leaves in the mind a sense of power and illumination and yet in detail it can be argued with. For instance, the poet begins with a statement,

> Deep conviction or preference can seldom
> Find direct terms in which to express itself,

and he says this because he wishes to show this "deep conviction" as imaged in the stones. But if on the other hand someone were to argue that deep conviction can sometimes appear as volubility what would this do to the value of the image that he has chosen to illustrate the statement by? And when he goes on to say:

> "I look at these stones and know little about them
> But I know their gates are open too,
> Always open, far longer open, than any bird's can be . . ."

is he not more or less in the same world as Teilhard de Chardin, that is seeing the universe in a way which is concerned with poeticism rather than poetry?

Later he goes on to say that it is easy to find a "spontaneity here", but that "it is wrong to indulge in these illustrations instead of just accepting the stones".

But why wrong? Is it because such illustrations do not fit his case? And is that therefore what he is doing, that is, making a case?

In another part of the poem he says:

But the world cannot dispense with stones
They alone are not redundant. Nothing can replace them except
A new creation of God.

For that matter does he or does he not believe in God?

In what sense is it true to say that the stones are not redundant? In what sense is it any truer to say this than to say that air is not redundant or water? In what sense also should one accept the statement:

Let men find the faith that builds mountains
Before they seek the faith that moves them. . . .

And he follows this with:

. . . Men cannot hope
To survive the fall of the mountains
Which they will no more see than they saw their rise,
Unless they are more concentrated and determined. . . .

In what sense, one wonders, would one's concentration be enough to allow one to survive the fall of the mountains? And what does the following statement mean?

These stones go through Man, straight to God, if there is one.

(And what, we feel like asking, if there isn't one?)

What have I been trying to say so far? I think I have been trying to say that the "poetry of facts" is not a poetry of facts at all, it is in fact a poetry of ideas with an intention aimed at us, in other words a poetry of propaganda and persuasion. Such a poetry allows the mind to construct opposites for what is being said. Intelligence is not the real source of poetry, nor is, I think, ideas. In a sense, between the passages of poetry the statements are used as connecting links and the strength of the poem as a whole must depend on our assent to the connecting links.

This poetry is different from the extended verse of Blake which is vaguer, less dependent on the muscularity of ideas, and is unreadable because of the private symbolism. It is not like the poetry of Milton either, for very often Milton embodies different ideas in different protagonists.

The strange thing about this poem is that though one may disagree with the ideas, the statements, the links, one finds in places a startling brilliance which convinces not so much by ideas but rather by a visionary illumination at the point where the stones are seen as themselves, nakedly confronting the poet. I find this, for instance, in the passage beginning:

Cold, undistracted, eternal, and sublime.
They will stem all the torrents of vicissitude forever
With a more than Roman peace.
Death is a physical horror to me no more.
I am prepared with everything else to share
Sunshine and darkness and wind and rain . . .

and later still, when MacDiarmid is talking of the artist, he writes:

By what immense exercise of will
Inconceivable discipline, courage, and endurance,
Self-purification and anti-humanity,
Be ourselves without interruption,
Adamantine and inexorable?

There are, for instance, passages of intense beauty and power but they seem to occur when the intellectual statements fall away and the poet sees the stones naked in front of him and yet at the same time as shining with the distance that is really between them and him. At those moments the poet is not being animistic, he is making no assumptions. The stones truly are distant, inhuman, and therefore they become a true image for the inhumanity that he feels he needs. This is not the "Wheelbarrow" of Carlos Williams gleaming in the rain; this is the true inhuman object staring back at that which wishes to be the same. At times like these the poem becomes a great one, when the intellectual statements fall away, when sentences such as "Truth has no trouble in knowing itself" die, and the poet is face to face with the reality and difference of the stones. It is in the difference between the stones and man that the true reality of the poem rests. It is in this stoicism, in this lesson learned from stones — "the rocks rattling in the bead-proof seas" — that we find MacDiarmid at his greatest. The conversation and ideas fall away. It is true that MacDiarmid says that he is not searching for an escape from life and he goes on to explain why

161

this should be so, why the inhumanity of the stones should not represent such a separation. But that is precisely where the weakness of the poem lies, in the explanations, as well as in the strange statements such as the following:

> I lift a stone: it is the meaning of life I clasp
> Which is death, for that is the meaning of death.

What my argument comes down to is this: if a poet has to use ideas in poetry then he has to be as rigorous in his ideas as any other person using ideas, e.g. the philosopher. I don't think the poet has any right to be unrigorous simply because he is a poet. This would apply as much to Lucretius as to MacDiarmid. I do not see that we should apply different criteria to poets, as far as ideas are concerned, from those we should apply to philosophers. MacDiarmid was in a different position from Dante, for whom there was already a system of ideas in existence. If a poet is going to use a system of ideas then he should be consistent within that system. It therefore does make a difference within a system of ideas whether a poet does or does not believe in God and it is not enough to say casually "whether He exists or not".

As far as this poem is concerned, the most powerful image that emerges from it is the confrontation of MacDiarmid with the stones and the lessons he learns from this confrontation. Many of the other statements he makes in the course of the poem are open to contradiction, but his confrontation as a human being with them is not. In this confrontation we are faced with the business of the poet which does not in the end depend on his ideas but rather on his imaginative power to create a convincing situation. And finally the pathos of the poem lies in the change that takes place in the poet for we sense that by this confrontation he has found the strength, as he says himself, not to be afraid of death anymore. What convinces us is the quality of the poetry at the point where this happens, and not by the statement of the idea as such. And in much the same way we are convinced by the change that occurred in Yeats at the point when he was writing *Easter 1916*. It is not, in other words, the stones that matter but the human being looking at the stones. No matter how much the stones are characterised, what technical terms are used, the centre of the poem is MacDiarmid himself: and this is as it should be.

MacDiarmid's Muses

RONALD STEVENSON

What I propose to present is no literary conceit, no mannequin parade of antique nymphs, but a high-relief frieze of the salient symbols in MacDiarmid's poetry.

And yet those nine Olympian ladies who sang at the banquets of the gods, led by Apollo Musagetes, must have symbolised realities in the Greek psyche. Their collective title — Muses — means "the thinkers". They were the daughters of Zeus and Mnemosyne, the personification of Memory. Calliope, with her wax tablet and stilus, was epic poetry; Euterpe, with her aulos or double flute, lyric poetry; Erato, with her small lyre, erotic poetry; Melpomene and Thalia, respectively the tragic and comic masks, each wreathed in ivy; Polyhymnia, veiled and pensive, the singer of sacred hymns; Terpsichore, the dancer with her lyre; Clio, with her scroll—history, the selective Muse, Memory's favourite daughter; Urania—astronomy, with her celestial globe.

The all have their counterparts in MacDiarmid's poetry. About which other contemporary poet could that be said? This in itself, at one swoop, shows MacDiarmid's range. He is the epic poet in his *Drunk Man* and *In Memoriam James Joyce*; lyric poet in *Sangschaw* and *Penny Wheep*; as erotic as any poet in *Wheesht, wheesht, ye fule*; he is tragedian in his translation of Rilke's *Requiem*, and grand comedian in *Crowdieknow*; secular psalmist in his *Hymns to Lenin*; verbal Terpsichorean in his dance-song *I heard Christ sing*; and in *The Bonnie Broukit Bairn*, like Dante long ago, he cocks a cosmonaut's eye at the earth, years befcre Gagarin or Armstrong: which poet alive has this range?

The Muses of classical mythology presided over the arts and sciences, the development of the *mind*. The development of the *body* was the concern of that other branch of Greek education: gymnastics. MacDiarmid telescopes the two of them in his concept of a poetry which includes *mental* gymnastics. He is a *funambulist* of language, walking a tightrope of a wiry line of words.

I've made my own tightrope in proposing that MacDiarmid's Muses number nine. But it is no artifical categorisation. I jotted down the different aspects of MacDiarmid's poetry and arrived at nine sub-headings. These different aspects interpenetrate, so I tried to delete some but found I couldn't. Neither could I add to them. So it seems that MacDiarmid, too, has nine Muses.

There can be no doubt about the first. She is Scotia. No nymph. She's a braw lass. Amazon. Rainbows her raiment. Birdsong her halo.

> Oor dourest hills are only
> Rainbows at a'e remove.
>
> Gowdfishes were rife on the Borders
> Till the eighteen-forties but syne
> Disappeared and didna come back
> Till the new century started . . .
>
> A cock siskin sings in a spruce,
> Crossbills are thrang wi' the rowans. . . .

This Scotia walks on a dropt heaven of flower-stars.

> Scotland small? Our multiform, our infinite Scotland *small*?
> Only as a patch of hillside may be a cliché corner
> To a fool who cries 'Nothing but heather!'
>   Where in September another
> Sitting there and resting and gazing around
> Sees not only heather but blaeberries
> With bright green leaves and leaves already turned scarlet
> Hiding ripe blue berries . . .
>
> . . . nodding harebells vying in their colour
> With the blue butterflies that poise themselves delicately
>   upon them,
> And stunted rowans with harsh dry leaves of glorious colour.
> 'Nothing but heather!' — How marvellously descriptive!
> And incomplete.

164

But MacDiarmid curses the *false* Scotland — the Scotland of the fitba fetish, tarted-up tartanry and Sir Harry Lauder bowdlerisation — just as much as he blesses what he feels to be the real, the true Scotland. This ambivalence is a manifestation of Professor Gregory Smith's concept of the "Caledonian Antisyzygy": the combination of opposites in the Scottish psyche. In his poem *Scotland's Pride*, MacDiarmid asks:

. . . who's done aught for you, Scotland? Who's tried?

. . . All your nobility can be stroked off first,
Titles they may have — but none to respect.

. . . Your divines come next. They may have served God,
But they have certainly rendered no service to man.

. . . As for your politicians, not a man of them's been
Other than a servant of your deadliest foe.

This cantankerousness suggests MacDiarmid's second Muse, the Thistle: the giant Thistle which seeds such a multiplicity of metaphors and similes in the *Drunk Man* that, magnified in the poet's imagination, it assumes the dominance of the Celtico-Norse Yggdrassil, the world-tree that binds heaven and earth and hell with its branches and its roots; uniting man with the Infinite. There are some forty-three thistle-symbols in the *Drunk Man*. A Whitmanesque catalogue of them staggers us by its prodigality of imagery. In the very first thistle-metaphor the drunk poet *is* the thistle. Then follow in rapid succession: the Thistle as the Gothic Idea; as skeleton; as bagpipe; its leaves as alligators; the Thistle as a gargoyle by a saint; as Mephistopheles in heaven; as all the fish of the sea nailed to the poet; as Leviathan, "its coils like a thistle's leaves"; the Thistle as the poet's tormented spirit; as the barren fig-tree; as a tattered ship's sail; as the man-in-the-earth (brother to the man-in-the-moon); the Thistle as spawner of a breeding-ground for — I ask you! — eels in the heavens; the Thistle as the miraculous rose-bearing plant (symbol of the General Strike); the Thistle as an exploded firework rocket; as crucifix; as a sparely flowering language; as a sunrise-tint in the grey of day; the Thistle as a pickled foetus; as the corpse of a liberated soul; as a snowstorm; as a flight of swallows (here, just over halfway

165

through the poem, the images rain and pelt); the Thistle as a swarm of midges; as a plague of moths; as a starry sky; the Thistle as a tree that fills the universe; as a dried, shrivelled herring; as a horse's skin, twitching beneath flea-bites; the Thistle as the Northern Lights; as a death-captured soul; as a spewed haggis; as a moon; the Thistle as the Platonic Idea; as the puzzle of a man's soul; as a many-branched candelabrum vying with the stars; the Thistle as an epileptic; as a web for the spider-world; as humanity's mind; as a giant weed, choking the sun's golden grain and the moon's white harvest; the Thistle as a heraldic horror; the Thistle as a Presbyterian growth, crucifying its own roses.

This enthistled waste land is the natural habitat of MacDiarmid's third Muse: Cencrastus or the Curly Snake. This creature crept into MacDiarmid's mythology from the pages of James Watson's *Choice Collection* of 1709, where it is described as "a beist of filthy braith": a perfect symbol for MacDiarmid the polemicist and political pamphleteer. It is, of course, the snake found in those involuted Celtic knot-designs; the snake coiled with its tail in its mouth, symbol of eternity; the same whose form symbolises James Joyce's *Finnegan's Wake*, the novel which finishes only to wake again, the last incomplete sentence stopping with the word "the", only to start again, like a continuous cinema-show. There was a Curly Snake (locally known by that name) on the outskirts of Langholm, MacDiarmid's birthplace in the Borders; a winding path (now overgrown) which he thought of, like Kierkegaard's Nook of the Night Paths in Grib Forest in North Zeeland, as the groundplan of his life's work: a twisting path that led him to the convolutions of the Celtic pscyhe.

And thence to his fourth Muse, the Gaelic Muse. He found her where the Irish Gaelic poet of the late seventeenth and early eighteenth centuries, Aodhagan O'Rathaille, left her: in the lonely glen MacDiarmid transplants in the gardens of verse he dedicated *In Memoriam James Joyce*.

> At last, at last I see her again
> In our long-lifeless glen,
> Eidolon of our fallen race,
> Shining in full renascent grace,

> She whose hair is plaited
> Like the generations of men,
> And for whom my heart has waited
> Time out of ken.

Recognition of the Gaelic Muse is basic to MacDiarmid's vision of a Union of Celtic Republics. Everywhere he extends a hand to Celtic brother-poets, whether he finds them in Wales in David Jones or Dylan Thomas, whether in Ireland in Yeats and Joyce, whether major or minor poets, in the Isle of Man in Hall Caine, in Cornwall in Charles Causely, or in Scotland in Sorley Maclean.

This is only the first ring in the water whose ripples take us to the shores where MacDiarmid's fifth Muse awaits us: the Muse of the five Continents and of World Language. Here MacDiarmid is the confrere of polyglot poets, Eliot and Pound.

MacDiarmid is a passionate lover of language and *all* languages. The best introductory study I know to his concept of language is the little-known, posthumously published and recently republished opuscule of Walt Whitman, *An American Primer*, which, in Whitman's original manuscript, was entitled *A Primer of Words*, which includes a typical Whitmanesque — I had almost said MacDiarmidian — catalogue:

> Words of the Laws of Earth,
> Words of the Stars, and about them,
> Words of the Sun and Moon,
> Words of Geology, History, Geography,
> Words of Ancient Races,
> Words of Medieval Races,
> Words of the progress of Religion, Law, Art, Government,
> Words of the surface of the Earth,
>   grass, rocks, trees, flowers, grains and the like . . .
> Words of Modern Inventions, Discoveries. . . .

For Whitman, language, to quote his memorable phrase, "rolls with venison richness upon the palate". And so it does for MacDiarmid. I well remember the first time I mentioned Whitman to MacDiarmid: he interrupted me. "Whitman!" he exclaimed. "One of my idols!" MacDiarmid was then in his mid-sixties. I admired the intensity, the fervour of his enthusiasm, such as few retain to that age. And he had it to the end of his life.

Whitman was the Poet of Democracy, a prophet of MacDiarmid's sixth Muse: the Muse of Marxism. MacDiarmid has little in common with the early poets of the October Revolution, with Essenine and Mayakovsky. *They* had more in common with the American tramp-poet, Vachel Lindsay, as indeed has Yevtushenko today. MacDiarmid is not a journalist-poet or a slogan-poet, as so many are in a revolutionary or post-revolutionary situation. The Marxist poets with whom he has most in common are two epic poets, the Chilean Neruda and the Nicaraguan Cardenal. This last name is not generally known in Britain. Ernesto Cardenal, a Trappist monk in his early fifties who has lived two years in Cuba, describes himself as a "spiritual Marxist". After reading Cardenal's long poem, *Homage to the American Indians*, MacDiarmid wrote to me: "Cardenal is an absolute find as far as I am concerned. He is like Pound but better than Pound in several quintessential ways."

The Marxist Muse links hands with MacDiarmid's seventh and eighth Muses: those of Science and Cosmos. MacDiarmid is the first poet known to me who referred to Einstein's space-time concept. This reference occurs in the last two lines of the poem *Empty Vessel*.

> The licht that bends owre a' thing
> Is less ta'en up wi't.

The bent light refers to the refraction of light which is a consequence of Einstein's Theory of Relativity. In the poem this bending light refers to the unheeding Universe — or God, if you like — less concerned with the death of a baby than the mother is.

Incidentally, the only other reference to Einsteinian space-time known to me in the work of any *younger* Scots poet occurs in Duncan Glen's *Time's Gane Oot* from his volume *In Appearances*, in the lines:

> Here's daurks and mists no bent
> or fixed by ony licht.

Science and Cosmos lead us to the music of the spheres. Lest this idea be dismissed as antique fiction, I refer to the book *Between the Planets* by Fletcher G. Watson of the Harvard Observatory, published in 1956. This gives Watson's findings on asteroids (those small interplanetary bodies). Observation of the orbits of asteroids controlled by Jupiter reveals that the period-time of their revolutions bears the same relationship to the large period of the planet, as overtones bear to a fundamental note.

Here we meet MacDiarmid's ninth Muse: the Muse of Music. No other poetry I know contains more references to music than MacDiarmid's. More than that, as a composer myself who has set to music many of MacDiarmid's poems, I attest that I have even found suggestions of musical techniques in the poetry itself.

The Greek word from which the word Music is derived (*mousikétechné*) means the art of the Muses and was used in antiquity to embrace all those arts and sciences over which the Nine Muses presided.

So we have come full circle.

When I reflect on MacDiarmid's achievement and how he has the power to transmogrify the old into the new, the commonplace into the cosmic; when I see him with his own Muses, as Homer had *his* — standing there by his Yggdrassilian Giant Thistle with Cencrastus Cornucopius coiled round it, the Whitmanesque leaves of grass like uttering universal tongues below it and the cosmic music above it; old Marx and Einstein in the background, nodding assent; and the Gaelic Muse and Scotia on each side of him — why then, I know that we may love him and his work, but we are not really his contemporaries. His contemporaries are those unborn.

Beyond the Stony Limits:
Two Poets Talking in Comfort

an imaginary dialogue

by

JOHN WAIN

Scene: The Hall of Welcome for Newly-Arrived Shades.

Time: an autumn evening in 1978 (measuring by Earth-time, that is: the Shades live in a continuous present, though their thoughts embrace the concepts of Past and Future).

A bright log fire is burning in the huge fireplace, its sparks whirling up into the empyrean to replace the comets that burn out. A wide-shouldered Shade, gap-toothed and combat-scarred as in life, is musing beside the fire. It is ROY CAMPBELL. He raises his head now and again, searching among the crowd of new Shades who move timidly forward. At length he sees the figure he is awaiting, rises, and goes towards it.

Campbell. Welcome, MacDiarmid.

MacDiarmid. I did not expect such a greeting from an inveterate opponent. Are all my experiences on this side of the Gulf to be as purely surprising as this first one?

RC. Sit down, old enemy, new companion. Pull a stool up to this fire. You'll find its warmth grateful notwtihstanding your altered physical nature. We still have all the innocent pleasures here.

HM. Oh? Is there whisky?

RC. That's served in permitted hours, as in Edinburgh. Six to eleven are the next set.

170

HM. It all seems very familiar. I shall soon feel myself at home. (*Pause*) But one thing isn't familiar. I'm looking at you, Campbell, and hearing your voice, without feeling any emotion of anger or hostility.

RC. You left those emotions outside the gate. They go back to earth to be re-cycled. That's why there are such huge quantities of them down there.

HM. You were my enemy: my favourite of all enemies. Wasn't it Jean Cocteau who remarked that friends come and friends go, but a good enemy is yours for ever?

You stood for everything I hated and opposed and you stood for it defiantly. Yet now I can sit and talk to you without acceleration of the pulse . . . does the pulse ever accelerate here, by the way?

RC. No. Our physical state is stable, except that aches and pains disappear. That's why my front teeth won't grow again. But my gammy leg doesn't trouble me.

Yes, you can talk to me peacefully. In human life we were what men call enemies. Here there is no enmity; and not much in the way of friendship either, in the old human sense. We look at life, at art, at history and individuality and experience, and see them in the spirit of a settled benignancy.

HM. Isn't that . . . well, rather dull?

RC. Not at all. One of the things you learn here is that positive feelings are actually more enjoyable than negative, and calm more creative than agitation. I'll teach you the ropes. I've been here since 1952, remember.

HM. Yes, as the older man I never thought to survive you by so many years. But you lived dangerously.

RC. It wasn't war, or the bull-ring, or breaking in horses, that killed me. It was driving a car along a road like any suburban gent. Somebody came out of a side turning. And anyway, you didn't survive me. You just tarried below for a few more years, while I waited for you up here.

HM. Waited for me? To continue our dispute?

RC. Not to continue it in any sense of tit-for-tat. But it might be amusing to run it through, like an old film, and this time

171

add a new soundtrack: a commentary from our present uncombative point of vantage.

HM.   Willingly, and yet I must tell you at the outset that I can't promise to agree with you any more than I did then.

RC.   It's not a question of agreeing or disagreeing, MacDiarmid. I was a Roman Catholic, a traditionalist, right-wing in politics to the point of sympathising with Fascism: at least I sympathised with the Fascist side in Spain in the 1930s to the extent of fighting for them and risking my skin, though a few years later I was fighting in World War II *against* the Fascist powers. I couldn't swallow Hitler, any more than Stalin.

HM.   I, on the contrary, could accept Stalin. He seemed to me the heir of Lenin, whom I hailed in his lifetime as the architect of a new order that was needed in the world.

RC.   But confess now, wasn't your Communism at least partly a Scottish radical's way of discomfiting the English ruling class? As I understood it, you thought they were a dead hand on England, which you hardly considered your business one way or another, and an even deader hand on Scotland, which they ruled in the interests of England: and that *did* concern you. You probably saw, with your shrewdness, that a Scotsman can proclaim himself Nationalist and Gaelic League as much as he likes without getting through the rhinoceros-hide of the English establishment, but to announce himself a Communist, and a hard-shell, Stalinist Communist at that, is to line up with a powerful enemy who threatens the destruction of the English way of life and has the power to carry out that threat. If you had really been a Communist in your heart, would you have lived in a grace-and-favour cottage on the estate of a Duke?

HM.   The cottage seems to me a trivial issue. The aristocracy might as well be milked in the few years left before modern forces destroy them. As for Communism, the materialist basis of its philosophy seemed to me a possible starting-point for speculation. As I put it in "Island Funeral",

172

> . . . if the nature of the mind is determined
> By that of the body, as I believe,
> It follows that every type of human mind
> Has existed an infinite number of times
> And will do so. Materialism promises something
> Hardly to be distinguished from eternal life.

RC. At any rate, one thing is clear: the distance between us on political issues was not a matter of one being populist and the other oligarchical. We both supported authoritarianisms, I of the Right, you of the Left. Frankly, now that egalitarianism is so much a fetish with the coming generation, I would expect to see a decline in the readership of your work with its continually expressed contempt for "the feck".

HM. Possibly, though you must remember that nationalism, the strongest force in the modern world, will always make the Scots read a poet who writes in their language and concerns himself with their issues, or at least make them talk about him and have his books on their shelves, which is as near as the feck are likely to come to reading any poet.

RC. I believed in tradition, the Church, the Catholic civilisation of Europe, and the self-respect a man might win and uphold by his own physical courage and hardihood. I had no respect for the ordinary inert, habit-ridden city populations with their mass entertainment and newspaper opinions. While you, if I am not mistaken, regarded these masses — at best — as material to be shaped and used by the few men of vision and strength who would rule over them. In your eyes, the common people were there to do as they were told, and no punishment was too harsh for them if they disobeyed.

HM. It's true that I loved stones more than men. Stones are emblems of metaphysical realities, which also interested me more than average humanity ever did.

RC. It particularly annoyed you, I think, that common undistinguished people should claim a great poet like Burns for their own, on the grounds of his sympathy for common humanity. In *A Drunk Man Looks at the Thistle* you

173

distinguish between the gifted individual and the many who have human bodies and nervous systems but are not important enough to have rights because

> They're nocht but zoologically men.

HM. Yes, I remember. The work of Burns, and anything that makes for greatness in the Scottish spirit, should be protected against these grunters.

RC. There were people, of course you know, who found that attitude unacceptably harsh.

HM. Yes, wishy-washy sentimentalists are as common as flies in a slaughterhouse.

RC. There is a fine passage in "On a Raised Beach" in which you describe the austere and lonely spirit that will actually achieve anything, actually move humanity forward towards truth and reality:

> It is a frenzied and chaotic age,
> Like a growth of weeds on the site of a demolished
>   building.
> How shall we set ourselves against it,
> Imperturbable, inscrutable, in the world and yet not in
>   it,
> Silent under the torments it inflicts upon us,
>   With a constant centre,
> With a single inspiration, foundations firm and
>   invariable;
>   By what immense exercise of will,
> Inconceivable discipline, courage, and endurance,
>   Self-purification and anti-humanity,
>   Be ourselves without interruption,
>   Adamantine and inexorable?
> It will be ever increasingly necessary to find
> In the interests of all mankind
> Men capable of rejecting all that all other men
>   Think, as a stone remains
> Essential to the world, inseparable from it,
>   And rejects all other life yet.
> Great work cannot be combined with surrender to the
>   crowd.

HM. (*nods, listening*)

RC. Now those lines describe the great artist and bring him vividly before our eyes. But, as of course people noticed, it describes equally well the inflexible tyrant, the Ghengiz Khan or Stalin, who can order the death of millions of people and sleep not the less soundly. *They* have "anti-humanity", *they* are "adamantine and inexorable": and no doubt their thought-processes appear to them as "self-purification" and their merciful impulses, if they have any, as temptations.

HM. I think I would accept that. What is called "common human sentiment" is seldom anything but a warm, confused muddle, and a great man must be lapidary: he cannot muddle, or the deeper design of the universe would never be advanced.

RC. Ah, you have the Scottish taste for metaphysics. It's evident all through your work. The ultimate issues, the eternal questions, are never far from your mind: if they were you would be no true voice for a nation of theologians and disputants.

HM. You mean you, with your Scottish name, were entirely indifferent to metaphysical questions? I don't believe it.

RC. I was a pioneer before I was a speculator. On the whole I took Nature and Man as I found them and handed over the questions to my religion. In any case, though my name is Lowland Scots, I had also Irish and Provençal blood in my veins. It's a mixture that makes for a mystical, rather than a speculative, turn of mind. We did, as you say, both support different versions of av 'ioritarianism. But our attitudes came from very different origins and roots. I supported the Franco side in the Spanish Civil War because of things that I saw happening in the street. I was never a theorist.

HM. That's true, and there you have the difference within the resemblance. I was always a man with a philosophy who drew strength from that philosophy. Yours was much more of a gut-reaction.

RC. Which is another reason why there was such antipathy between us. We were both men who, at different times, found ourselves recommending and supporting violence, but the violence in my life was mostly carried out in my own person. Yours was theoretical. I don't know whether that makes it better or worse.

HM.   I served in the First World War.

RC.   Yes, but in the Medical Corps. As far as I could discover you never fired a shot in anger or were shot at. I fought for what I wanted to defend because it was the only way I knew. I risked my neck fighting in Spain and then I came home and immediately joined up in the fight against Hitler and Mussolini, so I don't accept the label "Fascist". Authoritarian, yes. There are times when people don't respond to gentle persuasion and then you have to take a gun in your hand — in your own hand, not someone else's.

HM.   I don't think the difference is very great at that point. I helped the anti-Fascist cause with the fatigue and toil of my body. In the Second World War, well above military age, I worked in heavy engineering shops on Clydeside as part of the war effort. Life just never put me in the position of having to fight.

RC.   It never put me in anything else, growing up as I did in lonely, open spaces that had never been civilised or policed. If someone did something against you, there was no police station down the road where you could go and report the matter and then go home to afternoon tea. A man had to look after himself, to take and keep what he could and to defend what he could. My wife and I were in a Socialist part of Spain during a wave of intense anti-clericalism and we were Catholics — new converts, what's more, with the fervour of discovering a faith. Street-corner loungers used to spit tobacco-juice at my wife as she came from church. One man — I tell the story in *Light on a Dark Horse* — a man who made a living by gathering and selling edible frogs, working from a punt moored out in the estuary, met her in the street one day. He used to hawk his frogs around on a string, threaded through one foot. He pointed to this string of dead upside-down naked frogs and said to her, "That's what you'll look like when we've raped and killed you".

That night I swam out to his punt, using a breast-stroke so as not to splash and alert him, gave him a beating and overturned his punt so that he lost his stove and equipment; the punt itself floated away on the tide and was broken up. Throughout the operation I spoke no word so that he wouldn't be able to identify me from my voice. He went about afterwards saying that he had been attacked by a mad deaf mute. (*Laughing*) A mad deaf mute! What a description of a poet!

HM. Well, by the standards of the workaday commercial world we *are* mad. And for all the notice they take of us, we might as well be deaf mutes and not utter a word.

RC. Yes, I notice that you're quite unwavering in your opinion that the poet writes for the few. All that praise of your fellow-workers on Clydeside — I don't suppose their friendliness extended to reading what you'd written. You spoke for them, perhaps, but hardly *to* them.

HM. Oh, that's just because the educational system here is class-ridden. The bourgeoisie keep it to themselves. If you teach a worker to appreciate poetry, it doesn't make him any better able to earn profits for you. No, the links between us — that deep-down resemblance that made our quarrel so fierce, having as it did the true venom of *Bruderhass* — was that we both believed in strength and accepted authoritarianisms of different kinds. And you are right in saying that my attitudes involved a certain ruthlessness that gave offence to the weak. People who could tolerate mediocrity and selfishness couldn't tolerate blood. It was exactly that kind of person, sentimental about common humanity, who disliked my standing up in support of the Soviet invasion of Hungary. I had lapsed from membership of the Communist Party, but after the splendid display of strength and determination in Hungary I rejoined the party, as publicly as possible, to show my support for a firm policy. How that enraged all the sentimental populists! I remember one man, some kind of English writer, with a name like Payne or Fane, who seemed determined never to let me hear the last of it.

RC.   I believe I remember him. Used to hang about Oxford; we
      talked in a pub there, on one of my visits. He seemed polite
      enough.

HM.   Oh, he'd be polite. He was probably afraid that if he wasn't
      you'd give him a punch on the nose.

RC.   No, I think he really had some kind of admiration for me.
      He was very disapproving, I remember, when in *The Battle
      Continues* you went on attacking me after my earthly life
      was over.

HM.   Yes, he would have all those notions of Good Form and *de
      mortuis nihil nisi bonum* and the rest of it. But I settled
      Twayne's hash. I buried him under a fine load of abuse.

RC.   I remember reading it. We get the papers up here: the
      airmail editions, naturally.

HM.   I suppose people like him are still going about, spreading
      their sentimental twaddle about compassion and the rights
      of common humanity. Well, it won't make any difference,
      either to world politics or to my own reputation. My
      achievement in poetry was a major one and I can't imagine
      anybody denying that. These things are settled by the
      opinion of discriminating readers — fellow-poets, mostly,
      with a few sympathetic scholars — not by the vote of what
      Joyce called the rabblement.

RC.   Yes, when you put forth your powers in earnest you were
      quite content to leave the common man behind. You
      wouldn't have been afraid of that charge of "elitism"
      which the mob throws nowadays at anyone who doesn't
      locate his values simply in the counting of heads. In fact
      there are times when you seem to me to be courting
      obscurity, going out of your way to use a language that the
      ordinary reader won't understand.

HM.   If you're referring to my poems in Scots, I had better point
      out—

RC.   No, I'm not. Pardon my interrupting you, but even with
      eternity in front of us I didn't want to go down what would
      at the moment have been a blind alley. I was thinking of
      some of your flights of learning and speculation. That same
      poem "On a Raised Beach", for instance — it must be one

of your best-known, certainly one of the most admired by
the connoisseur of your work. Since one of the privileges
we have here is instant recall of everything we've ever
written (very useful to people like Dickens — he often
gives recitals from his novels, always well attended), I'd be
obliged if you would repeat the opening passage of that
poem — the first couple of dozen lines.

HM. All is lithogenesis — or lochia,
Carpolite fruit of the forbidden tree,
Stones blacker than any in the Caaba,
Cream-coloured, caen-stone, chatoyant pieces,
Celadon and corbeau, bistre and beige,
Glaucous, hoar, enfouldered, cyathiform,
Making mere faculae of the sun and moon,
I study you glout and gloss, but have
No cadrans to adjust you with, and turn again
From optik to haptik and like a blind man run
My fingers over you, arris by arris, burr by burr,
Slickensides, truité, rugas, foveoles,
Bringing my aesthesia in vain to bear,
An angle-titch to all your corrugations and coigns,
Hatched foraminous cavo-rilieva of the world,
Diectic, fiducial stones, chiliad by chiliad
What bricole piled you here, stupendous cairn?
What artist poses the Earth écorché thus,
Pillar of creation engouled in me?
What eburnation augments you with men's bones,
Every energumen an Endymion yet?
All the other stones are in this haecceity it seems,
But where is the Christophanic rock that moved?
What Cabirian song from this catasta comes?

RC. Thank you. The illustration speaks for itself, I suppose. You
surely don't expect the man in the street to comprehend all
those petrological terms, or go to the library and look them
up, for that matter? He'd rather switch on the television.

HM. Of course I don't expect him to understand it. But it works
just as well if he doesn't. The poem contains a good many
philosophical reflections, some of which the reader is going

to find unfamiliar and perhaps startling, and that exordium
is deliberately meant as a steep lyrical flight, lifting him up
into a new and strange region of thought. What it conveys
to the uninstructed reader — who might just as easily be
someone highly literate, very well-read in poetry, as a son
of toil — is the richness and strangeness of the world of
stones. If I don't convey that at the beginning, there's no
point later in writing a passage like

> These stones go through Man, straight to God, if there
>   is one.
> What had they not gone through already?
> Empires, civilisations, aeons. Only in them
> If in anything, can His creation confront Him.
> They came so far out of the water and halted forever.
> That larking dallier, the sun, has only been able to play
> With superficial by-products since;
> The moon moves the waters backwards and forwards,
> But the stones cannot be lured an inch further
> Either on this side of eternity or the other.
> Who thinks God is easier to know than they are?
> Trying to reach men any more, any otherwise, than
>   they are?
> These stones will reach us long before we reach them.
> Cold, undistracted, eternal and sublime.

RC.   Very fine, and, as usual with you, remote from all
compromise. But, just before we leave the subject for
others more interesting; you would deny, then, that your
Communism had anything to do with annoying the
English?

HM.   You and I each had an attitude to the English. One can't
write in English — any version of it — and inhabit the
British Isles, without having one. You defined yourself
against them, consciously using their traditions and
attitudes as a backdrop. The young adventurer from the
bushveldt with his outdoor bearing and wide-brimmed hat,
who also had a rich gift for words — you fascinated them,
and their fascination only increased when you lampooned
them. *The Georgiad* may have made you some personal
enemies, but it wasn't the kind of satire that arouses

genuine hatred and fierce opposition. You were, I think, what T. S. Eliot said Blake was, "a wild pet for the super-cultivated". There's no great harm in this: a man has to define himself against *something*. But my quarrel with England was older and bitterer. It goes back to Flodden and forward to Cumberland's butcheries. And I had a solid, settled literary tradition behind me, which an English-speaking South African has not. The writers who came to England from South Africa, the William Plomers and the David Wrights and the Angus Wilsons, have usually shed all trace of South Africa and simply written as Englishmen. No Scot could do that if he tried. The tradition itself is strong enough to take the pen out of his hand and write for him, if he tried to ignore it.

And now, since we are in a dimension of peace and reconciliation, and since we shall be seeing one another regularly throughout eternity, let us speak of our affinities.

RC. Gladly. Our backgrounds, totally contrasting in physical terms, are very similar in their emotional and imaginative aspects. We are neither of us city-bred or willing to adapt to the frills, the gadgetry and the affectations that seem natural in megalopolis. My bushveldt is as stark, as totally uncompromising and demanding, as your rocky coastline and islands.

HM. Yes, that shared starting-point impelled us both to seek finality, to try to state problems in their ultimate terms, to cut away ornamentation, to be done as fast as possible with the adventitious and the incidental. The numerous passages about stone in my work are similar in spirit to your praise of the bare boughs of winter-stripped trees in that fine lyric that begins,

> I love to see, when leaves depart,
> The clear anatomy arrive;
> Winter, the paragon of art,
> That kills all forms of thought and feeling
> Save what is pure and will survive.

RC. Yes, that is something we share. Your poems about rock and light and water, and bare basic forms of plant life such

181

as sea-lichens, address themselves to the same area of experience as my descriptions of physical toil, of blinding heat on rock and daunting vegetation, of the immense silences of the bush, and of simple, deeply tenacious forms of human life.

HM. Like the Zulu girl.

RC. Yes, the Zulu girl or for that matter the poet as Africa bred him. Remember how I put it?—

> We shall grow terrible through fear,
> We shall grow venomous with truth,
> And through these plains where thought meanders
> Through sheepish brains in wormy life,
> Our lives shall roll like fierce Scamanders
> Their red alluvium of strife.

And I have always known that if you had been familiar with some of the landscapes in which I made my home at various times — the Camargue, for instance — you would have recreated them in your work as memorably as ever I did, though in a different idiom.

As a matter of fact we even came close together, at one point, in our choice of environment. Your island home at Whalsay, described by your son as "a self-induced Scottish Siberia that allowed no compromise" — meaning, I suppose, that you lived there in the style of Zhivago at Varykino, gathering the harvest of your mind oblivious of the wolves who howled at the edge of the clearing — was hardly different at all from the steep coast of North Wales where my wife and I, almost penniless young people but happy in our creativity and our rich makeshift, anchored for a time in the 'twenties, up on those cliffs near Aberdaron that stare across the deep turbulent channel to Bardsey Island. Your admiration for the islanders you knew was much the same as the comradeship I found with the isolated and untamed breed who inhabited Bardsey in those days (all gone now!) and who, in gratitude for some service I had been able to do them one wild winter night at the risk of drowning, called me "Africa bach" and left presents of a lamb or a basket of eggs at our cottage door.

182

HM. The difference being that Bardsey was a Christian shrine, a place of pilgrimage where Christian saints and would-be saints had journeyed to lay their bones. My Scottish islanders derived their spiritual values from their deep, inarticulate — no, unarticulated — Gaelic tradition; they had never been, like the Welsh, deeply Christianised.

RC. I find great love and understanding in that poem you quoted, "Island Funeral".

HM. Yes, that is a tribute to a breed of human being who gave me, and will continue to give me, hope for the race.

RC. It also offers, I think, a good characteristic sample of one of the kinds of poetry you wrote — one, I say, because unlike my work, which is always within hailing distance of a fairly evident centre, your work is highly diverse. But there are enough poems roughly similar to "Island Funeral" to make it a good exhibit. I shall say what I admire in it, and what I feel more reluctant to praise.

HM. Do. I shall hear you without contention.

RC. I admire the boldness, the strength and range of thought, and the unexpectedness. One of the characteristics that links your work with classical "modern" poetry, as written in English or French or German or Italian, is the audacity of the leap it makes, every so often, from one crag to another. In "Direadh III", for instance, another of those discursive poems, you pass from the water-crowfoot and the flight of a rock-pigeon to "the first line of the loveliest chorus in *Hippolytus*": then follows:

> Here where the colours—
> Red standing for heat,
> Solar, sensual, spiritual;
> Blue for cold—polar, bodily, intellectual;
> Yellow luminous and embodied
> In the most enduring and the brightest form in gold—
> Remind me how about this
> Pindar and Confucius agreed.
> Confucius who was Pindar's contemporary
> For nearly half a century!
> And it was Pindar's 'golden snow'
> My love and I climbed in t' 't day!

183

The jump from nakedly observed nature to one of the
traditional high points of European culture, then to the
Orient, roping the two peaks together, and the sudden
movement across to the personal — these are the marks of
your poetry and they are marks you share with other
important poets in the modern tradition. Not that, as a rule,
you share their difficulty. The only poem of yours I find
completely baffling is "Harry Semen"; I can't make out
whether it is a monologue uttered by a spermatozoon, or a
man contemplating his origin in human seed, and in any
case I find it difficult to follow what the poem is telling me.

HM. Persevere. At least here you will have plenty of time.

RC. Certainly. To go back to "Island Funeral": who could ever
have guessed that when you looked round for a parallel to
the spiritual tradition of these islanders, their unique
contribution to the world, you would find it in the cornet
playing of Bix Beiderbecke? It seems a combination that
could only form itself in one mind — yours; but the poem
argues it convincingly.

> This clear old Gaelic sound,
> In the chaos of the modern world,
> Is like a phrase from Beiderbecke's cornet,
> As beautiful as any phrase can be.
> It is, in its loveliness and perfection,
> Unique, as a phrase should be;
> And it is ultimately indescribable.
>
> Panassié speaks of it as 'full and powerful',
> But also as 'so fine
> As to be almost transparent',
> And there is in fact
> This extraordinary delicacy in strength.
> He speaks of phrases that soar;
> And this, too, is in fact
> A remarkable and distinguishing quality.
> Otis Ferguson speaks of 'the clear line
> Of that music', of 'every phrase
> As fresh and glistening as creation itself',
> And there is in fact
> This radiance, and simple joyousness.

That, as I say, is convincingly argued; but I use the word "argued" partly to indicate a misgiving. It is expository, like a passage in a lecture, complete with quotations (and who would have guessed that Hugues Panassié, the pioneer European critic of jazz, would be cited as one of your oracles along with Blok, Joyce, Zamyatin, Beethoven, Melville). But I miss the impulse to song. Such passages— and they are many, and long — are interesting as an essay is interesting, rather than arresting like a poem.

HM. I could defend that point. Both of us were makers rather than theorists. To the artist, praxis is all — what is legitimate is what works. My expository poems, the ones that treat discursively of ideas, express themselves in the idiom of the lecture, the essay, the sermon, because they find themselves at certain moments doing the work of the lecture, the essay, the sermon. I've never been afraid of that — especially since people whose primary demand on the poet is for lyrical expression will find themselves well catered for in my pages.

RC. You were, as everyone saw, an undisputed master of the lyric. And it might well be urged, as you seem to be urging, that a man who has written much fine lyric verse, and proved his mastery of it beyond doubt at all periods of his productive life, has the right to be prosy when he wants to be. But that would be a moral argument. Rights exist in Heaven, not on Parnassus. I still find too relentlessly prosy a quality in a passage like this:

> A little priest arrives; he has a long body and short legs and wears bicycle clips on his trousers. He stands at the head of the grave and casts a narrow purple ribbon round his neck and begins without delay to read the Latin prayers as if they were a string of beads. Twice the dead woman's son hands him a bottle and twice he sprinkles the coffin and the grave with holy water. In all the faces gathered round there is a strange remoteness. They are weather-beaten people with eyes grown clear, like the eyes of travellers and seamen, from always watching far horizons. But there is another legend written on those

185

faces, a shadow — or a light — of spiritual vision that will seldom find full play on the features of country folk or men of strenuous action. Among these mourners are believers and unbelievers, and many of them steer a middle course, being now priest-ridden by convention and pagan by conviction, but not one of them betrays a sign of facile and self-lulling piety, nor can one see on any face 'a sure and certain hope of the Resurrection to eternal life'. This burial is just an act of nature, a reassertion of the islanders' inborn certainty that 'in the midst of life we are in death'.

HM. You have rendered my verse as prose.

RC. And very good prose it is. That would be an excellent passage in a novel about island life.

HM. I must insist again that I wrote that passage as verse and you have presented it as prose.

RC. I defy you, simply from memory, to reconstruct the lineation.

HM. Reconstruction is a futile exercise. As I remark in "On a Raised Beach", there are many ruined buildings in the world, but no ruined stones. The reason my discursive poems are constructed in a prose-like manner is because the force that is in them is the force of ideas. Convictions, paradoxes, intellectual realities, nuggets of fact whether historical, geological, etymological or hagiographical, are woven into a carpet stout enough to be put down on the floor and walked across, back and forth, for a lifetime.

RC. I concede that, and it answers my objection. But let us go on to speak of these ideas.

HM. No; I refuse that invitation. If we are to speak of my work it must be *in toto*. I did not have, and I doubt if any poet has, "ideas" that can be extrapolated and talked about. They have their life in the poems where they occur. They are inseparable from their expression.

RC. What comes across is an attitude of mind, a sternness and boldness: you are for sweeping the cupboard bare. With all your knowledge of history and your interest in its patterns, you were always determined not to be dragged at the heels of history. We had to be as indifferent to time as the stones themselves.

HM. Yes, the stone was always my basic metaphor: hardly a metaphor at all, in some ways. *There are no ruined stones —* think of that, and then ask why we should tolerate ruined ideas.

RC. The stone is the key to the love and admiration your work has inspired, and also to the fear it has aroused in some minds. To some onlookers — to the Englishman Swain, for instance — there are times when you come close to embodying the truth of Yeats's lines in *Easter 1916* about the political single-mindedness that breeds the fanatic:

> Hearts with one purpose alone
> In summer or winter seem
> Enchanted to a stone
> To trouble the living stream.

To him, the stone was something to be feared:

> Too long a sacrifice
> Can make a stone of the heart:
> Oh when may it suffice?

HM. Yes, and my friend Sean O'Casey has a character cry out in *Juno and the Paycock*, "Mother of God! Take away our hearts of stone and give us hearts of flesh and blood!" That same fear of the stone as something that doesn't respond in a human way. But we have been responding to things in a human way for aeons and how far have we got? We are, as a race, nowhere near the perception of truth and the reason may be that our minds have too much of the frailty of flesh and blood and too little of the certainty of stone. My own prayer might be, "Take away our minds of blood and tears and give us minds of calmly enduring stone, fit for our destinies to be inscribed on".

RC. That destiny you never saw in Christian terms, as I did. Yet there is in one poem of yours, a lyric from your earliest book, which shows a deep perception of the tragic profundity of the Christian vision.

HM. Which one is that?

RC. "The Innumerable Christ".

187

HM. Ah, that lyric which takes off from a statement by a scientist, J. Y. Simpson's "Other stars may have their Bethlehem, and their Calvary too".

RC. The permitted hour has come for the drinking of whisky. I shall conduct you to my favourite bar (there are many here) and stand you your first glass of single malt on this side of the Gulf.

(They are instantly there, by pure volition, with glasses in their hands.)

And now, by way of a toast, I shall repeat to you, while you drink, that lyric of "The Innumerable Christ".

(In his strong voice, South African twang and all, Campbell recites:)

> Wha kens on whatna Bethlehems
> Earth twinkles like a star the nicht,
> An' whatna shepherds lift their heids
> In its unearthly licht?
>
> 'Yont a' the stars oor een can see
> An' farther than their lichts can fly,
> I' mony an unco warl' the nicht
> The fatefu' bairnies cry.
>
> I' mony an unco warl' the nicht
> The lift gaes black as pitch at noon,
> An' sideways on their chests the heids
> O' endless Christs roll doon.
>
> An' when the earth's as cauld's the mune
> An' a' its folk are lang syne deid,
> On coontless stars the Babe maun cry
> An' the Crucified maun bleed.

HM. *(listening and drinking; looks up at the end)* In this I bury all unkindness.

Acknowledgement of quotations:
Those from MacDiarmid are taken from *The Hugh MacDiarmid Anthology*, ed. Grieve and Scott, Routledge and Kegan Paul, 1972.

Roy Campbell's poems are quoted in too short extracts to need copyright permission, I believe; the lines beginning "I love to see, when leaves depart" I quoted from memory, and "Poets in Africa", the other poem quoted, occurs I believe in *Sons of the Mistral* (Faber and Faber).

Grieve

IAIN CUTHBERTSON

Editor's note:

At Hugh MacDiarmid's funeral on 13 September 1978 in his native
Langholm, Norman MacCaig delivered an oration, and, for once,
no other word is adequate. It reverberates in the minds of all who
heard it, but no text remains. It was born out of the emotions of
the moment; there was no script and no recording. MacCaig
himself has no precise recollection of his own words. We should
like to have been able to print them in this book; but since that is
impossible, we include a poem in which Ian Cuthbertson speaks of
his reaction to them.

My last memory is my clearest:
Norman's voice as dissentient as his
(His hair wild in the wet)
Uttering in a quiver all our bony thoughts,
Translucent, driven and intransigent.

He was, *nota bene*, fastidiously accurate
In his pick of words not a fraction out.
But we mourners stood various and splay-footed,
Blubbery under Earshaw Hill.

Norman was bang on. For me that was intractably Chris—
When all is said and done—a man most timeous:
He hated the unchronometric, the indefinite article,
The hot undetermined air of wetnosed men;
Never once did he doubt his origins but,
Against Scottish national apathy and philistinism,
He sustained them as living organs of his intellect;

He spent several lifetimes in Barlinnie
In thrawn alliance with convicted outlaws,
Hardlabouring his vocabulary, his standpoint refined;
He saw the fat established view change daily and altered with it,
Contradictive, controversial and contumacious.
After all, the truth was thin and lay in opposition.

It was his bounden duty to himself to be a panepistemon:
To know all these orra folk by name at least, these familiars;
To make out that Montaigne and Spinoza both played centre-
    forward
For Langholm Juniors (at different times, of course)
Means that you know your man and you know your team.
If you know these intelligentry well enough they'll do anything
    you say.

Likewise, it should not be beyond the power of man to con
The spare parts of a late sixteenth-century Spanish cuirass
Or a Russian telega, have them at the fingertips,
As in the anatomy of a macrosporangium.
Ah, high spring tides at Scrabster more than two hours before
The state of affairs at Kirkwall. This affects joint-tenancies.
He was steeped in pawnee history, versed in the branches
Of mongolic stock, observed their curious interweave,
Just like the average bloke who knows who eats the gibbous
    wrasse
In quantity or who the raccoon-oyster and why.
To be a polymathic polyhedron heid is a fair and reasonable
    ambition.
Dammit, if a Scot cannot understand his situation in the
    worldscene
Who the hell else can? Certes, no the English.

A man's identity is the sum of his active knowledge:
Behind that jar of honey lie stacked a range of hills,
Each a pile and mine of information
For which that little jar is a front reference.
A typical 'product of our educational system'

190

Buys the jar, eats the honey and throws away the empty jar.
He has learnt nothing, has not begun to. It's just a jar.

For all this philosophical deep-talk of Chris
It would be a blunder in the extreme if we were ever
To separate him from his politics. It has been tried
Time and time over by the whitewasherwomen, *sans succès*.
Like Yeats' Crazy Jane, when you take me you take the lot.
Therefore Chris, you cannot be summarised. Each biography
Is a joke. Yet when you see them all lined up and say,
"Is that that?" The answer's "Yes." The joke is over

And we are back in that graveyard under Earshaw Hill,
Legless for lack of you. There is no record of what Norman said.
But it was right: bang on. We must spend the rest of our lives
Making up for and living up to your illumination.

191

Part III

MacDiarmid and Scotland

EDWIN MORGAN

MacDiarmid's concern with Scotland scarcely needs to be underlined; even the titles of his prose books — *Contemporary Scottish Studies, Scottish Scene, The Islands of Scotland, Scottish Eccentrics* — hammer the point home. But his poetry, it seems to me, could still stand a fair amount of examination on this theme.

In the 1920s MacDiarmid began from a position not unlike that of James Joyce in Ireland when he began writing *Dubliners* — an intense exasperation with the state of the country, focused especially on the apathy or indifference of the people. A favourite word is "aboulia" — apathy — which is very like Joyce's "paralysis"; Scotland, like Ireland, is held static by some paralysis of the will. This apathy or paralysis shows itself, he thinks, in a general wershness in the quality of Scottish life as well as in more specific things like the insufficient support given to figures like John MacLean whose ideas and life's effort are allowed to drift into the sand. In *A Drunk Man Looks at the Thistle* he begins on a light, amusing note, saying that even the whisky is not what it used to be:

> A' that's Scotch aboot it is the name,
> Like a' thing else ca'd Scottish nooadays
> —A' destitute o' speerit juist the same.

The pun on "speerit" helps him to announce very clearly in the poem that something is wrong with the soul of Scotland, and this (as it emerges) is seen to be a matter not solely of politics and economics.

> And in the toon that I belang tae
> —What tho'ts Montrose or Nazareth?—
> Helplessly the folk continue
> To lead their livin' death!

Without quite saying that he is Jesus Christ, he suggests that it may take a miracle or two to shake people out of their unaware and lethargic condition. Some of the things that he sees as being wrong with Scotland are of course identifiable. There is nothing obscure about "To Any Scottish Laird" (1932):

> Your land? You fool, it hauds nae beast
> Or bird or troot or tree or weed
> If they kent you as owner but
> 'Ud leave it empty as your heid.

If the grip of the feudal past is still strong in Scotland, the political effects of the Union of 1707 are also attacked, as notably in "The Parrot Cry" from *To Circumjack Cencrastus*:

> Tell me the auld, auld story
> O' hoo the Union brocht
> Puir Scotland into being
> As a country worth a thocht.
> England frae whom a' blessings flow
> What could we dae withoot ye?
> Then dinna threip it doon oor throats
> As gin we e'er could doot ye!
> > My feelings lang wi' gratitude
> > Ha'e been sae sairly harrowed
> > That dod! I think it's time
> > The claith was owre the parrot!

The poem is effective because it is well controlled, and does not fall into the hectoring tone that MacDiarmid sometimes uses; it keeps a mocking satirical stance and yet leaves us in no doubt about the feeling behind it, the feeling that (as the refrain tells us) it is time for questioning and overthrowing the repeated assertion that the Union saved Scotland — the poet is sure that this time has come and that it is his duty as poet and prophet to announce this to other people. He cannot accept the superficially attractive argument that Scotland has had the best of both worlds, that it has preserved its cultural identity without having all the troubles and responsibilities of political identity. On the contrary, he says, the voice of the parrot, the unionist voice, has been so loud and so persistent that it has silenced other, more truly native voices; it has given only the illusion of cultural health. MacDiarmid saw the lack of cultural health in Scotland particularly in philistinism, and some of his bitterest poems — as well as some entertaining ones — direct their attack either at kailyard culture or at what he sees as even worse, indifference to culture. And the attack is continued into the world of education, and especially the universities, where he says the wrong kind of culture is being taught, at the expense of important native traditions. In "Glasgow 1960" (published in 1935), an amusing and well-turned sonnet, in which crowds throng the buses to Ibrox Park not for football but for an intellectual debate, and other eager citizens snap up a newspaper special which has Scottish authors' opinions of a "Turkish poet's abstruse new song", his target is the lumpen unimaginativeness and backwardness not only of the public but of its cultural representatives. A more angry and contemptuous poem, "Allelauder" (1932), gives a two-pronged attack on the entertainer Harry Lauder and the politician Ramsay MacDonald, Lauder in particular being presented as the very worst kind of Scot, upholding a sentimental and unthinking patriotism which would make people contented with their lot and would in *Sir Harry Lauder's* own case show him as being hand in glove with the old feudalism and paternalism that MacDiarmid wanted to break.

> The little man with the enlarged heart
> Can only make us wholly forget
> All the horrors of war and peace
> With which mankind's beset,
> Every so-called crisis disappears
> — 'He's made us happy for fifty years!'
> Honour to Ramsay MacDonald who
> Sees and proclaims this fact,
> Knowing that pawky patter does more
> Than an Ottawa or O-to-hell pact.
> Dire necessity and foul disease
> Are vanquished by a variety act . . .
> With a waggle here and a wiggle there
> The world will soon be rid
> Of all its trouble and doubts and fears
> *-Happy for good as for fifty years!*
> Allelauder, Allelauder,

Let the grateful millions raise
Their starving mouths and helpless hands
In great Sir Harry's praise . . .
Oh, Lauder is bad enough, but we
Might have been happier still
If MacDonald every now and again
Hadn't figured too on the bill
—The cross-talk duo, it appears,
Toplining these fifty filthy years.

As for education, he makes his attack in places like the section "Oor four Universities" in *To Circumjack Cencrastus*, where the staff are more familiar with Czech and Sanskrit than with medieval Gaelic poetry, and where students cannot tell him "Where Trenmor triumphed/Or Oscar fell". It does not really mean that he wants no one to learn Czech or Sanskrit (if a "Turkish poet" has an "abstruse new song" we ought to know about it), but rather that he is ashamed to think of how an educational system can deliberately foster neglect of a part (here, the Celtic part) of its own culture.

When he looks round at the general life of the cities in Scotland, he is not much encouraged by what he sees there either. He has many poems about Glasgow, a few about Edinburgh. Neither place comes in for much admiration, to put it mildly, but Glasgow receives a stronger criticism because it is a larger and more obvious target. MacDiarmid always claimed that he had no patience with back-to-the-landism and that he was on the side of the urban proletariat, but from his poems about cities one would hardly ever have that claim confirmed. In one of the Glasgow poems, "Personalities and the Machine Age" (1936), he does say that it is to Glasgow's credit — it is the only thing to Glasgow's credit — to have an abundance of machines—

crankheads flashing rhythmically between
Twin column hiding flying crossroads and thrusting silver
    rods;
The starboard shaft oiled and shining in the blaze of electric
    lights
Turning its eighty revolutions a minute. My sympathies
Are with the workers, not the country clods.

But that passage is quite exceptional; usually he presents Glasgow
as if he had just been looking through Doré's illustrations to
Dante's *Inferno*:

> The houses are Glasgow, not the people—these
> Are simply the food the houses live and grow on
> Endlessly, drawing from their vulgarity
> And pettiness and darkness of spirit
> —Gorgonising the mindless generations,
> Turning them all into filthy property,
> Apt as the Karaunas by diabolic arts
> To produce darkness and obscure the light of day.
> To see or hear a clock in Glasgow's horrible,
> Like seeing a dead man's watch, still going though he's dead.
> Everything is dead except stupidity here.
>
> Where have I seen a human being looking
> As Glasgow looks this gin-clear evening—with face and
>   fingers
> A cadaverous blue, hand-clasp slimy and cold
> As that of a corpse, finger-nails grown immeasurably long
> As they do in a grave, little white eyes, and hardly
> Any face at all? Cold, lightning-like, unpleasant, light, and
>   blue
> Like having one's cold spots intoxicated with mescal.
> Looking down a street the houses seem
> Long pointed teeth like a ferret's over the slit
> Of a crooked unspeakable smile, like the Thracian woman's
> When Thales fell in the well, a hag
> Whose soul-gelding ugliness would chill
> To eternal chastity a cantharidized satyr. . . .

("Glasgow")

The curious rhetoric of the poem, by which the city is personified
only to become less human, produces a strong but mixed effect —
part anger, part disgust, part black comedy. The "soul-gelding
ugliness" is the ugliness of a large industrial city during the decline
and neglect of the inter-war years, before the days of smokeless
zones and stone-cleaning; the corpselike devourer of the
"mindless generations" is a city that has been slow to attain the
consciousness which serious writers might give it; but the way in

197

which the images and comparisons proliferate towards fantasy suggests much less an observer's social-critical eye than the turbulent basic rejection of someone whose stamping-ground this place is not and would never be. In so far as "Scotland" is the central and western industrial belt, this is a Scotland with which he did not come to terms. Nor was it natural that he should, since the countryside and the small town were in his bones and the city was not; and he had the problem, as a poet, of reconciling his progressive and materialist ideas with his natural feeling for country life, and indeed for simple uncluttered life (despite the paper clutter of books, notes, and cuttings). The way he moved around and into this problem is of great interest.

The method is imaginative. Although the first insistence is on the reality of detail in describing or evoking or enumerating the varied aspects of life or landscape in the whole country, and on reminding people of the nature, the actuality of Scotland, islands and mainland, history and present, the matter is then moved out into another dimension, where the poet as seer, with his feet firmly on the ground, can nevertheless invite his readers to consider the entire meaning and destiny of this country, this place, Scotland. Rather like Walt Whitman with America, he demands that you know the country first, and he wants to shame you into admitting how ignorant you are about Scottish geography and history, but then you must not stop at contemplation — though contemplation is important — but must use your knowledge to help this place, this country, into the right forward streams of future history. "My aim in regard to Scotland," he said in *Lucky Poet*, "was to be like the sword with which Sergeant Troy bedazzled Bathsheba, which seemed to be anywhere and everywhere!" In one poem he will list uncommon Scottish place-names; in another he will describe and celebrate some local way of life — perhaps in an isolated community — as in "Shetland Lyrics" or "Island Funeral"; in some poems he will link features of landscape into personal life (as in "Of my first love" where the waterfall called the Fall of Coul in Sutherland reminds the speaker of the cascade of hair of his first love when she let him undo it thirty years ago); or sometimes he will bring unexpected praise to features of the land which he wants us to think about in a new way

198

— perhaps metaphorically. The poem "Bracken Hills in Autumn" describes in minute detail a very Scottish scene, but also meditates on two seemingly opposed things, the elemental and even menacing indifference to man that is shown in the profuse spread of bracken, and the fact that bracken can be used if you know how to use it; the bracken beds "nurse the thunder", but:

> cast
> Cartloads of them into a pool where the trout are few
> And soon the swarming animalculae upon them
> Will proportionately increase the fishes too.
> Miracles are never far away
> Save bringing new thought to play.

He also uses country scenes and figures, as Burns did, to focus some of his many ideas about Scotland, as in "A Vision of Scotland", where a girl becomes an allegorical representative of her country, and the point is made, through the oblique way in which she is shown, that even if she is found in a city like Glasgow or Dundee there is something about her which should remind you of country rather than town; and indeed as an instance of the recurring Celtic theme, she seems to reach right back through the Scottish highlands to the Irish countryside:

> Every now and again in a girl like you,
> Even in the streets of Glasgow or Dundee,
> She throws her headsquare off and a mass
> Of authentic flaxen hair is revealed,
> Fine spun as newly-retted fibres
> On a sunlit Irish bleaching field.

But finally he wants something more than a revitalized Scotland, revitalized politically and economically, knowledgeable and aware in poetry and the arts. As he says in *A Drunk Man*,

> He canna Scotland see wha yet
> Canna see the Infinite,

and in another passage,

> I wad ha'e Scotland to my eye
> Until I saw a timeless flame
> Tak' Auchtermuchty for a name,
> And kent that Ecclefechan stood
> As pairt o' an eternal mood.

In some of his poetry he is very impatient with nationalist practical politics; in fact he makes merry in some sharply satirical pieces with the ardent lover of causes, including the nationalist cause—

> Juist as I thocht; your slogan is:
> Ilka worm lo'es its ain wriggle best.

This impatience may seem strange, coming from someone who was one of the founders of an organised nationalist movement in Scotland; but it comes from the visionary side of MacDiarmid, which was very strong and which emerges in some of the best of his poems. He often uses the old traditional device of climbing a mountain to receive or to give a prophetic message. It will be of course a Scottish mountain (we have no shortage), Liathach or Sgurr Alasdair or the Inaccessible Pinnacle or the cliffs of Foula, a real place which can be described and which may be relatively familiar, but then it becomes something else:

> The north face of Liathach
> Lives in the mind like a vision.

This "something else" is what unfolds gradually in a series of meditations, linked only by tenuous associational material, on time and history, on the economic future, on Scotland's relation to other countries in the world, on the nature of national character, on human will and evolution, on the kind of universe that Scotland and the world belong to, and on many other things which the heresy of paraphrase is hard put to it to extract. "Here," as he says in "Direadh III" — and "here" means "here on the page" as much as "here on a mountain-top", which brings a subtle irony to his claim that the mountain's inhuman beauty "seems the antithesis of every form of art"—

> Here near the summit of Sgurr Alasdair
> The air is very still and warm,
> The Outer Isles look as though
> They were cut out of black paper
> And stuck on a brilliant silver background,
> (Even as I have seen the snow-capped ridges of Hayes
>   Peninsula
> Stand out stark and clear in the pellucid Arctic atmosphere
> Or, after a wild and foggy night, in the dawn

Seen the jagged line of the Tierra del Fuego cliffs
Looking for all the world as if they were cut out of tin,
Extending gaunt and desolate),
The western sea and sky undivided by horizon,
So dazzling is the sun
And its glass image in the sea.
The Cuillin peaks seem miniature
And nearer than is natural
And they move like liquid ripples
In the molten breath
Of the corries which divide them.
I light my pipe and the match burns steadily
Without the shielding of my hands,
The flame hardly visible in the intensity of light
Which drenches the mountain top. . . .

I am possessed by this purity here
As in a welling of stainless water
Trembling and pure like a body of light
Are the webs of feathery weeds all waving,
Which it traverses with its deep threads of clearness
Like the chalcedony in moss agate
Starred here and there with grenouillette. . . .

This is only the setting of the scene, the place of meditation. And I
think the point is that whatever material the author is using,
whatever imaginatively fused mixture of his reading and his
experience and observation, he has brought together through the
comparisons, and especially from the imagery of light and water, a
magic construct, a magic place, a place where everything is as real
as it is in a surrealistic painting, and yet at the same time as real as
it would be if one was actually there in "real" life. It is Scotland all
right, but another world seems to be only a few steps away. What
MacDiarmid always argued is that without some sense of this
larger world, whether one can define it or not, our sense of
Scotland will remain mediocre and crippled.

The Nationalism of Hugh MacDiarmid

STEPHEN MAXWELL

By listing Anglophobia among his hobbies in a notorious *Who's Who* entry, MacDiarmid did more to type-cast himself as a chauvinistic "Wha's like us?" Scottish nationalist than anything his critics and traducers ever did or could have done. Whatever its psychological source — and MacDiarmid would have it that a strain of Anglophobia was part of the inheritance of anyone born and bred on the Scottish side of the Border — MacDiarmid's mature nationalism was "sui generis". It scorned sentimental nationalism whether of the Burns Club or Hampden Park variety. It learned to reject the traditional categories of literary nationalism — country, land, people, even in the end language — both as sources of inspiration and as subject. It was a nationalism at once realist and idealist, seeing Scotland as she was and setting out to remake her in the image of several, complementary ideas of what she ought to be. It was this mental construct, more MacDiarmid than Scotland, which became the inspiration and the subject of his nationalism. It was a nationalism which sought, finally, to transcend nationality and to present Scotland not as the possessor of distinctive national qualities but as an exemplar of universal intellectual and aesthetic qualities which rendered trivial all lesser distinctions.

In the April 1923 issue of the *Scottish Chapbook*, which he edited from Montrose, MacDiarmid recommended a poem by the "Scoto-Russian" poet Lermontov as an example of the attitude which Scottish poets should adopt towards Scotland.

> I love my country but with strange love.
> This love my reason cannot overcome.

'Tis not the glory bought at price of blood,
Nor quiet, full of haughty confidence,
Nor dark antiquity's untouched traditions
That moved in me a happy reverie,
But I do love, which I know not myself,
The cold deep silence of my country's fields,
Her sleeping forests moving in the wind,
Her rivers flowing widely like the sea.

The poem goes on to evoke the autumn landscape of Russia with its parching harvest, silver birches, its train of waggons on the steppes, its happy, drunken peasantry. But MacDiarmid misjudged the direction of his own development, for while he followed Lermontov in rejecting the traditional Romantic sources of attachment to nation described in the early lines of the poem, his own response to Scotland embraced few of the elegiac and Virgilian strains which dominate the poem. A poem addressed by Henrik Ibsen to his fellow Norwegian, the composer Edvard Grieg, more accurately describes MacDiarmid's relationship with Scotland.

Orpheus woke with crystal tones
Souls in brutes; struck fire from stones.

Stones there are in Norway plenty;
Brutes far more than ten or twenty.

Play! so stones spark far and wide
Play! to pierce the brutes' thick hide.

Only occasionally does MacDiarmid adopt the literary convention of addressing the spirit of Scotland as a person. More characteristically he approaches Scotland as an intellectual problem, a challenge to the imagination, as in "Scotland" (*Lucky Poet*, 1943):

Scotland! Everything he saw in it
Was a polyhedron he held in his brain.
Every side of it visible at once
Of knowledge drawn from every field of life
—Polyhedrons everywhere! He knew
There was a way of combining them he must find yet.

In his intellectual autobiography, *Lucky Poet*, MacDiarmid claimed that he had written hardly more than a dozen lines of nature poetry conventionally understood. His aim had always been to interpret nature "in terms of human activities, being alert to the historical processes and careful to avoid the heresy of separateness". The Scottish landscape is celebrated less for its imminent qualities than for its capacity to uncover for the observer an ultimate human reality. "The North Face of Liathach" (*Collected Poems*, 1962):

> The North Face of Liathach
> Lives in the mind like a vision
> . . . Not of my mother
> But of many other women I have known
> As I could not know her.
> It is with them that I have found the soul most exposed
> Something not of this world,
> Which makes you tremble with delight and repulsion.

The people of Scotland were even less qualified to serve as the inspiration of MacDiarmid's nationalism than the conventional literary props of country or land. He occasionally celebrated Scottish types like the East Lothian bailiff in "Direadh II":

> With a voice that could carry nearly all over
> The six hundred acres of his farm
> And a whistle that would carry
> Even further than his voice

or the Border characters in the Coldingham Inn in the same poem, but he found little virtue in the Scottish people as a whole. As in *A Drunk Man Looks at the Thistle*, his characteristic attitude is one of contempt:

> I micht ha'e been contentit—gin the feck
> O' may ain folk had grovelled wi' less respec',
> But their obsequious devotion
> Made it for me a criminal emotion.

MacDiarmid sounds more like the conventional nationalist in his early pronouncements on the potential of the Scots language in the *Scottish Chapbook* than in almost anything else he wrote about nationalism. In the first issue of the *Chapbook*, published in October 1922, he wrote ". . . the value of the Doric lies in the extent to which it contains certain lapsed or unrealised qualities, which correspond to 'unconscious' elements of distinctively

Scottish psychology". The suggestion here of belief in the existence of a Scots national "Geist" preserved in the Scots language is developed, in phantasmagoric imagery, in "Gairmscoile" (*Penny Wheep*, 1926), a poem which includes references to the "spirit of the race" and "Scotland's hidden poee'ers":

> . . . And ther's forgotten shibboleths o' the Scots
> Ha'e keys to senses lockit to us yet
> —Coorse words that shamble thro' oor minds like stots,
> Syne turn on's muckle een wi' doonsin emerauds lit.

If at this stage of his nationalist development MacDiarmid borrowed from the National Romanticism of the nineteenth century, he rejected from the beginning any suggestion that the quality of Scottish thought or feeling was defined in the Scots language beyond the possibility of growth. In the same issue of the *Chapbook*, he insisted: "Whatever the potentialities of the Doric may be, there cannot be a revival in the real sense of the word — a revival of the spirit as opposed to a mere renewed vogue of the letter — unless those potentialities are in accord with the newest and truest tendencies of human thought. . . . The real enemy is he who cries 'Hands off our fine old Scottish tongue!'. If all that the movement is to achieve is to preserve specimens of Braid Scots, archaic, imitative, belonging to a type of life that has passed and cannot return, in a sort of museum department of our conscious-ness — set apart from our vital preconceptions — it is a movement which not only cannot claim our support but compels our opposition."

MacDiarmid's interest in the potentialities of Scots as a literary language was reinforced by his knowledge of the development of cultural nationalism in nineteenth-century Norway. Both his poetry and his prose contain admiring references to the leading Norwegian cultural nationalists of the century — Henrik Wergeland in the first half of the century and Bjornsterne Bjornson in the second. What especially aroused MacDiarmid's admiration was the way in which the two Norwegians combined their literary nationalism with radical and progressive views on the political and social issues of their times. Wergeland — whom MacDiarmid enrolled in his pantheon of Scottish cultural heroes

205

by virtue of a remote family connection with Scotland — had been a stern critic of the historical and antiquarian literary romanticism which he had encountered in Denmark and Germany — whence it had spread from the Scotland of Macpherson and Scott — declaring in words which MacDiarmid could have adopted as his credo: "Real poets do not shut their souls into closets. Their field of action is world history, and they find their place in the world, formerly as leaders of hosts and teachers of kings, now as leaders of ideas and teachers of people." In a later essay — "Charles Doughty and the Need for Heroic Poetry" (1936), MacDiarmid quotes Bjornson's description of the poet's role as his own ideal:

> A poet's is the prophet's call;
> In times of need and travail-throe
> His faith the gleam they seek can show
> To those who strive, and striving fall.
> Now ringed by champions from of old
> Now marshalling the new-enrolled,
> Mid whispering hopes, he hears the cry,
> He sees the dreams, of prophecy.

MacDiarmid's knowledge of the part played in Norwegian nationalism by the "landsmaal" movement must have encouraged his belief in the capacity of a Scots vernacular literature to meet the intellectual challenge of the twentieth century. In an obituary in *New Age* (August 1929) of the Norwegian writer Arne Garborg, MacDiarmid recommended Garborg's achievement in using the synthetic "landsmaal" created from Old Norse and regional dialects in the mid-nineteenth century, to write about the social and cultural problems of his age.

In the *Scottish Chapbook* MacDiarmid used two slogans to summarise the direction he believed the Scottish revival had to follow — Nietzsche's "Become what you are" and "Not Tradition—Precedent". Nietzsche's slogan was an apt summary for this early, linguistic phase of MacDiarmid's nationalism, expressing at once his judgement of the unfulfilled potential of the Scots language and his sense of the balance between the past, present and future necessary to the healthy development of the Scottish revival. But it was the second slogan — "Not Tradition —Precedent", carried on the cover of the *Scottish Chapbook* —

which was to prove the more accurate guide to the development of MacDiarmid's nationalism in the 1930s and 1940s.

Ironically it is MacDiarmid's greatest poem in Scots, perhaps the greatest of all his poems, which previews the development of his nationalist ideas beyond this linguistic phase. At the beginning of *A Drunk Man Looks at the Thistle*, the narrator outlines his strategy for leading his countrymen out of the Scottish Waste Land to a full realisation of their spiritual potential.

> To prove my saul is Scots I maun begin
> Wi' what's still deemed Scots and the folk expect
> And spire up syne by visible degrees
> To heichts whereo' the fules ha'e never recked.

But the spiritual pilgrimage does not lead the narrator to a clear perception of Scottish identity. On the contrary he is driven to despair of ever finding a common identity for the scattered fragments of history which go under the label "Scotland".

. . . and syne I saw

> . . . and syne I saw
> John Knox and Clavers in my raw,
> And Mary Queen o' Scots ana',
>
> And Rabbie Burns and Weelum Wallace,
> And Carlyle lookin' unco gallus,
> And Harry Lauder (to enthrall us).
>
> And as I looked I saw them a',
> A' the Scots baith big and sma',
> That e'er the braith of life did draw.

His cry of protest:

> But in this huge ineducable
> Heterogeneous hotch and rabble
> Why am *I* condemned to squabble?

is an admission that Scotland's past does not offer the basis for a Scottish revival. Indeed the poem goes on to suggest that there may be no hope to be found anywhere within a recognisably Scottish experience. The narrator's alter ego — perhaps more accurately his super-ego — pronounces the uncompromising judgement:

A Scottish poet maun assume
The burden o' his people's doom,
And dee to brak their livin' tomb.

Mony ha'e tried, but a' ha'e failed,
Their sacrifice has nocht availed . . .

Ye maun choose but gin ye'd see
Anither category ye
Maun tine your nationality.

Faced with this choice between a thankless, indeed spiritually fatal, duty and a rejection of his nationality, the narrator seeks consolation in the thought "Yet ha'e I Silence left, the croon o' a'", and beyond that in the prospect of Jean's debunking response "And weel ye micht . . . efter sic a nicht!".

Yet for all the pessimism of its argument about Scottish identity, *A Drunk Man Looks at the Thistle* is in the end a poem of hope, and not just because it is itself a demonstration of the potential of the Scots language. Growing out of its pessimistic argument, like the flower out of the thistle, is a liberating vision of Scotland as part of a larger reality which subsumes the conventional distinctions of nationality.

Whatever Scotland is to me,
Be it aye pairt o' a' men see
O' Earth and o' Eternity

Wha winna hide their heids in't till
It seems the haill o' Space to fill,
As t'were an unsurmounted hill.

He canna Scotland see wha yet
Canna see the Infinite,
And Scotland in true scale to it.

It was this perspective which sustained MacDiarmid's hope — and his imagination — when the reality of Scotland, in both its historical and its contemporary aspects, proved intractably hostile.

In an age of crisis MacDiarmid's appreciation of the crisis facing Scottish culture served to integrate Scotland with international developments. The narrator of *A Drunk Man* comments sardonically on Scotland as an acute case of the wider crisis facing Western culture:

> T. S. Eliot—it's a Scottish name—
> Afore he wrote 'The Waste Land' s'ud ha'e come
> To Scotland here. He wad ha'e written
> A better poem syne—like this by gum.

In calling for precedents not traditions, MacDiarmid was responding not just to a Scottish need but to a need felt by many Western intellectuals in the inter-war decades when dramatic economic and political changes were felt to be rendering traditional canons obsolete.

Although "Not Tradition—Precedent" was formulated to summarise a cultural doctrine, it also provides an apt summary of the direction in which MacDiarmid's political nationalism was to develop. In its political as in its cultural application, it symbolises MacDiarmid's concern to integrate Scotland with international developments.

MacDiarmid's interest in nationalism had been stirred by the official Allied doctrine that the First World War was a war fought for rights of small nations, and by the international acceptance at the Versailles Peace Conference of the principle of national self-determination. The immediate beneficiaries in Europe were peoples whose nationalism had been sustained by distinctive cultural traditions, including linguistic traditions, which in many cases had been restated in the nineteenth century. But the second wave of progressive nationalism in the twentieth century was among peoples subject to Western imperialism and with a far weaker sense of cultural identity. In contrast to the European nationalist movements, these national liberation movements were inspired not so much by the ambition to recover a national identity based on language as by the need to create an identity in the very process of the struggle for political and economic freedom. By force of circumstance, these were nationalisms of precedent rather than tradition.

MacDiarmid's nationalist fervour continued unabated when, roughly from the publication in 1932 of *Scots Unbound and Other Poems*, his use of Scots became spasmodic. At roughly the same time, while maintaining the Janus pose characteristic of European nationalists — scouring Scotland's past for themes which might help to mould Scotland's future — he became less interested in the historical antecedents of the "traditions" he discovered than in their formative influence. His nationalism came to owe less and less to Scotland and more and more to MacDiarmid himself, as expressed in a later poem, "The Poet as Prophet" (1953):

> Scotland felt at that moment
> That no man ever personified her,
> Ever would represent her,
> As he did,
> And she grew in glory
> And was transfigured with pride.
> It was not a Scottish moment;
> It was a universal moment.

It was a nationalism which, foreswearing the conventional categories of nationality, envisioned Scotland variously as a field of heroic intellectual effort, as an inexhaustible source of all the data required to feed the artist's imagination, as a starting point for the people of Scotland in their search for the synthesis of science and art in a "poetry of facts". Above all it was an exhortatory nationalism which challenged the people of Scotland to take the van in the urgent work of cultural recovery facing the West.

MacDiarmid gave expression to this heroic, exemplary nationalism through his advocacy of four "master ideas" — the Caledonian Antisyzygy, the Gaelic Idea, the Social Credit doctrine of C. H. Douglas and Scottish Socialism. Although at different stages of his development one or other, or some particular combination, of these ideas tended to dominate, each exerted a lifelong influence on his political and cultural thinking.

MacDiarmid's belief in the role of the Caledonian Antisyzygy and of Scotland's Gaelic culture developed from his acceptance, acknowledged in the *Scottish Chapbook* of March 1923, of Spengler's theory of the growth and decay of cultures. The classical, Apollonian mind — dogmatic, unquestioning, instinctive — represented in the modern world by England and Germany — had exhausted its creative potential. Dostoevsky had been the precursor of the era of the Faustian mind — "ever questioning never satisfied, rationalistic in religion and politics, romantic in art and literature". MacDiarmid embraced the Faustian mind as a "perfect expression of the Scottish race", and declared: "The 'canny Scot' tradition has been fulfilled in the Spenglerian sense: and the future depends upon the freeing and development of that opposite tendency in our consciousness which runs counter to the conventional conception of what is Scottish."

The opposite tendency to the "canny Scot" tradition was summed up for MacDiarmid by the concept of the Caledonian Antisyzygy. The originator of the term, Professor Gregory Smith, used it to describe a distinctive quality of the Scottish imagination — its capacity to juxtapose disparate, apparently contradictory ideas, to jump from the sublime to the ridiculous, from the real to the fantastic, from the sacred to the profane. In this interpretation, the concept served as a theoretical support for MacDiarmid's literary work in Scots. But as MacDiarmid's views developed beyond his early interest in Scots, he transformed the concept in his imagination into a polemical scythe which he used to clear away traditional definitions of Scottish nationality, if not the very possibility of defining Scottish identity, leaving the Scottish spirit capable of "countless manifestations, at absolute variance with each other, yet confined within the 'limited infinity' of the adjective 'Scottish' ".

MacDiarmid retained these ideas as a framework for his growing interest in Scotland's Gaelic culture. Writing in November 1927 in the first issue of the *Pictish Review*, the periodical of the Gaelic revival edited by Erskine of Marr, he concedes that the promising developments in Scots literature of the previous six years had come to a "virtual standstill" and suggests that Scots vernacular is too vulnerable to stand alone against the threat of standardisation posed by industrialism and cosmopolitan finance. The only chance of recovery for Scottish culture — and hence in his Spenglerian perspective for Western culture as a whole — lay in the rediscovery of the long-neglected

"Ur-motives" of the race. These were preserved in their most vital and accessible form in Scotland's Gaelic culture.

The fullest development of this medley of ideas is in an essay on "The Caledonian Antisyzygy and the Gaelic Idea" published in 1931. The Russian Idea represented earlier by Dostoevsky had now assumed what appeared to MacDiarmid in these pre-Communist days the less attractive Soviet form which denied the relationship between "freedom and genius, freedom and thought". Only Gaeldom offered a dynamic counter-idea "that does not run wholly counter to it, but supplements, corrects, challenges and qualifies it". Gaeldom offered a way back beyond the Renaissance which had drained Western culture of its imaginative energy, to a classicism flowing directly from the "Ur-motives" of the race. In political terms, Gaeldom's potential is symbolised for MacDiarmid by its repudiation of usury in favour of Social Credit and by the high social prestige it accorded to poets and scholars.

The validity of these cultural metaphysics is less important for our purpose than the light they throw on the evolution of MacDiarmid's conception of Scottish nationality. No sooner has MacDiarmid declared his faith in the world role of the Gaelic Idea than he is asserting his indifference to the status of the historical claims he makes for it. "It does not matter a rap whether the whole conception of this Gaelic Idea is as far fetched as Dostoevsky's Russian idea. . . . The point is that Dostoevsky's was a great creative idea — a dynamic myth — and in no way devalued by the difference of the actual happenings in Russia from any Dostoevsky dreamed or desired."

MacDiarmid's view of the spiritual mission of Scotland's Gaelic idea is best expressed in "Lament for the Great Music" (*Stony Limits*, 1934). Inspiration flows not from "that instinctive love of a native land" but from a "mystical sense of the high destiny of a nation".

> . . . It is now the duty of the Scottish genius
> Which has provided economic freedom for it
> To lead in the abandonment of creeds and moral compromises
> Of every sort and to commence to express the unity of life.

Intimations of that "unity of life", of a "cosmic consciousness", are provided by the "Ceol Mor", the art of the pibroch as exemplified by the great pipers of the MacCrimmon family, whose playing gives the poet a glimpse of:

> . . . my beloved Scotland yet
> As the land I dreamt of where the supreme values
> Which the people recognise are states of mind
> Their ruling passion the attainment of higher consciousness.

MacDiarmid's interest in the restorative potential of Scotland's Gaelic culture stimulated his interest in the implications of a political revival among the suppressed Celtic nations of Europe. In the essay on "The Caledonian Antisyzygy" he looks forward to Scotland, Ireland and Wales combining to reduce England to its "proper subordinate role in our internal and imperial affairs", a theme to which he periodically reverted, sometimes adding Brittany and the Isle of Man to the line-up of Celtic nations.

Among the Celtic nations, Ireland provided MacDiarmid with a frequent point of reference. The achievement of the Irish literary renaissance in adapting English to its own purposes, including the expressing of Celtic themes, was a source of encouragement when his early faith in Scots began to wane. But while he admired Irish nationalism, he was not willing to adopt Ireland as she had developed by the 1930s as a political model for Scotland. In "At the Sign of the Thistle" (1934) he argues that Scotland has something to contribute to Europe's history to which Irish developments were a "mere preliminary". That contribution went beyond the reduction of England's imperial role to encompass the grandly apostrophised "Defence of the West", to be achieved by another Scottish master-idea — the Social Credit doctrine of Scots-born Major C. H. Douglas.

Douglas believed that the economic problems facing the Western countries between the wars was a problem of distribution not production. Under the capitalist system, the costs of the credits used in the creation of capital assets, including the means of production, were absorbed into the selling price of the goods produced. This meant that the public was paying twice for its goods — in the form of consumption foregone at the stage of capital formation and through higher prices at the moment of purchase. As a result purchasing power was steadily falling behind productive capacity and unemployment was rising.

Douglas proposed a system of consumer credits or discounts on the purchase price as the solution, the credits to be paid in the form of a national dividend which he calculated in the late 1920s could be worth about £300 to each Scottish family.

MacDiarmid seized on Douglas's ideas as a "substantive manifestation of the Scottish genius which would signalize Scotland's re-emergence into the arena of world affairs with a contribution of consequence to all humanity". They offered to free mankind from its subjection to productive forces which were technically capable of meeting all his material needs, and of ushering in the age of Liberty, Leisure and Culture. In *Scottish Scene* (1934) he looked forward to Douglas's "Plan for Scotland" — "the only document of the slightest importance to have come out of Scotland since the Declaration of Arbroath" — aiding in the defeat of the vicious "commercial Calvinism" which had been largely responsible for Scotland's decline. And in a notable example of dynamic myth-making he related Douglasism "to certain features alike in the old Gaelic commonwealth and in subsequent pre-Union Scottish policy".

MacDiarmid gave conflicting accounts of the relationship between Social Credit and Communism, reflecting his own ambivalence towards Communism in the early 1930s. Douglasism is presented at one moment as an alternative to both Fascism and Communism — which he sees as equally hostile to the emerging Leisure State which scientific progress has made possible, at another as an urgent alternative to Fascism and, like the Gaelic Idea, the "complement and corrective of Communism". Not until *The Company I've Kept* (1966), after many years as an avowed Communist, did he present it as a transitional stage to "integrated Communism".

Although MacDiarmid saw politics strictly as a means to a cultural end, political figures such as Lenin, Connolly, and Maclean, were accorded their place as heroes of their time along with the greatest creative artists. MacDiarmid was himself a political activist as well as a political myth-maker. The history of his involvement in organised politics reflects a lifelong dialectic between nationalism and socialism which achieved its synthesis only in his own world of ideas.

In an essay on "The Poetry and Politics of Hugh MacDiarmid" written by himself in 1952 under the pseudonym Arthur Leslie, MacDiarmid claimed that his working-class childhood in the Borders — when he was fed on an "out-and-out Radicalism and Republicanism" — had made him a man "naturally fitted for Communism". Certainly his political loyalties lay with the Left from his earliest days. He joined the ILP at the age of 16, played a leading role in the Edinburgh University Fabian Society, where he sometimes described himself as an Anarchist, and at twenty served on a Fabian Society Committee on agriculture, supplying the extensive Scottish sections of the committee's report. Returning to Scotland in 1912 after a period of journalism in Wales, where he met Keir Hardie and other Socialist pioneers, he rejoined the ILP in Clydebank. In 1922 he was elected as an Independent Socialist councillor in Montrose. But from this point his relations with the Socialist movement in Scotland were increasingly influenced by his developing nationalism, in the form first of cultural nationalism, then of a more clearly focused political nationalism.

The fullest account of MacDiarmid's political views in the 1920s is contained in *Albyn, or Scotland and the Future* (1927), where he identifies five developments in Scottish life which offer hope for the future — the growth of Scottish Socialism, the somewhat slower growth of the Scottish Home rule movement, the impact on Scotland of the immigrant Irish community, the Catholic revival, and the Scots and Gaelic cultural movements.

The emergence of the ILP in the West of Scotland represented for MacDiarmid a modern restatement of the challenge which Scottish radicalism and republicanism had traditionally made to the conservatism and constitutionalism of English politics. MacDiarmid looked forward to an alliance between the ILP with its commitment to a Scottish Parliament, and the growing Home Rule movement, led by the Scottish Home Rule Association— which had extended its aim to embrace fiscal autonomy for Scotland and the Scots National League committed to full independence.

215

To MacDiarmid, however, these developments in the political field, encouraging as they were, were mere epiphenomena. Under the influence of his theories of literary nationalism, MacDiarmid believed that political nationalism could succeed only where it drew on a distinctive psychology. Whatever the future of literary Scots, the survival of spoken Scots testified to the "subterranean continuance of all manner of distinctive states and potentialities". What was more, those potentialities were at last being stirred. The immigrant Irish element in Scotland's population was reinforcing Scotland's Catholic tradition as well as her Celtic identity, so helping to undo "those accompaniments of the Reformation which have lain like a blight on Scottish arts and affairs". The Scots and Gaelic revivals were meantime challenging the cult of Burns and the Kailyard. "Art and religion," declared MacDiarmid, "if these can be national-istically stirred we have the conditions we have hitherto lacked for the creation of a dynamic Scottish nationalism."

Although MacDiarmid became a founder member of the National Party of Scotland in 1928, just one year after the publication of *Albyn*, he had already criticised nationalist organisations for attempting to build their campaigns on what he paraphrased as a "distinction without a difference". A nationalism which simply predicated the transfer to Scotland of the political institutions and values of England, was condemned to failure. Nationalism must "represent something fundamentally different and answering to the unexpressed needs of the Scottish spirit". But MacDiarmid's own offering — a cocktail of socialism, republicanism, Social Credit, Scots and Gaelic revivalism — was too exotic to win the support of the established nationalist organisations. And as his own views moved further to the left in the early 1930s in response to economic and political developments in Britain and abroad, he became increasingly scornful of the conservatism of the nationalists, particularly the moves to form a broad nationalist alliance which resulted in the fusion of the National Party of Scotland and the Scottish Party in 1934 to form the Scottish National Party. He gave vent to his frustrations in a series of bitter poems in 1932 and 1933 attacking such Establishment nationalists as the Duke of Montrose and excoriating the moves for amalgamation as in "The Noble Seventy-Four":

> Cathcart Tories, Cathcart Liberals,
> Scotland's in the cart all right.
> Just let Will Fyffe and Lauder
> Their forces with ours unite,
> And Rothermere and Beaverbrook,
> And we'll win by hook — or crook!

It can have come as no surprise when that author of poems whose spirit is summed up in such titles as "The Scottish National Yo-Yo Contest" and "Yellow Belly" was expelled from the National Party prior to its amalgamation with the Scottish Party.

By the mid-1930s MacDiarmid was ready to admit that the hopeful tendencies which he had identified in *Albyn* in 1927 had failed to come to fruition. In *Scottish Scene*, which he co-edited with Lewis Grassic Gibbon in 1934, he had despaired of conventional Scottish politics. He wrote: "It is in fact impossible to imagine a 'Political History of Scotland 1908-1935'. . . . Whatever our politicians are they are not Scottish politicians: Scottish politics have still to be created or an effective substitute found in relation to them for what all other countries still apparently need and call politics, and in lieu of which Scotland so far only has foisted on it an alien fraud and a farce." While the nationalist movement had turned its back on Douglasism — that idea which was Scotland's chance to vindicate herself in the eyes of the world — the Scottish Socialists had assisted, in growing numbers, at Scotland's humiliation in Westminster. "The most extraordinary example of all this was the way in which the Scottish socialists with not only a majority of the Scottish seats at Westminster but a majority of the total Scottish poll allowed their mandate — the majority will of the Scottish people — to be vetoed by an English majority of a reactionary character. If there had ever been any substance in their repeated declarations in favour of Scottish Home Rule — any real desire, and sense of opportunity, to promote anti-Imperialism — any urgent wish to apply the social reforms they advocated on behalf of the Scottish people, that was their opportunity. . . . But that is Scottish politicians all over; futilitarians, openers of bazaars and star turns at Bands of Hope and Pleasant Sunday Afternoons."

MacDiarmid joined the Communist Party in 1934 but the significant development of his views appears to have occurred between 1934 and 1936. As we have seen, in the 1920s and early 1930s MacDiarmid argued that a cultural renaissance drawing its energy from a distinctive Scottish psychology was the necessary preliminary to an effective political revival. In retrospect (*The Company I've Kept*, 1966) he claimed that he had felt a growing disillusionment with the Scottish Renaissance movement at least in the later years of this period. Most of those associated with the Renaissance had been unable to outgrow the "distortions" to which they had been subjected in their social and college days. A statement by MacDiarmid in 1936 leaves little room to doubt that "distortions" were social and political in origin.

MacDiarmid's 1936 statement, reprinted in *Lucky Poet* (1943), announced his conversion to John Maclean's programme of a Scottish Socialist Workers' Republic. MacDiarmid argued that in a world imminently menaced by fascism, social and national revolution must go together. He invoked Lenin and Marx, as well as Connolly and Maclean, against those who argued that the identity of interests of the workers of England and Scotland precluded a socially progressive Scottish nationalism. On the contrary, within the British Empire, Scotland, with its "persistent tremendous radicalism (leading more than once to over-all Socialist majorities) of the Scottish electorate vis-a-vis the English" equipped Scotland to take the van against capitalism and imperialism — "as Scotland has hitherto failed to do in the work of world revolution".

MacDiarmid declared that this "Red Scotland" line marked the "end of Scottish Nationalism and the beginning of Workers' Republicanism". But it was the movement and the strategy, not the cause, which was being repudiated. The "separatist and anti-imperialist line" would put an end to the "sinister association in the Scottish cultural movement of abstract highbrowism and politics which have no concern with the cause of the workers". Scotland's cultural future was henceforth to depend on the "self-education of the Scottish proletariat in their revolutionary tasks with the aid of their own intelligentsia", while her political future was to depend on the revolutionary will of the Scottish working class rather than on the sort of politics represented by "anachronistic 'Lost Cause' movements like latter-day Jacobitism, the narrow parochialism of the Scottish bourgeois nationalists themselves, and the suspect and factitious pseudo-nationalism, doffed and donned as occasion demands, of politicians interested only in securing Scottish votes for their own English-controlled parties". Indeed the statement looked forward to an autonomous Scottish republic enjoying the same freedom to provide for Scots and Gaelic as, following Lenin's teaching, the republics of the Soviet Union had to provide for their own national cultures. Against these statements, MacDiarmid's further assertion that his new line represented a "complete break with recent Scottish cultural developments" must be understood as a rejection not of the aim of a Scottish cultural revival but of his earlier belief that radical political developments in Scotland had to wait on a cultural revival. The motive force of radical change had henceforth to be sought in Scotland's political needs rather than in her distinctive linguistic or cultural heritage.

This development in MacDiarmid's view of the relative roles of political and cultural activity as agents of radical change did not affect his views of the relative status of politics and culture. Political activity continued to have importance only as a means to a cultural end that lay beyond politics. As he expressed it in "Second Hymn to Lenin" (1935):

> Sae here, twixt poetry and politics
> There's nae doot in the en',
> Poetry included that and su'd be
> The greatest poo'er amang men.

MacDiarmid expressed this philosophical conviction most graphically in his response to Grassic Gibbon's avowal in *Scottish Scene* that he would welcome the "end of Braid Scots and Gaelic, our culture, our history, our nationhood, under the heel of a Chinese army of occupation if it could cleanse the Glasgow slums". To MacDiarmid this was a "purple passage of emotional humanism — the very antithesis of the way these evils can be

219

overcome. I on the other hand would sacrifice a million people any day for an immortal lyric. I am a scientific Socialist. I have no use whatever for emotional humanism."

It is significant that MacDiarmid does not speak here as a Scottish nationalist concerned to defend the specifically Scottish traditions which Gibbon attacked but as a scientific socialist, who held not only that socialism was inevitable but that it finally freed mankind from all practical concerns, indeed all merely human concerns, leaving him free to concentrate on the development of his intellectual and aesthetic faculties. It was the aesthetic experience itself — the product of . . . "the terrific and sustained impact of intellect upon passion and passion upon the intellect" (*The Kind of Poetry I Want*, 1961) — which was the aim of all MacDiarmid's endeavour, cultural and political. In a poem entitled, surely with conscious irony, "The Caledonian Antisyzygy" (*Collected Poems*, 1961), MacDiarmid makes clear his belief that the achievement of that aesthetic ideal takes precedence over all doctrines of linguistic nationalism:

> I write now in English and now in Scots
> To the despair of friends who plead
> For consistency; . . .
> Yet the nightingale remains supreme,
> The nightingale whose thin high call
> And that deep throb,
> Which seem to come from different birds
> In different places, find an emotion
> And vibrate in the memory as the song
> Of no other bird—not even
> The love-note of the curlew—
>   Can do!

"Red Scotland" is the fourth of the master-themes on which MacDiarmid drew, in one combination or another, for the rest of his life to illustrate the exemplary role which he believed Scotland ought to play in the world. But if his conception of Scottish nationality remained relatively stable from the mid-1930s, his own involvement in politics became increasingly volatile. In 1938 he was expelled from the Communist Party of Great Britain for attacking in the spirit of his "Red Scotland" beliefs, the inadequacies of its policy for Scotland. He joined the Scottish National Party in 1944, only to leave four years later. In the General Elections of 1945 and 1950 he stood as an Independent Scottish Nationalist for the Glasgow Kelvingrove constituency, issuing on both occasions an election address which made no mention of either socialism or republicanism and which would have been acceptable to the average member of the SNP. As a writer and polemicist, however, MacDiarmid, while ready to welcome SNP electoral success as evidence of reviving Scottish morale, was consistent in denouncing the party as a bourgeois nationalist party intent on maintaining in Scotland the main features of British capitalist society. In 1957, in a gesture of ideological solidarity with the Soviet Union at a time when it was facing world-wide condemnation for its invasion of Hungary in 1956, he rejoined the Communist Party. In the 1964 General Election he stood as Communist candidate for Kinross and West Perthshire against the Prime Minister, Sir Alec Douglas-Home, subsequently petitioning the Scottish Election Court to declare Sir Alec's election void on the grounds that he had encouraged the BBC and the IBA to incur expenses on his behalf by presenting him in Conservative Party election broadcasts. Shortly before his death, loyal to the spirit of the narrator's declaration in *A Drunk Man* — "I'll ha'e nae hauf-way hoose but aye be whaur Extremes meet" — he let it be known that as a believer in separation he intended to vote against the Labour Government's proposal to set up a Scottish Assembly with limited powers in the referendum due in 1979.

In the "Second Hymn to Lenin", MacDiarmid asks:

> Are my poems spoken in the factories and the fields,
> In the streets o' the toon?
> Gin they're no', then I'm failin' to dae
> What I ocht to ha' dune.

Such was his early ideal of the poet's public role. His mature expectation is summed up in the sardonic "Glasgow 1960", in which an exile returning to the city is told that Ibrox is filling up for a debate on "la loi de l'effort converti" between Professor MacFadyen and a Spanish party.

I gasped. The newsboys came running along,
"Special! Turkish Poet's Abstruse New Song.
Scottish Authors' Opinions" — and, holy snakes,
I saw the edition sell like hot cakes!

MacDiarmid's impact on Scottish political opinion has been slight. In the formative years of Scottish nationalism in the 1920s and 1930s, his leadership of the Scottish Renaissance movement assured him of an influence among the literary intellectuals who assisted at the founding of the National Party of Scotland in 1928. But as the Scots vernacular movement lost its impetus and as the nationalist movement itself tried to widen its political base, the cultural nationalists were superseded by figures like John MacCormick whose talent was for organisation and manipulation, not theorising or polemics.

Since the Second World War MacDiarmid's contact with Scottish opinion has been even more tenuous. Following the British fashion, political nationalism as represented by the SNP has eschewed the heroic ideological commitment favoured by MacDiarmid for a wabbit social democratic consensus of little relevance to Scotland's deep-rooted social and economic problems. Scottish literary intellectuals have been even less inclined than their English counterparts to claim a political role or even to write about political themes. Where such writers of the inter-war decades as Neil Gunn, Grassic Gibbon and Fionn MacColla, as well as MacDiarmid himself, explored explicitly national, if not nationalist, themes, post-war writers with few exceptions have found their material in social themes or in a purely individual experience. Literary nationalism has withered while a pragmatic, political nationalism has waxed strong.

Yet MacDiarmid's achievement is such that it is absurd to attempt any final estimate of his influence on the evidence of a few decades. By successfully overturning the traditional definitions of "Scottish" he challenged Scots to face the whole range of their contemporary experience without any of their familiar, comforting alibis. He demonstrated by his own achievement that the survival of a vital sense of nationality depends on a continued process not of restatement, not even, as the conventional theories would have it, of redefinition, but of exemplification, or attempted exemplification, of values which transcend nationality. To MacDiarmid, Scottish nationalism was concerned ultimately not with the form or content of Scotland's experience but with Scotland's will and capacity for experience itself.

MacDiarmid and Politics

NEAL ASCHERSON

MacDiarmid was his own custodian. He recognised early in himself a great cultural monument, for which he willingly took responsibility. It would be tempting to argue that he did so because nobody else, certainly until his later years, understood his genius, but this is not really the case. To the end of his life, MacDiarmid's work always acted on critics like a tongue of Pentecostal fire, inspiring them to write about him with a brilliance which they might never find again (how many of the most penetrating judgements on MacDiarmid have been passed in student publications by writers whose names mean nothing to us today?). Not lack of recognition in Scotland and elsewhere, but his awareness of his own unique qualifications turned him into a guide to the monument. He understood it better than anyone else. He had a sharp eye for vandals, approaching with some critical spray-can. He knew the points on the guided tour at which visitors were tempted to yawn or give up.

There is undeniably something comic in this. It's impossible not to laugh over "Arthur Leslie's" grand oratorio of praise to "the politics and poetry of Hugh MacDiarmid" when we know who "Leslie" really was—and as recently as 1952. The point at which the author quotes Trotsky's hymn to Marx and Engels as personalities and adds: "Almost all the writers who have appraised MacDiarmid's personality and poetry have realised that that quotation fits him like a glove" is specially tasty. MacDiarmid was wonderfully boastful — but he was not vain. The "Leslie" essay is not in itself an exaggeration of his own gifts, and provides the most interesting and helpful summary of his political and poetic attitudes. He is aware of the puzzles he sets, and endeavours to solve them. In the end, there is nothing absurd and much which is admirable about the separation of Grieve and MacDiarmid. The fact is that we take MacDiarmid at Grieve's own valuation still, and have found no important grounds to question it.

The closer we come to MacDiarmid, indeed, the more solid his boasts appear. I suspect this is true also of the element in his work which generates the strongest tendency to mutiny and scepticism in the reader — his sources. Perhaps the best example is the famous introduction to the *Golden Treasury of Scottish Poetry* (1940), with its cataract of references to obscure books and theses sometimes in obscure languages, a bombardment of the reader with the receipts of learnedness. The temptation is to see this as a defensive trick, an angry and nervous pre-emptive strike against some super-educated reader, the compensating truculence of the autodidact. Well, maybe not. I have not done the long work of going back to these sources, of checking whether MacDiarmid quoted them correctly, or understood their meaning properly, or even read them at all. But there are hardy students who are doing this. And a casual talk with one of them provided an insight which was almost frightening. It looks as if the man read what he quoted, and — for example, in philosophy and aesthetics — mastered the systems which lie behind those endless references. There are books coming which will make MacDiarmid even taller.

These opening thoughts are meant to show that it is dangerous to dismiss his own account of his own views in politics, as dangerous as to dismiss his own estimate of his significance as a poet and of his intellectual breadth and depth. These accounts, written and spoken in so many different versions, are not of course the end of the matter. MacDiarmid changed emphases, left out episodes which became inconvenient, perhaps interpolated here and there. But they remain not only pretty accurate accounts but penetrating analyses. The gaps are substantial; as Sorley Maclean writes elsewhere in this book, we don't know off-hand how he reacted to the Nazi-Soviet Pact or to the Communist line on the war between 1939 and 1941, or (which is the same question) how he reacted to those Nationalists who rejected participation in a British war even against Hitler. The brush with fascism in the

twenties and early thirties is intriguing, but again unexplored, and
one can argue that his attitude to Mussolini and to aspects of the
Nazi "Volksgemeinschaft" concept were more significant than
his direct reaction to political events outwith his control. The
retreat to Whalsay may have become, after 1939, an evasion of
choices he did not wish to make.

Communist and Nationalist. The very words are supposed to be
at war, and yet MacDiarmid made out of their collision a fusion.
He did not, as far as I know, develop any conventional Marxist
argument to justify his position. He observes, superbly, that any
problems which arose with the Communist Party of Great Britain
over his nationalism were "very minor points" and arose from the
"unfortunate limitations" of a few Scottish Communists rather
than from any real ideological problem.

The CP nonetheless chucked him out. They did not consider
nationalist deviation a minor point at all, and surely they were
right. Nearly fifty years later, we are beginning to discuss more
openly the weakness of the conventional Marxist approach to
nationalism, but in the thirties the question was much more
roughly put. The proletariat were the class whose mark was
universality. The nation-state, in its final phase, was the creation
of the bourgeoisie. Nineteenth-century struggles for national
independence led by bourgeois nationalists before the emergence
of the proletariat had possessed objectively progressive
significance — sometimes, crucial significance. But not in the
nineteen-thirties. The torch of history had passed from the
bourgeoisie to the proletariat, from the class whose badge was
aggressive nationalism and militarism (the symbols of 1914-1918)
to the class whose badge was internationalism and the
transcending of nation-state boundaries. Scottish nationalism in
1930 could only mean — in this view — sabotaging the struggle of
the British section of the working class.

Today it is possible to see through this dogma. We know more
about the difference between working-class solidarity across
frontiers and the argument that socialism and internationalism
belong together. Nationalism, in Tom Nairn's phrase, has a double
Janus-face, one looking back into a sinister past of bloodshed and
reaction, the other forward to political and social revolution and

to the destruction of outworn relationships of domination (Basque and Catalan resistance to Franco providing good illustrations of this brighter face). Nairn, indeed, has gone on to suggest that there has always been something spurious about the concept of socialist internationalism itself, a pious pretence that the Marxist revolutionaries could provide a new category to transcend the nation just as they could provide socialism to transcend capitalism.

MacDiarmid's early political formation was, in contrast to these problems of theory, very simple and direct. He was born into the working class in a society where cultural and social differences were not generally sorted into different baskets. There were "we" and there were "they". "They" spoke differently, relied upon a much more anglicised interpretation of history and even of heaven, and were at the same time the exploiters. The young Grieve thus shared the very obvious perception of all Scottish socialists of his generation: the more working-class you were, the more Scots you were. The idea of bourgeois decay was no mere abstraction, but a sight in the street: Scots who had become de-cultured but who could not become re-cultured English-men. ". . . . It had never been my aim to rise above the class into which I was born — it had, indeed, been my vigilant determina-tion to see that I allowed nothing to come between me and my class . . . where others were concerned to rise, I, on the contrary, was determined to strengthen and develop my organic relationship to the Commons of Scotland by every means in my power" — and this was the explanation for his "regression to Scots" in his writing. (Note that word "organic", by the way. Nothing would have made Chris Grieve more furious than the suggestion that he wrote Scots in order to be more easily understood by the Commons of Scotland; that would have been the prostitution of his gift. The relationship was to the culture, not in a direct, political sense to the man in the street.)

He was an ILP socialist who later became a Communist. But he's concerned to dismiss any idea that this was a "conversion"; the logic of his birth and his beliefs, Grieve states, led him easily and naturally into the Communist Party in a way which a bourgeois intellectual might have envied. Such is his version. But there must have been more to it. He has written about his disgust after the first world war, fought and ostensibly settled for the sake of small nations, which left Scotland so injured and abandoned. An old order had been restored, at least in Britain. But in Russia, a new order had burst through: the "out-and-out Radicalism and Republicanism" of his family upbringing could only encourage him to revel in the triumph of the Russian Revolution, while the poet in him was aware of the creative eruption of the first Bolshevik years, a "cultural revolution" in a sense which was not the sense Lenin or Mao gave to the phrase. MacDiarmid's intellectual relationship to Marx and Lenin was not a particularly intimate one, however. Engels clearly appealed to him, because of those very expeditions carrying the dialectic into the natural world which many Marxist scholars now find embarrassing. Lenin seized MacDiarmid's heart for the man he was, for the statue he made, even for "the eternal lightning of Lenin's bones", but "Leninism" as a theory of revolutionary organisation mattered less. Marx . . . that is a hard question to answer satisfactorily. My own feeling from MacDiarmid's work is that it was the colossal scale of the Marxist theory which appealed to him, the way in which — especially in the hands of Engels — all of the universe, its gas, its floating scintillas of shattered planet, its human beings, its stones were related in one solemn music. It was the cosmology, in all its boldness and comprehensiveness, which drew him. He had, from the beginning, sought a total interpretation of this kind or, perhaps more accurately, sensed the relationship of all creation dead and living. The early Scots lyrics, swinging vertiginously between abstract and concrete, the roof of the byre and the stars, God and his smallest creations, showed this sense. From this instinct sprang his interest, long antedating his formal Communism, in what one might now call the "fringe" philosophies of Shestov or Solovyev. His 1923 essay on "A Russo-Scottish Parallelism", examining Solovyev's curious system of Logos, Ether and Sophia, displays MacDiarmid's fascination with a theory which glorified chaos and contradiction as the raw material on which the Logos plays and from which is extracted some ultimate harmony. Joy in such chaos and contradiction was to remain an abiding element in his writing, as every MacDiarmid reader knows. But Solovyev could not embrace the imperative to political and social revolution, and MacDiarmid's own version of dialectical materialism was in the end more satisfying.

MacDiarmid was certainly no orthodox Communist. He could, as we have seen, refer with approval to the un-person Trotsky when he felt like it, and he simply brushed aside views of nationalism which were not welcome to him. But he does not seem to have experienced problems with Stalin. With the class determinism and the respect for Marxism as a cosmology there went a respect for revolutionary authority: MacDiarmid was not immune to the "Führerprinzip", and could be thoroughly callous to the protests of "bourgeois liberalism". He accepted Stalin's theory of nationalities on its face value, and wrote with approval of the way in which national minority cultures were protected and encouraged in the Soviet Union. After the Soviet intervention in Hungary in 1956, he characteristically decided to rejoin the party, apparently more impressed by the need to march in the opposite direction to the appalled emigration from the party than by any considerations for the fate of another small nation and its culture. In Russia, he counted among his friends deplorable conformists like Alexei Surkov, wrote gladly of the "trend of poetic effort towards the heroic" and praised the way in which he fancied that the Russian language was being cleansed of Latin and French roots — a policy carried to its conclusions by Nazi Germany rather than by Stalin's Russia.

MacDiarmid took from Communism what he needed and fancied. He was wilfully casual about the realities of Stalinism. He was heretical when he chose, as his long interest in Major Douglas and the theory of Social Credits suggests (a theory much more appropriate to a petty-bourgeois nationalist movement like the SNP of the thirties and forties than to "scientific socialism"). Most striking of all, as Sorley Maclean brings out, MacDiarmid in the main stood aside from the central experience of a whole generation of Scottish socialists: Spain and the defence of Europe against fascism. Whether he was in the Communist Party or temporarily out of it, this was an extraordinary lack of interest: even party orthodoxy, in the late thirties, instructed him to shelve distaste for non-Communist allies in that struggle.

His Scottish nationalism was enduring. It was also Protean. At different times, and sometimes simultaneously, he argued for national independence as the only way to cultural salvation, as the path to socialist revolution, as the shrewdest blow to English imperialism, as the remedy for Scotland's economic miseries. He argued for it because it *must* come, and also — voluntaristically — because morally it *should* come. He joined or gave his sponsorship and support to the most heterogonous list of nationalist groups, from the aristocratic leaders of the late twenties to far-left republican outfits who detested Stalinism as deeply as they hated the British state. At the same time, his nationalism had an ultimate, transcending quality which was unique; no man was harder on his own country and people, and yet he believed that this, as it often seemed and seems, craven little nation so unwilling to look further or higher than the next penny on the rates or the next advance factory, contained an incredible destiny: no less than the chance of transfiguration into a race of fulfilled human beings in control of all that life could offer. As John MacLean said: "We are out for life, and all that life can give us".

How can this contradiction be explained, between his violent, impatient contempt for the "foul stupidity" of Scottish society as he knew it and his faith in such a destiny? Perhaps we have to go back to the last words of Renwick, the Covenanter saint, on the Edinburgh scaffold: "Scotland must be rid of Scotland before the delivery come". No Scottish writer raised in the Presbyterian tradition, however early he or she rejects it, can be entirely free of Calvinist notions of redemption. The election is sure, but before assurance of that grace can be received, there must intervene an utter self-abnegation, an admission that the will and the flesh are corrupt, a purging of the old self through the fire from which the new, God-guided phoenix-man arises. I think that MacDiarmid expressed a version of this faith on a collective, national plane. He certainly expressed it in some remarkable images; none more seizing than his short poem on "Why I am a Scottish Nationalist" in which Scotland appears as a sullen woman in bed, slowly and unwillingly brought to passion as "the muirburn tak's the hill". MacDiarmid saw independence as the result of a dialectical process, the collision of contradictions, rather than as the

230

consequence of a genteel, linear advance towards political self-government. Here his revolutionary Marxism and his Scottish theology of grace came powerfully together, and it was natural that his view of the SNP should have been so ambiguous. Even in the mid-seventies, when the nationalist tide was running so strongly, MacDiarmid predicted collapse; the party's horizons were too narrow, their portrait of a future free Scotland resembled all too closely the British state which they intended to disrupt. He was, as one would expect, prepared to see violence used. He said in 1968, for instance: "No one in his senses wants warfare, but if we are determined to be absolutely independent, it may be, and almost certainly will be forced upon us . . . we have a great deal of violence in Scotland today. I only wish that it were possible that it could be channelled in better directions." He did nothing much about this, seeing little contemporary possibility for the use of force in ways which were not clownish, but it was one of his fundamental complaints against the SNP that they were not prepared to face the idea that armed struggle might one day be necessary. They were too constitutional, too respectable. An independence obtained without real struggle and overcoming would not be worth having, and indeed would not be independence at all in the almost sacramental sense he attached to the idea. He feared that this would also be true at the social level at which independence would affect the lives of "the Commons of Scotland", and he would have agreed with Yeats's sinister couplet:

"Parnell came down the road, and said to the cheering man:
'Ireland shall have her freedom, and you still break stones'."

MacDiarmid's Anglophobia rends every fig-leaf. His sweeping dismissals of the English literary tradition, not only in his own time but in history, are often absurd. And MacDiarmid is close to so many pugnacious Scots in claiming that every device of real use or value on earth was conceived or perfected by a Scot (a form of chauvinism shared by the Russians). He regarded the English as uncultured, ignorant, ruthless and imperialist, and was accordingly obliged to argue that the Scots were the reverse of all these adjectives. A hard job: his efforts to present Scotsmen in the

Empire as sensitive men of feeling who understood the native point of view are not convincing — least of all to anyone who can remember that tropical empire and the enthusiastic rôle as merchants, policemen and non-commissioned officers which the Scots played in it. They were to the Pax Britannica as the Croats were to the Austro-Hungarian Empire and the Corsicans to the French: closer to the native than the governing caste, but closer, too often, at the length of a malacca cane or a sjambok. (And, like the other two races, ready to rebel against the imperial power when its empire was gone.) MacDiarmid is on much surer ground when cursing English insularity and aloofness. His faith in the Scottish genius for foreign languages, which he obtained from vast reading of travel journals, has something to it, but typically he derives this too far: "Neitzsche, Rilke, Kierkegaard, Kafka, Leontiev and Martin Buber were being translated and written about by Scottish writers before they began to be mentioned in England . . .".

In a way, England did block MacDiarmid's view. He realised that Scotland was a more European nation than England, and he turned with marvellous energy to German, Russian, French and even Czech sources, knowing that it was across the North Sea rather than across the Border that lines must be laid to connect Scottish literature, once again, to its sources of energy. But in politics he wasted time trying to prove Scotland's superiority over England, when he should have been emphasising what historians know with increasing clarity: that England is the exception of Europe. England's particular Reformation, its enclosures, its weird social cohesion and deference, its gentleness, its archaic institutions descending from a revolution which happened too early, all make England an impossible object for crude comparisons with "normal" European nations. This is not a matter of size, not to do with any absurdity in the sight of a five-million nation sticking out its chest and telling a fifty-million nation that it can flatten them any way they care to mention. It is just that Scotland must take its differences from England as constituting, not a challenge, but an "English problem" which Scotland shares with France, Ireland, Norway, Poland and so forth — all countries which have more in common with each other than with the land of Hampden and Harold Wilson. MacDiarmid, while plainly aware of this way of looking at the matter, probably thought it insipid. To him, English imperialism was still advancing over his own land and people, and they were still succumbing to a resentful acceptance of English superiority. This must not be, and if the quickest morale-booster was to claim that Scots genius had invented the electric toothbrush, then the claim should loudly be made.

MacDiarmid was, for much of his life at any rate, a racist. This is a bad word. But it seems to me ridiculous to deny it, another fig-leaf which won't stay on. It is perfectly clear that he thought that heredity could determine national culture, and he said so repeatedly. This did not mean that he thought white men superior to black, or subscribed to notions of the Judaic World-Enemy (although, I am told, there are anti-Jewish flashes in some of his papers, possibly to do with resentments of the London publishing world). But it meant, for example, that MacDiarmid could hold against England that it partook "too much of Teutonic and Mediterranean influences; it is a composite — not a 'thing-in-itself'", that he insisted (against the evidence) on the Celtic nature of *all* Scotland as a source of cultural salvation, and that he summoned up the grand "Gaelic Idea" which would dominate western Europe, supplant the three decadent "culture-nations" of England, France and Italy, and "complement the Russian idea which has destroyed the old European balance of north and south and produced a continental disequilibrium which is threatening European civilisation and, behind that, white supremacy"

What can we make of this astounding remark, this choking mouthful of hot ideology? It comes from the famous 1932 essay, "The Caledonian Antisyzygy and the Gaelic Idea". The first thing to say is that the "culture-nation" concept is far older than fascism, and that MacDiarmid is drawing on nineteenth-century Russian thought rather than on twentieth-century German at this point. It is a racist concept, when you get down to it. But it is not therefore and precisely a right-wing thought. The lifelong socialist Grieve is talking about "complementing" the Russian idea, not crushing it as some Asiatic threat to the Christian West. I am not sure what he meant by the off-hand "and, behind that, white supremacy". The implication that European civilisation of his day rested on white supremacy in the colonial world is plain. But was he saying that the Russian threat to white supremacy must therefore be resisted — or that this was the inevitable and welcome development of history?

The uncertainty remains, and itches. The same essay contains a celebrated and perilous swerve along the border of Nazism (written, it should be remembered, before Hitler took power but at a moment when the savagery of National Socialism was already well understood). This is MacDiarmid's approving reference to "Blutsgefühl", which is "a keyword of the Hitler movement" and denotes the drawing-together of people of one race and culture "through bodily attraction". MacDiarmid here was trying to rebut the anti-nationalist class-based politics of what he called the "Labour-cum-socialist electoral majority in Scotland" as a false internationalism. He observed: "Hitler's 'Nazis' wear their socialism with precisely the difference which post-socialist Scottish nationalists must adopt. Class-consciousness is anathema to them, and in contradistinction to it they set up the principle of race-consciousness." What MacDiarmid was really talking about, I think, was the Nazi notion of "Volksgemeinschaft" (folk community), which demanded equality of esteem in society without insisting on equality of reward or power. This was of course an attempt to replace class solidarity by national and racial solidarity. Queer company for a Marxist to keep.

He was being contrary, once again. If class politics were to mean anglicisation for Scotland, then he would invoke another politics which did not. But there is certainly no evidence that this brief expedition among fascist ideologies had any lasting effect. Indeed, the fact that MacDiarmid did not become, even for a time, a fascist is remarkable in itself. Many writers of his stamp and times, and even of his socialist background, did so. Pound, whom MacDiarmid revered, went that way, and MacDiarmid shared with Pound (and Yeats) a profound élitism in addition to his rather genetic sense of national destiny. But he remained, on his own terms, a socialist and — except for the period when the party banned him for nationalist deviation — a Communist.

His élitism, unlike that of Pound or Yeats, was not aristocratic. He was a Lowland Scot, pretty impervious to Jacobite sentiment or to mourning for deserted palaces and noble families dispersed. But he was not, in common parlance, a democrat either. He believed that in the world he saw around him, the vast mass of ordinary people lived and died with the insignificance of flies. Their tastes were mostly manipulated and vulgar, certainly not to be pandered to. He wrote of his "fight against ignorance and anti-intellectualism, and the incessant cry of stupid socialists and communists that nothing should be written save what is intelligible to the mass of the people". His own work was a lifting-up, an insistence on perfection. He jeered often, and with serious purpose, at the Scottish notion of "the untutored ploughboy", the cosy thought that everyone could be his own poet with a bit of education: he saw the poet as being at once raised above the human race and committed to intellectual struggle. MacDiarmid, as he always repeated, wanted an "intellectual poetry" which wrestled with the universe, not a sweet sound. He even scorned the post-war revival of popular song, inspired by Hamish Henderson and Norman Buchan, because it was giving numen to what he affected to regard as the doggerel of drunken gamekeepers.

Turning from MacDiarmid's hot, tangled prose arguments to his verse is plunging from a crowded shore into the sea: suddenly, there is lucidity and joy. All these things have been written by the poet:

"I am horrified by the triviality of life, by its corruption and
   helplessness , , ,
No passion without satiety. Yet life could be beautiful even
   now.
But all is soiled under philistine rule. What untouched
   spiritual powers
Are hidden in the dark and cold . . ."

and, later on in the same passage of "Lament for the Great Music", there comes:

"A state composed exclusively of such workers and peasants
As make up most modern nations would be utterly
   barbarous.
Every liberal tradition would perish in it. The national and
   historic

> Essence of patriotism itself would be lost, though the
>   emotion no doubt
> Would endure, for it is not generosity that the people lack.
> They possess every impulse; it is experience they cannot
>   gather
> For in gathering it they would be constituting the higher
>   organs
> That make up an aristocratic society . . .",

and later yet:

> "Civilisation, culture, all the good in the world
> Depends ultimately on the existence of a few men of good
>   will.
> The perspective will converge upon them yet."

In verse like this, the contradictions of MacDiarmid's politics are carried away in a single tide. Here is the perceived need for revolution, here the distrust of the mass, here the outraged democratic spirit which sees that the folly of the Demos has been deliberately brought about by those aristocratic "higher organs". And here, also, is the patriotism: MacDiarmid said that his country had given to the world the idea of political freedom, in the Middle Ages, and then through the Industrial Revolution the chance of freedom from economic necessity as well. This carried a responsibility: Scotland could lead mankind to a third age of freedom:

> "The struggle for material existence is over. It has been won.
> The need for repressions and disciplines has passed.
> The struggle for truth and that indescribable necessity,
> Beauty, begins now, hampered by none of the lower
>   needs . . .
> . . . It is now the duty of the Scottish genius
> Which has provided the economic freedom for it
> To lead in the abandonment of creeds and moral
>   compromises
> Of every sort and to commence to express the unity of life. . . ."

More than Communist, more than Social Creditist or Shestovian or Nationalist, MacDiarmid drew his politics from what was at the centre a coherent view of human bondage and emancipation, of the relationship of consciousness to material condition, of the function of the mind not as an idea-creator by itself but (Calvin again!) as an organ through which the Universe might choose to distribute its ideas. It was a spectacular thought-structure, belonging in some respects more to the nineteenth century than the twentieth and absolutely un-English in its language and references. The political attitude which he brought out of all this was that of a Red Republican. Even a Communist is only one of many descendants of the Red Republicans, the ancestors of all revolutionary projects, the giants who spoke through Rabaud de St. Etienne and said: "Il faut tout détruire, oui, tout détruire, puisque tout est à récréer . . .". They are extinct now, and I do not think we can breed back to them. And yet we have lived with one, for MacDiarmid remained on earth long after his great tribe had departed, like Oisin leaving the Fenian heroes in their heaven to stay again for a while among the small men of the succeeding age. "Oisin d'eis na Feine"—Oisin after the Fianna, which MacDiarmid said was a phrase with "more than Virgilian tears".

Like Oisin, he often felt lonely in a country which was less than it had been or should be. But both, by staying on behind, were able to pass on the great music.

Prose and Polemic

OWEN DUDLEY EDWARDS

> ". . . I envy him his enthusiasm."
> —Christopher Murray Grieve,
> speaking of Hugh M'Diarmid
> *Scottish Chapbook,* I, 3 (October 1922)

> All who should help to open the way for true expression
> —The teachers, the ministers, the writers—are living like
>   maggots
> On dead words in an advanced state of decomposition,
> Big words that died over twenty years ago
> —For most of the important words were killed in the First
>   World War. . .
> —Hugh MacDiarmid, "Talking with Five
>   Thousand People in Edinburgh"

> O Thou, whose beautiful embittered speech,
> Radiant and effortless, made such war on
> All topics that your tireless tongue could reach
> In endless evenings at the Café Caron.
> —C. M. Grieve, "J. K. Huysmans"
> (*Scottish Chapbook* I, 2 (September 1922))

At the beginning we should say that there is no separating Grieve and M'Diarmid (later and hereinafter MacDiarmid), his Lallans and his English, his prose and his poetry, his history and his literature, his politics and his culture, his youth and his age, his

Scotland and his universe, his anger and his love, his comedy and his tragedy, his creation of himself and his creation of modern Scottish creativity.

After which, we proceed to separate them, but no sum of parts is equal to the whole. I could take it farther and say (and say it without blasphemy, an appropriate word when we deal with a poet of some of the most moving lines about Christ yet written and he a firmly professed atheist) that there is no separating in him the Redeemer and the lunatic who cried that his name was Legion "for we are many". And any man who set himself the tasks that Grieve set Grieve and the even more daunting ones that he set Hugh MacDiarmid when he had created him, was at once Redeemer and lunatic to have undertaken them even with the assistance of his self-created new identities. In brief, he set himself to bring back to life in Scotland a language, a culture and a nation.

There is a compelling unity in all that he wrote, yet more than most artists there was an astonishing diversity, linguistic, cultural, stylistic, methodological, topographical, emotional, metaphorical. There was everything to be done, and there were so many ways to be thought of to do it, so many art-forms to be chosen from, so many instruments to be fashioned and tuned, so many musicians to be created or found and when found trained — and he the sublime conductor.

And let us hope, speaking as pig spokesman for pigs, that his spirit entered into us.

As my epigraphs imply at the outset, it began with C. M. Grieve, first working with influences of the 1890s and bringing into conjunction with the aesthetic revival of the sonnet in that decade a new force, didacticism and humour. But even there a demand for a vernacular was expressing itself: in paying his homage to Huysmans he insisted on a Scotsman's pronunciation of "Caron" instead of the careful parrot-French intonation of the 'nineties. But the 'nineties could not content him for long, for all of his devotion to their greatest Scottish poetic genius, John Davidson, nor his occasional kindly word for that more remotely Scottish sonneteer of flashes of genius and storms of self-destruction, Lord Alfred Douglas, nor his fury at William Sharp alias "Fiona Macleod", nor his joyful attempts to prove that J. M. Barrie's verses on the death of Robert Louis Stevenson as a totality constituted the worst poem in English literature, despite all that had been said for the rival claims of Cornelius Whur. There was much to be learned from the 1890s, including its false dawn of Scottish literary revival, and there was much to be forgotten.

Hugh MacDiarmid was not born until 1922 to do the work his creator Grieve demanded, but the origins of his birth lie, appropriately, in holocaust. Perhaps the single best line on the effect of that war that has ever been written is the last quoted in my second epigraph. It was pre-eminently the war of words, the words that called men to slaughter with all of the boundless beauty and destructiveness of the Sirens, the words that assured Socialists the workers would not kill one another, the Scrap of Paper, the Fourteen Points, the epitaph for Rupert Brooke, the Torch — be yours to hold it high — the Rendezvous with Death. Paul Fussell's *The Great War and Modern Memory* brilliantly recaptures so much of the mood of conviction and its sequel disillusion, and rightly quotes Hemingway's *A Farewell to Arms*:

> abstract words such as glory, honor, courage were obscene beside the concrete names of villages, the numbers of roads, the names of rivers, the numbers of regiments and the dates.

But Fussell is, I think, wrong in implying such a thought could not be uttered until eleven years after the war was over, Hemingway's date of composition. MacDiarmid's artistic, cultural, social and economic crusades were born within four years of that peace, even if he was not to articulate it in "Talking with Five Thousand People in Edinburgh" until many years later and then, perhaps, with Hemingway's lines in mind. You could sum the thing up by saying that for all of its objective hyopcrisy in smothering the betrayal of the dead by the cult of their sacrifice, Armistice Day at least offered an awful symbolic truth in The Silence.

Into that Silence Hugh MacDiarmid was born of Christopher Murray Grieve that there be new words, to live in a language at once old and new; but there were also new words — important words — to be written in English.

II

"The teachers, the ministers, the writers . . .", Grieve was all three: minister in the dual sense of preacher and priest of the new Scottish culture. The work of the teacher demands rather more elaboration than the other two, for we think of MacDiarmid primarily as a poet, and a poet's teaching in his poetry demands huge thoughts in small space: it is for the pupils to dig for them and the work of art stands for itself in their despite. But the prose of Grieve, and later of MacDiarmid, is teaching from the marrow of the bone, using every device that could come to a great craftsman's hand to waken up his pupils and keep their noses to the grindstone. He confronted a world that was hedonistic, disillusioned, xenophobic, bankrupt of the vocabulary of idealism. He got to work.

It was for this reason that he invented MacDiarmid and all of those other minor pseudonyms, and plugged their messages in various forms. His ironic comments as Grieve on the poetry and linguistic crusade of MacDiarmid were but one aspect of it. He needed to be two people, and Grieve was a little in awe at the task he had set MacDiarmid and the boldness with which MacDiarmid tackled it. The prose-writer, truculent and unrepentant as he portrayed himself, saw the poetry, I think, as part of another identity. There is nothing very unusual in this. Prose invites much more self-doubt than poetry, when the poetry is successful. In any case, Grieve was one of the most modest men I have ever known. His pride in the causes for which he fought never prevented him from turning a compliment to a young writer with a self-deprecating codicil. He boasted apparently of himself but actually of the art he had brought to life apparently from nowhere. If he had to remain permanently embattled for apparently hopeless causes, he had to appear self-congratulatory: pupils had to be encouraged that the fight had got as far as it had, and if it often seemed as though only he, or one of his identities, had been the main fighter, the lesson was to study the art-form in which the fighting had been done. Poetry, especially poetry in a language many found alien, had to have its prose evangelist. So much of his prose writing — like Shaw's prefaces — is a matter of the artist being his own evangelist: listeners have to be lured to and instructed in the significance of the poetry. He did find other evangelists, one of the very earliest being John Buchan (some of whose own important words had also died in the First World War, however much his Tory face seemed to belie it). And his gratitude to Buchan — which he never lost sight of — found early expression in his dedication of *Annals of the Five Senses*: "TO JOHN BUCHAN — For the encouragement and help he has given to a young and unknown writer (as young as it is possible to be in the Twentieth Century, and almost entirely unknown, at least to himself) . . .". MacDiarmid had been by then born for a year although *his* first book (for the *Annals* was Grieve's) did not appear until 1925 — with Buchan's introduction. Underneath the evangelisation Grieve had to try to understand MacDiarmid, and it was not whimsy for him to show some problems in doing so: in Macaulay. He revelled in hurling before his audience quotations, conducted a form of introversion in extrovert terms with far more confidence than he may actually have had about it.

It was for this reason, too, that MacDiarmid is one of the most extraordinary name-droppers in all prose writing, and name-dropping invariably with teaching intent. In this he resembles Macaulay, who likewise discharges names in machine-gun-like bursts with the similar effect of informing his audience and stimulating it to get the original shot into his sight on an epigram. But MacDiarmid had a much more documentary approach than Macaulay. He revelled in hurling before his audience, quotations, sentences, paragraphs, criticisms, fulminations, imbecilities, profundities of others. A single page may present an obscure line of rich poetry, a fatuous statement from a small town clerk, an even more fatuous pomposity from a Fellow of the Royal Society, an insight by an eminent critic, a Philistinism from an Aberdeen newspaper, a hard-bitten assertion from a Canadian economist, three lines from an ancient Gaelic poem of which the rest is lost, a ferocious denunciation of C. M. Grieve by a Kailyard giant, an extract from the proceedings of the General Assembly of the Church of Scotland. And all are there to teach. He presents his evidence, often with extraordinary economy in his own comment. His remarkable essay on Christopher North, for instance, in *Scottish Eccentrics*, contains eight pages of quotation to three of his own. He wanted his readers to read (a) him, and (b) as much else as he could possibly get them to lay their hands on.

But he knew exactly how to select quotation for what it would instruct, both in content and in style. He could give a victim enormous lengths of rope with which to hang himself from his own mouth, to mix a metaphor on a MacDiarmid recipe. He also had, both as a magazine editor and as a prose writer, a remarkable gift for digging out the ludicrous from newspapers, speeches, sermons, official proceedings and the Lord knew what, and making them do their own instructively self-destructive work: H. L. Mencken was to perform some of the same service for America, and it is a nice thought for graduate students to consider who might have learned from whom and how much. Grieve's *Scottish Chapbook* was appearing before Mencken's *American Mercury* but the Voltaire of Baltimore had had the earlier apprenticeship of the *Smart Set*, and the use of news quotation in MacDiarmid's and Lewis Grassic Gibbon's *Scottish Scene* suggests some refinement of a separately developed method from study of Mencken either in the *Mercury* or in its spin-off volumes of *Americana*.

The intentions of Mencken and of MacDiarmid, however, were significantly different, although there are surprising similarities. Both were fascinated by language, and both made powerful cases for languages separate from English in their countries: Mencken by his lexicography, MacDiarmid by his poetry. Both bitterly resented English élitist cultural and critical domination of their countries, and even more savagely assailed the cringing acceptance of it on the part of their own country's alleged intellectual leaders. Both were liberated in their comments on sex and its place in culture, although not without a wry and somewhat self-critical male chauvinism. Both enjoyed and extolled alcohol and berated the hypocrisy of its opponents. Both were implacable foes of clerical tyranny, which they saw as designed to keep the masses in fear of original self-discovery. Both had a bitter hatred of injustice, and a roaring delight in comedy. Both were ashamed of the cultural and social disgrace of their countries. But Mencken, in the last analysis, was an urban patrician and a Nietzschean, finding it more congenial, or at least more productive, to use his pen for destructive purposes.

243

MacDiarmid could denounce Scotland in language Jeremiah might envy, but he never lost sight of the goals of Jeremiah and to him they had the same sacred significance. I thought of rewriting that sentence, but decline to: MacDiarmid *was* recalling his people to a God of Scotland to whom they had turned their backs in order to achieve preferred provincial status in the spiritual empire of Baal.

MacDiarmid also differed from Mencken in the multiplicity of his methods. Mencken usually supplied a witticism per sentence, often at the cost of the force of his general argument, if any; MacDiarmid would keep the customers waiting for pages for his *coup de grace*, and in reading his prose one often finds that there Langholm he exposed in its narrowness and hypocrisy in his final view, and the oftener the better) the whole thing proves to be one. They did resemble one another in being able to use any subject, from a politician to a lexicographical problem, as a text on which to fit a sermon enough to bring the audience from their seats, frequently with a strong desire to fling them at the speaker. But again the distinction arose on topographical matters. Mencken was a sophisticated eastern urbanite who made a virtue of his detestation of the country. MacDiarmid was in his element in anatomising a city with all too pertinent emphases on its cancers while unexpectedly catching glimmerings of soul, but he also showed a mastery of the country genius. His awareness of the strengths, pettinesses and pulls on loyalty of a small town recalls not Mencken but his friend and protégé Sinclair Lewis. His native Langholm he exposed in its narrowness and hyopcrisy in his final act of being buried there in the envenomed teeth of lace-curtain-cloaked opposition from the city fathers, but he immortalised the dead of his community in "Crowdieknowe" with more sardonic love than has ever been shown in a piece of such brevity and integrity. Towards the dying Gaelic civilisation of the islands he showed, perhaps, rather more romanticism: but his work on it asserted the totality that he brought to the understanding of the Scotland he wished to liberate and redeem.

He again resembled Mencken in his insistence on teaching by exaggeration. Both men, like their mentor Shaw, woke the customers up by shocking them, and to do so it often became necessary to overstate a case. This in its turn induced hyperbole, and an ultimate danger to credibility. MacDiarmid, having started his audience into attention, could lose them again when he failed to vary his pitch (in all senses). Christopher Harvie, reviewing one essay of his, termed it "a MacDiarmidden" (the distinguished author more privately described it as "lousy") and at times Constant Reader was in danger, not of throwing up, but of going down for the thirty-third time. The more serious danger was that, once the MacDiarmid method of incessant documentation, seemingly endless denunciation, and gems of knowledge had been repeated sufficiently to a lazy audience, he was in danger of being dismissed as the mixture as before. In fact audience rejection was more an indictment of itself than of him. Take, for instance, the introduction which he wrote to *The Scottish Insurrection of 1820* by P. Berresford Ellis and Seumas Mac A' Ghobhainn in 1970, when he was seventy-eight.

Structurally, the thing is a little masterpiece, and a clarion-call to historians. The authors had opened up a lost insurrection (or Red Scare) and raised some important points about it. MacDiarmid was nice about them, but from the very first hurled a far larger canvas in space and time before the reader. The study, he points out, must be regarded as preliminary. What is needed is much more detailed historical work on the relations between Scottish, English and Irish radicalism in the thirty years preceding the event. No more valuable opening remark could have been made by the profoundest professional historian: he reached the heart of the problem of historical ignorance on the issue at once. He wanted his Scottish history internationalised, as it has not been: even where it is integrated with English developments (sometimes to the point of obliteration), the failure to examine the interactions on the English periphery and to compare the several responses to England on that periphery remains one of the greatest unfulfilled tasks of Scottish historians. He then jumps to his expulsion from the C.P.G.B. in the late 1930s on the issue of nationalism, sardonically comments that on his readmission he was assured the party had learned much on the question from him, and salutes John MacLean, grasping the nettle of his alleged insanity in his last years by citing documentary evidence. "In my view what finally broke him was less his admittedly great sufferings in prison than his feeling that most of his friends had repudiated his teachings and were committed to courses which must prove disastrous — as indeed they have proved." Then he cites two other Scottish radicals as examples of neglected historical figures on the Left: John Murdoch and John Swinton. Here, once more, historians can only cheer — and blush. John Murdoch, of the *Inverness Highlander*, was the crofters' journalistic leader in the wars of the 1880s who used his Irish experience and acquaintances to integrate the agrarian struggle in the two countries: his manuscript autobiography still lies unpublished in the Mitchell Library, Glasgow, although subsequent to MacDiarmid's adjuration it has begun to receive editorial attention, and the full story of the war in which he was so deeply involved only received its first major scientific history in Dr James Hunter's *Making of the Crofting Community* six years after the old man's call. John Swinton is a critical link between Scottish and American labour history: it is an irony which would have sourly amused MacDiarmid that with all of the intellectuals of the British Labour Party stressing their internationalism in their Socialist ideals, they have played virtually no part in stressing the international character of Scottish working-class history beyond their own island and, occasionally, its imperial possessions. Swinton was a splendid labour journalist on the *New York Sun* who wrote an important book on his travels in Europe and ultimately set up his own paper, *John Swinton's Paper*, in the mid-1880s, until forced to abandon it by increasing blindness. It is still the major newspaper source for the history of American labour in that decade, perhaps the most crucial in the development of American labour politics. As MacDiarmid pointed out, Swinton had been a friend of the South Carolina blacks before the Civil War as well as of Walt Whitman, and knew Marx (though I was delighted to discover in reading the files of his paper that, true to the principles of Americanization, he invariably referred to him as "Dr Charles Marx").

From these stimuli to future historians, the old man goes on to quote extensively from Philip Mairet's life of Patrick Geddes as to the hatred of the establishment for ideas of real improvement of society. Here, perhaps, age and piety brought him to overdo the art of judicious literary economy: Geddes's ideals and work would be far less familiar to his audience than he may have assumed. Yet am I right? If his readers were to complain that he failed to tell them what were the great proposals and achievements of Geddes, would that not lead them to find out for themselves? He then goes on to cite a case of a young historian, warned off the case of the radical of the 1790s, Thomas Muir, by archivists on the ground that all that could be known had been written, then discovering manuscripts in the Kilmarnock Museum which proved invaluable. Again, even the most conservative academic historian could hardly object to a plea to the researcher not to sign off from his digging because of informed gossip, but to find out and keep at it. This leads MacDiarmid into a comment on the same young man's discovery as to Burns's radicalism in the Dumfries Volunteers, followed by wry remarks on the readiness of Burns votaries to have accepted the assumption that he had sold out. In other words, to MacDiarmid, history is a matter of keeping on looking. Characteristically, he cites the work of Major M. V. Hay of Seaton, whose *Chain of Error in Scottish History* had pointed up falsifications in the commonly accepted national story, and from the discoveries of the Catholic apologist analogised that Socialists had many similar chains of error to expose. This, also, was characteristic. MacDiarmid was interested, both as poet and as prose-writer, in the Catholic rejections of Protestant common-place assumptions about the Scottish experience, and, wiser than his anti-Catholic Socialist colleagues, showed what could be learned by looking at one form of questioning of the conventional wisdom. He throws in some words on MacLean's obligations to Gaelic thought and closes with a few well-chosen curses on espionage activities in modern nationalist movements as in the 1820 insurrection. With a few minor changes, it would have made an admirable inaugural lecture for any professor of Scottish history anxious to set on foot new directions of research and analysis in his field.

I single this *tour-de-force* out because I am a historian: other teachers will find its equivalent in their fields. It is traditional MacDiarmid with its teaching urgency, its sense of the importance of studying cultural heritage to inform the conduct of the present, its constant impetus to get its audience to study in as many directions as possible. But it is also very much of 1970 and beyond. For all of the inflexibility of its dogma, it is fully in key with the latest developments in historical study, given its stress on the comparative method, its emphasis on the pursuit of obscure source-depositories, its demand for rethinking of medical assumptions of an earlier age in the light of additional evidence, its insistence on the study of national, social and economic history in an international context, its sense of the relevance of allied case-studies in similar societies, its pursuit of out-of-way literary and journalistic sources, its advice to study methods of historians with divergent interests with a view to improvement of one's own, its reminder that the great neglected books of the past can open up entirely new fields to the students. MacDiarmid believed that an educated Scotland would make itself a progressive and a free Scotland, and, with this belief, he as a teacher was constantly urging an opening-up of aspects of Scottish history which the agreed conventions sealed off. History, *pace* Napoleon, was never to be the agreed lie while he was around. From this standpoint MacDiarmid has to be recommended to the student of Scottish civilisation not only for his cultural priorities and achievements but also for the tremendous new light his most casual remarks throw on the Scottish past. And what I have gleaned from this single essay has its counterparts in the historical matter in *Scottish Scene*, in *Scottish Eccentrics*, in the autobiographical volumes and in countless other works. He had, after all, three of the best gifts a historian can have, as a great researcher (which the reviver of Lallans had to be), a great artist and a great teacher. He fulfilled the dictum of Professor Archibald Cary Coolidge of Yale: "Young man, to be a histowian, you must wead, and wead, and wead." And because he was fighting so hard for the future, he was in love with the past. It told us what we had been, and what we might yet be.

II

C. M. Grieve's prose style changed remarkably little in fifty years: many writers' do not, perhaps. Hugh MacDiarmid's poetic style has vast diversities from his very first quinquennium when he moved between lyric and epic, and his English poems, when he came to write them, differed greatly from one another and from the few poems we have from C. M. Grieve. But the Grieve-MacDiarmid prose also altered little in *method*. Virtually everything he wrote in prose can be classified as polemic in one form or another, though the art-forms themselves might be topography, biography, history, criticism, lexicography, literary criticism, correspondence public and private, and what his endlessly adventurous spirit might will. Various reasons can be assigned. With him, prose was always secondary to poetry, and his great experimentalism in style and method was reserved for the latter. Prose as a form of communication was necessary for the less receptive pupils. A reader who could enter into communion with the poet of "The Watergaw" or "To Circumjack Cencrastus" did not need the repetitions and explications of prose. Even when at his most discursive and hortatory in poetry (as in "Talking to Five Thousand People in Edinburgh") he still demands a receptivity and initial commitment from his audience, and he still practises a literary economy. In prose he might be constrained by reasons of space, but there is little substantial difference between the methods of *Lucky Poet*, with its range of near-500 pages, and those of his two-page editorials in small magazines. Admittedly, he never seemed to have enough space: such economics as he practiced in prose were dictated by space, not by art-form — he reluctantly pared down *Lucky Poet* to one-quarter of the size of the manuscript originally given to the publishers, casually remarking that wartime restrictions on print and paper dictated the cut. This brought two different effects. In one way, his satisfaction with the style and method he had developed in 1920 and was happy to employ in 1970 meant that his prose always possessed a triumphant youth about it. With MacDiarmid as prose-writer, far more than with most other writers, one has an eerie sense of the author always remaining the same age. The volumes of reading he devoured, the new authors and new discoveries he embraced, the new controversies into which he leapt, the political Odysseys he so hardily sailed, the friends he continued to make of any age, added to the totality of what he was saying, but did not alter the way of saying it. He was fond of repeating himself, and indeed believed it to be his sovereign and God-sent duty so to do, but in fact his receptivity to ideas was very marked throughout his life. He amused himself by pretending to be very party line during part of his time in the Communist Party, but he was much more concerned to ensure that the Communist Party would be MacDiarmid line where he troubled himself about it at all. This did not prevent him from mischievously saying to Hamish Henderson on a film, when the latter sought to persuade him to join Jim Sillars's Scottish Labour Party, that it would depend on what the Communist Party would think about such a step, but any Communist who assumed that such a statement was an acceptance of dictatorship of the apparatchiks would have found the hungry churchyard strewn with his bones when he recovered ideological consciousness.

But the other effect of the timelessness of his prose was that his sense of prose craftsmanship was formed in a more leisurely age when writing was the only means of continuous publication open to the literate, and readers' receptivity was formed accordingly. Although his first literary decade almost exactly spans the 1920s, he was not a 'twenties figure as a prose-writer, save in content. The important words might have been killed in the First World War, but he had known them before their deaths. And Scottish prose moved slowly, slower than the norm: it was still moving with a confident and leisured dignity, whether its content was drivel or genius, at a time when Anglo-American cultural civilisation spoke the literary equivalent of "23-skidoo, no change". MacDiarmid took the Scottish pomposities and stood them on their heads, but he remained ready to extol, say, the wisdom of Andrew Lang (where Andrew Lang was wise) when to most of the English-speaking world Lang was no more than a memory of archaically-presented fairy-stories, which lacked the eternal appeal of Andersen or the Grimms. I have mentioned his awareness of the 1890s as a literary influence, and in certain ways his prose is that of the last of the Victorians. Even the Edwardians will not do: it is impossible to think of polemic on the titanic scale MacDiarmid conceived it, whether his remit was two pages or two thousand, coming from the Edwardians. The Forsyte Saga is at least ostensibly fictional.

He certainly dropped one or two devices. The Victorians and Edwardians made much of the dialogue or of its variants, and the young Grieve played with it, especially for nationalist purposes. (Arthur Clery, in Ireland, had used it to some advantage in that direction.) But it was cumbersome, and was losing its audience. It was a child of the drawing-room recitation, a form with which by nature he had little in common. In any case, as he became more famous, his opponents provided the weaker sides of the dialogues and he was left with the part he wanted to work on — his own. But his use of the documentary method throughout his life, his vehement search for enemies and allies on his own printed page, testifies to that interest in maintaining a number of voices before the reader rather than monolithic Ciceronean oratory.

In some ways his methods are even older. There are resemblances to Benjamin Franklin, so curious that one wonders if he was indeed an influence on the omniverous MacDiarmid. The poet certainly knew his great Americans: as Professor George Shepperson has shown, MacDiarmid used his Melville. In Franklin's case the ambitions are oddly similar, those of educating a country awaiting political and cultural emancipation, and using a whole variety of communications methods which are at heart polemic. The Franklin evangel was, at bottom, hedonistic, the MacDiarmid, all through, cultural, but the approaches resemble one another at significant points. Franklin also had the trick of getting his methods across by the use of a number of pseudonyms, and getting them to comment on and explicate the teachings of one another: Father Abraham, Poor Richard, and so forth, much as C. M. Grieve, Arthur Leslie and others discussed the significance of what Hugh MacDiarmid was seeking to do. But even at his most impassioned, there was a scientific blandness about Franklin which could never do for MacDiarmid. It is another eighteenth-century author whom he resembles more in the temper of his writings: "Use the point of your pen," proclaimed Swift, "not the feather."

One factor which gave this strangely pre-war character to his writing is that books had for Grieve a sacred quality which means very little to persons grown up in a well-to-do society, and one which takes its written culture in doses administered by disposable

251

paperback. The hunger for books, the privations endured to achieve long-sought items, the threadbare friendships with book-collectors of better means, the searches for revered quarries both scarce and elusive of those with slender pockets, the unbelievable rapture of personal publication, the long tramps with a single volume in hand — it is a lost world to us now. Naturally, what was available on cheap second-hand stalls was often Victorian and Edwardian, the mind was set in its prose by the private battles and alliances with reading matter and the product was conceived in its literary terms.

The fact that Grieve's first friends and enemies were printed pages dictated much of his controversial future. It could lead to anachronism: the strange thing is that it induced so little of it. My examination of the preface to the *Scottish Insurrection* shows a man not behind his times but well before them, whether seventy-eight or not. But he shaped his discovery of the future in the light of a past which still dominated him, and it was one much more remote in time than most of his contemporaries would realise. This again informed his polemics with urgency. To him the printed word possessed its own sanctity, and profanations were not merely ordinarily wrong, they were a pernicious waste of a scarce commodity. If he had few restraints on the ambitions of his length of utterance, he believed himself to have Pelions upon Ossas of Error to drown in the ocean of his rhetoric. He was highly traditional as a Scotsman with his fascination for books: the two greatest nineteenth-century passages on love of writing are from authors of Scottish antecedents — Macaulay's lines on the friendship of dead writers in the opening passages of his essay on Bacon, and Conan Doyle's tribute to the favourite books of his life, *Through the Magic Door*. Where he differed from them was that his sense of books and writing as enemies was as urgent as his sense of them as friends. There is nothing racist in asserting the Scottish-ness of this: it is the natural attitude of literary men deriving from a poorer society with a sense of the omnipresence of a richer one.

Grieve's book-learned polemic had its advantages: in a discourteous and vocabulary-weakened world it gave him a dignity and range lacking even to his exact contemporaries. On the other hand, the fact that he, as MacDiarmid, was producing poetic experiments in the vernacular far more demanding and elaborate than the revolution currently under way in the United States with its new insistence on American and not English prose, was an insurance against any charges of undue academicism. His prose, then, was suited for any age between twenty-eight and seventy-eight partly because he conceived it in terms where it could oppose his seniors in a deeper seriousness and yet show his juniors that a belief in older forms had an idealistic iconoclasm beyond their own.

A further point needs to be made on his maintenance of prose forms throughout his literary career. At the time of Hugh MacDiarmid's birth, C. M. Grieve was powerfully aware of the plethora of revolting "dialect" literature in Scotland, unscientific in its methods, demeaning to its subject and conceived to expose its alleged users to the indulgent sneers of more sophisticated consumers. One cannot always fault its accuracy of reportage: indeed, the Irish equivalent in the magazines which carried the Kailyard School, the short stories of Somerville and Ross, are conspicuous for the extraordinary, almost scientific accuracy, of their use of Anglo-Irish and post-Gaelic syntactical forms and peculiarities of pronunciation. But Grieve was, as I believe, appalled by the thought that any prose writing by him in his painfully-built Lallans would simply be equated with hated Kailyardism and produce the amused patrician response to which the English readership was by now attuned with respect to dialect writing. He was by no means the only one: Wodehouse, in one of his earliest novels, was bitterly to denounce the dishonour of dialect writing. So Hugh MacDiarmid was born in part because poetic genius alone could carry the newly-resurrected Lallans to an audience which might see it as the product of a great and different culture, not as an invitation to prompt snobbish amusement at the expense of the poor provincials. Hence Grieve was condemned to write in English, and when MacDiarmid — who alone could liberate in Lallans — came to write prose, he was obliged to forsake his early Lallans. Prose to Grieve was a battleground where one of the most important citadels had been lost. Because of his work in reasserting the grandeur of Lallans, later prose writers could attempt to employ a vernacular, but one always retains the uneasy question as to whether they are closer to the *Drunk Man* or the Kailyard in their results, and in the audience-reception of those results.

IV

Belatedly, we may turn to the question of content, and the constants and variables of ideology with which Grieve/ MacDiarmid polemic preoccupied itself. To chart the constants and variables from his poetry would have to be the precursor of any attempt to disentangle them from his prose, and any attempt to do it the other way round would be fatal. MacDiarmid, time and again, made it clear that his prose was for people too stupid to understand his poetry, and while he also wrote for those who did understand it, they would also be expected to understand that his prose did not represent the 100 per cent commitment that his poetry did. And this forces one to recognise a critical problem about his prose. He was an educator; he knew that shock was one of the earliest ways to blast an opening in the thick crania of his audience by which he might be able to filter sense in; therefore he said things whose purpose was to shock, to challenge comfortable nostra in his audience, to force the foundations to give way that something real might find a place within them. I am not saying he wrote hypocritically: he was incapable of it. But he did say things he believed with only part of his mind, usually the uppermost and most superficial part. I recall only one conversation with him on Ireland, a subject on which he was very inclined to take a position as extreme in favour of unification as could be managed. I said, with some trepidation, that I disagreed with him. He said that we needn't talk about it, I knew much more about it than he did. It was characteristic. I knew more about what this meant when I saw from his early prose writing that wanting to make Scots think about the idea of freedom was what attracted him about the Sinn Féin cause in the early 1920s, and about its extreme votaries during the Irish civil war. But it was not really about Ireland that he was talking at all: he wanted to waken Scots up. He was deeply engaged with the Ireland of letters, of Yeats, of Joyce and of Shaw. He admired and loved Sean O'Casey. He knew about Irish censorship and the exclusion of unwelcome ideas and (Irish) attempts to seek cultural originality: he knew all too well that his Scotland was very capable of doing the same thing, and without being unkind enough to bring in the analogy of what independent Ireland was doing, he showed in his fierce words how much he feared for a Scotland independent of England politically but tied to English economics, English cultural fashions and English bourgeois manners. In a way, to see what Hugh MacDiarmid really thought about Ireland, one has to look at his endless crusade against Scottish Philistinism and apply his comments to Ireland. His own testimony was to remind us of the importance of comparison and interconnection, two things Sinn Féin, by its name and behaviour, denied.

"The only way way to write", observed MacDiarmid's editorial to *The Voice of Scotland* in December 1946, "is to consider the reader to be the author's equal", as he did with poetry, but not, I insist, with prose, apart from those who could be trusted to read it judiciously, critically and conscious of the larger audience whom in no sense the author considered his equal. Sometimes, of course, he might believe something wholeheartedly and be in error for want of fact. Thus, when in the same article, demolishing the fears of those concerned about adverse theatre criticism from *The Scotsman* in the search for new ideas, he states "*The Scotsman* has never had any critical standing whatever" he was unjust: its reputation in the later nineteenth century was deservedly held. It was only in the twentieth century that it became identified with puffing the safe and sure literary bets — one thinks of A. E. Housman's "the punctual praises of the *Scotsman*". But it does not matter whether MacDiarmid knew his remarks were open to pedantic revision or not. What was at stake was that *The Scotsman* had become an image of driving out cultural experimentalism by means of fear and MacDiarmid, like Franklin Roosevelt, was telling his audience the only thing they had to fear was fear itself — fear that they would rouse up entrenched interests, fear of what those interests were capable of doing, fear of appearing ridiculous in an effort to realise themselves, fear of moving too far from what might be the acceptable literary fashion in England. Like Roosevelt, MacDiarmid's first task was to rebuild national morale.

The incident is wholly characteristic. The young revolutionary playwrights of Scotland were in danger of putting their lights under their bushels for fear of scaring off a generous grunt (*sic*) from the Arts Council. MacDiarmid's method was to tell the Arts Council what its duties really were and are:

> They are not commissioned to act as dictators of policy. It will come as a surprise to most people to learn that they do attempt to exercise a covert censorship of this sort and are in a position to load the dice against those who have different views as to artistic policy and different political leanings. That the Arts Council is empowered to exercise any such controlling influence — or that its assistance is contingent upon applicants toeing the line in this way — is simply not true. . . . That in fact this is no isolated instance but the regular practice of the Arts Council is highly probable, of course, and shows the danger of quasi-governmental patronage of this kind. But the fact remains that the Arts Council cannot be allowed to get away with it in this most important instance.

It was, in fact, the Arts Council, and not MacDiarmid, which was ultimately forced to bow the knee. His later prose had the advantage that he became so great that he could not be ignored. But it was the fight against fear in this and similar instances which put the establishment on the defensive, and ultimately to observe the spirit of its own charter, whatever the double-think in which that might have been conceived.

Turning over *The Voice of Scotland* I am amused to find my pedantic remarks about *The Scotsman*'s lost critical acceptability being comprehended by the editor, in April-July 1957, by remarks on the *Glasgow Herald*. He was quoting with approval from a remonstrance uttered to that paper by one of his poetic contributors, Andrew Tannahill:

> ". . . In the music hall and on the pantomime stage the Scots language has suffered the slings and arrows of the comedians. To join in the denigration with a 'Scots comic' of its use is surely unworthy of a newspaper with the standard of the *Glasgow Herald*."

All this is excellently said by a real authority on the matter, save for the last few words. If the *Glasgow Herald* ever had a standard it was a very long time ago. It is now completely acultural, viciously anti-Scottish, and staffed by malignant nitwits.

Constant Reader might wrinkle his brows over the superlatives and vehemence, yet it was impossible to see MacDiarmid hurl his lance against the Pillars of Society without breathing a freer air.

The main, unending target of MacDiarmid's invective in prose or poetry was neither England nor any other country save Scotland itself, the Scotland of cringe, of what in Ireland is called "shoneenism", of lusting for crumbs from the metropolitan table. Of the Scottish literary tradition MacDiarmid wrote in the same editorial: "Other countries all over the world — including England itself — are eager to see such a tradition successfully recreated; it is only Anglo-Scots who are implacably imposed to any such achievement." The "Anglophobia" which he paraded as his "Recreation" in *Who's Who* was not a hatred of England; it was a hatred of Scottish cultural suicide in the pursuit of English credentials. The whole thing was, in any case, absurd in itself: England, frequently tottering on the edge of cultural bankruptcy, had every reason to hope that Scots would do their own thing and thereby pump new blood into anaemic English literary veins. MacDiarmid did not say so in so many words here, but his citation of F. R. Leavis's admiration for his own work in Lallans proves the point. As ever, he liked his documents to play their own part.

"For God's sake, be yourselves." This was surely MacDiarmid's message to the literary Scots and their readers. It was wholly a characteristic that from the first he did so by burying them in an avalanche of international data. Scottish achievement, Scottish possibilities, could be asserted by showing the expectations of the great Europeans for cultural liberation emerging from the example of a small country — and he would cite, as he did in "English Ascendancy in British Literature", the preface of Laurie Magnus to his *Dictionary of European Literature*, Keyselring's *Europe*, and Spengler's *Decline of the West* — a book with a profound influence upon his thought, though initially he preferred to give it its German title, perhaps because he liked the poetry of words whose most literal translation is "The Going-Under of the Evening-Countries". Spengler's thesis had every relevance to the apocalypse of World War I; it was MacDiarmid's mission to ensure that Scotland was not an "Evening-Country". To do so he sought to awaken it to the promise of hope in countless belittled civilisations from Iceland to Russia, and he clearly hoped that a culturally free Scotland would rejuvenate the going-under countries by its achievements and example. It has been said that Scotland enjoyed a national identity in the reign of James IV, who called himself King-Emperor: MacDiarmid wished Scotland to return to its destiny, not simply of nationalism, but of cultrual export and international infection. Meanwhile, in the votaries of an English uniformity, he saw the destruction of all non-English and English cultures in the British Isles: he knew enough of one of his targets, St John Ervine, to cite him in reply to his insistence on the English norm as an example of the decline of a playwright who abandoned the Ulster cultural heritage whence he had initially written so well. The English, like Orwell, might understandably resent the anti-English tone of MacDiarmid's writing, ignorant as they were of the pernicious effects of Scottish voluntary enslavement to English cultural domination: but they could not protest that MacDiarmid did not know them and their origins.

MacDiarmid's prose has the advantage of enabling us to chart his ideological waxings and wanings where his poetry is necessarily silent. He could beat out his tremendous admiration for Lenin into three tremendous hymns (the third published when most people, particularly Stalin, were content to have forgotten that Lenin ever existed in real terms), but the receptivity and internal debate which produced ultimately the volcanic fires of his poetry require a study of his prose. In certain most important respects, of course, it will not. Some of his greatest lyrics have their origin in poetic perception, in deeply personal crisis, and in other matters on which his prose is silent. Prose, even correspondence, was for him a public vehicle, and his comparatively low opinion of it make the clues to his poetic development crude for the most part.

Perhaps the enthusiasm which evokes least reaction in MacDiarmid's audience today is that for the Social Credit philosophy of Major C. H. Douglas. Douglas's career, as writer and as government adviser, ultimately declined into sad expressions of paranoia about international conspiracy, and his frustrations and failures tragically led him into anti-Semitism among other aberrations. But when MacDiarmid so enthusiastically took him up he seemed like a harbinger of a great new economic justice, and MacDiarmid's receptivity to him is characteristic of the poet's hunger for new ideas which might rejuvenate the arthritic culture and society against which he raged. And it is worth looking at some of those reflections on Douglas's theories, particularly as asserted in *Scottish Scene*, to see the significance of the Douglas challenge and why MacDiarmid responded to him. In a disintegrating world it seemed to a giant that it was a choice between economic obliteration for conventional ostriches or search for new solutions which would harness economic instruments now apparently about to destroy their inventors. He extolled the poetry, so to say, of Douglas's economics much as the Second New Deal embraced what had hitherto been seen as the heretical doctrines of Keynes. But *Scottish Scene* has another lesson, and an important one. MacDiarmid's collaborator, Lewis Grassic Gibbon, was in important ways his counterpart, sometimes in agreement, sometimes in confrontation. Gibbon was an anti-nationalist expatriate, but Gibbon was as assertively Scottish and radical as his friend, and the Douglas study by MacDiarmid ("The Builder") is intended to complement Gibbon's on James Ramsay MacDonald ("The Wrecker"). To MacDiarmid, as to Gibbon, MacDonald had dishonoured Scotland, Socialism, the working class and the human intellect. It was characteristic of MacDiarmid that he (unlike Gibbon) had to place a constructive alternative Scottish inspirational figure before his audience instead of merely contemplating the ruins of one. Gibbon worked his visions through assertion of the ideas of Marxism and mysticism: MacDiarmid insisted that he had to educate by human vehicles, and threw formidable energies into the cults of Lenin, Davidson, MacLean and, for a time, Douglas.

I am tempted to stop here — editor and publisher suffer from that temptation in even more virulent form — and remark with the author of *Lucky Poet* that this subject requires about 750,000 more words which I hope to produce shortly. But let me end on

Lucky Poet itself, and on MacDiarmid's more general auto-biographical writing, equally classifiable as polemic. Inevitably, it challenges comparison with his Irish contemporary, Sean O'Casey, with whom Orwell and other commentators often compared him. Both were at various times Communists and nationalists, although O'Casey was much more alert to the dangers of violent nationalism than MacDiarmid was: O'Casey had seen Irish Socialism consumed by the Irish revolution on which it had sought to ride into power. Both were bitterly hostile to the clerical establishments in their own countries, and from a curiously alien standpoint — O'Casey because his people were Protestant, MacDiarmid because the religious belief which most attracted him was the Roman Catholic, and both of them because they were atheists. As autobiographers, both are artists, and on a creative level O'Casey much more so: after all, his artistic triumphs had been in prose, albeit the prose of plays. But taken cumulatively the effects of both are astonishingly different. O'Casey makes one the witness of far more events than does MacDiarmid. O'Casey is concerned with ideas, but also with his own discovery of them, MacDiarmid with ideas and with others' reception of them from him. O'Casey deals with himself in the third person, MacDiarmid, for all of his pseudonyms, with a thunderous repetition of the first. But in fact the final verdict is that O'Casey shows himself persistently preoccupied with his own grievances to the point of whining, and MacDiarmid's work is happy work, in which his battles are discussed with confidence and optimism, however painful the privations he endured in order to fight them.

Edmund Wilson's *To the Finland Station* entitles two of its chapters, "Trotsky identifies history with himself", and "Lenin identifies himself with history". I think I would use that classification to distinguish O'Casey from MacDiarmid, provided we accept it that MacDiarmid's self-identification with "history" required a use of the word embracing Scotland, and poetry, and extended to the end of time.

Haud Forrit

To Hugh MacDiarmid, on his eightieth birthday.

Over the years you've dreamed your dreams
And as always
You go back to your past
In Langholm — your tap-root.
Sometimes the past flows beside you
Like the Esk when partly hidden in the mist
Then there are these meetings in dreams—
Strange how sad they can be
Like Heine's grey ghost
That walked beside him
As he talked
Then again it's like a journey
In the sun and you look back
Over eighty years
Rather like looking back
After a long day's walk
Over Tarras Moor
And always in the background
The rivers Ewes and Wauchope
The sound of the Esk in high spate
Rising high and spilling over
Like you, MacDiarmid, ginny-truckled
Now you're awake
And find you're not an astronaut
Just a poet
Thousands of people and switches
Put Neil Armstrong on the Moon
You gripped the curly snake Cencrastus

And made it alone
Scars there will be in plenty
Let's hope they will be in their natural creases
For your home-town is silent and moonstruck
Reaching out you find no welcoming hand.
Hell! What need have you to care
You are meeting your eightieth year
Head held high, haud forrit MacDiarmid
Like Muhammed Ali—you're the greatest.

VALDA TREVLYN
From *The Scotsman*, 12 August 1972.   (Mrs Hugh MacDiarmid)

Notes on Contributors

SORLEY MACLEAN

Scotland's most distinguished living poet, he is generally regarded as the greatest Gaelic poet for more than 200 years. Born in Raasay in 1911 and educated at Portree High School and Edinburgh University where he took a first in English and also studied Celtic. He became a schoolmaster and did a great deal for the teaching of Gaelic in secondary schools. He retired as headmaster of Plockton High School in 1976. Subsequently he was Writer in Residence at Edinburgh University for two years. He now lives in his great-great-grandfather's house in the Braes district of Skye, overlooking Raasay Sound.

He is an Hon. LL.D. of Dundee University (1972), an Hon. D.Litt. (Celtic) of the National University of Ireland (1978) and an Hon. D.Litt. of Edinburgh University (1980).

His publications include: *Seventeen Poems for Sixpence* (with Robert Garioch), 1940; *Four Points of a Saltire*, Gordon Wright, 1970; *Barr Agus Asbhuain* (Selected Poems), Canongate, 1977.

J. K. ANNAND

Native of Edinburgh, where he has lived and worked except for the war years at sea and a short spell in Galloway. Had same teacher of English at Broughton School as C. M. Grieve. While still a schoolboy reviewed, in 1925, *Sangschaw* in school magazine, and corresponded with Grieve from 1926 till 1977. Edited *Early Lyrics by Hugh MacDiarmid*. Author of six books of verse. Formerly edited *Lines Review*; currently edits *Lallans*.

DUNCAN GLEN

Duncan Glen's pioneering work, *Hugh MacDiarmid and the Scottish Renaissance*, was published by Chambers in 1964 and since then he has written extensively on MacDiarmid and edited *Selected Essays of Hugh MacDiarmid* (Cape 1969) and *Hugh MacDiarmid: A Critical Survey* (Scottish Academic Press 1972). He is also well-known as a poet and as the editor of the poetry magazine *Akros*. His most recent work of poetry is the long 192-page *Realities Poems* (Akros Publications 1980). He is presently working in Nottingham where he is Head of the Department of Visual Communication in Trent Polytechnic.

ALAN BOLD

Alan Bold was born in Edinburgh in 1943 and since 1975 has lived with his wife and daughter in rural Fife. He has published many collections of poetry including *To Find the New, A Perpetual Motion Machine, The State of the Nation* and *This Fine Day*. He has edited *The Penguin Book of Socialist Verse, The Martial Muse, The Cambridge Book of English Verse 1939-75, Making Love* and *The Bawdy Beautiful*. He has also written critical books on *Thom Gunn and Ted Hughes, George Mackay Brown* and *The Ballad*. He has had many exhibitions of his Illuminated Poems (pictures combining an original poetic manuscript with an illustrative composition).

TOM SCOTT

Tom Scott was born in Glasgow in 1918, son of a Clydeside boilermaker. He went to Thornwood School, then Hyndland Secondary, but as a result of the 1931 slump the family moved to St Andrews where he went to Madras College for a year-and-a-half. He worked for a year or so with a butcher firm, then as a builder's labourer-cum-apprentice. His real but frustrated interests were in nature, books and singing. At the outbreak of war he was called up and served in Nigeria from 1941-43, during which time he wrote and published some poems, notable chiefly, he says, for their intense but wet lyricism, very much the product of the nightmarish times. Since his discovery of his Scots voice, he has published several books of verse, edited three anthologies, written critical works, and one or two books for youngsters. After a year at Newbattle Abbey in Edwin Muir's time, he took an Honours degree and Ph.D. at Edinburgh University.

DAVID DAICHES

David Daiches, M.A.(Edin.), D.Phil.(Oxon.), Hon. D.Litt. (Brown University, University of Sussex, Edinburgh University). Doctor *honoris causa* (Sorbonne), D.Univ. (Stirling).

Has held academic posts at Oxford, Chicago, Cornell, Cambridge and Sussex, at the last of which he was Professor of English and Dean of the School of English and American Studies from its foundation in 1961 until his retirement in 1977. Author of some forty books, including *The Novel and the Modern World, A Study of Literature, A Critical History of English Literature, Robert Burns, The Paradox of Scottish Culture, Scotland and the Union, Sir Walter Scott and his World, Edinburgh,* etc. Now Professor Emeritus of the University of Sussex and lives in Edinburgh.

DAVID MURISON

David Murison was born in Fraserburgh, where he has now retired. He is a graduate in Classics of the Universities of Aberdeen and Cambridge and has been a lecturer in all the four older Scottish universities, ending as Reader in Scottish and English Languages at Glasgow. He succeeded Dr William Grant as editor of the Scottish National Dictionary in 1946 and completed the ten-volume work in 1976. He has broadcast and contributed articles on Scots to various books and periodicals and is the author of a short handbook, *The Guid Scots Tongue.*

GEORGE BRUCE

Of George Bruce's first collection of poems, *Sea Talk* (1944), Kurt Wittig wrote in *The Scottish Tradition in Literature*: "His 'English' is, in its own way, totally unlike that of Southern English; its consonants are more prominent and it is firmer and more distinctly articulated." Bruce's awareness of a distinctive Scots-English, and also of the distinctive vitality of Scots, may be recognised in his several essays on MacDiarmid, as well as on other Scottish poets. It has a special application to his essay in *The Age of MacDiarmid*, which is based on a personal encounter with MacDiarmid and Muir. In the past decade Bruce's publications include *The Collected Poems of George Bruce* (1970), *Neil M. Gunn* (1971) and *William Soutar* (1978) — essays commissioned by the National Library of Scotland, *Anne Redpath* (1974) — a monograph

265

of the Scottish artist, and *Festival in the North* (1975) — a history of the Edinburgh International Festival.

KENNETH BUTHLAY

Kenneth Buthlay wrote an influential book on Hugh MacDiarmid for Oliver & Boyd's *Writers and Critics* series in 1964, when he was Professor of English Literature at the University of Sao Paulo, Brazil. He has edited a collection of MacDiarmid's prose, *The Uncanny Scot*, written critical studies of his poetry in various periodicals, and contributed an essay to Gordon Wright's pictorial biography of MacDiarmid. He is presently Senior Lecturer in Scottish Literature at the University of Glasgow.

IAIN CRICHTON SMITH

Iain Crichton Smith was born in 1928 on the island of Lewis. Completely bilingual in English and Gaelic, he has written novels, poetry, short stories and plays in both languages. He is married and is a former English teacher, a position from which he retired in 1977 in order to take up full-time writing.

RONALD STEVENSON

Ronald Stevenson, Scottish composer/pianist, was a friend of MacDiarmid for the poet's last twenty years and has set to music many of the later poems, chiefly the song-cycle *Border Boyhood* (commissioned and performed by Sir Peter Pears and the composer at the 1972 Aldeburgh Festival). Stevenson has extended to music MacDiarmid's vision of a world language, in such works as his *Passacaglia on DSCH* (published by O.U.P. and recorded by E.M.I.), his Second Piano Concerto (*The Continents*—London Proms 1972), and his Violin Concerto (commissioned by Yehudi Menuhin). As pianist, Stevenson has performed all over the world, including a tour of Australia in 1980.

JOHN WAIN

Born 1925. Novelist, poet, critic. Professor of Poetry, University of Oxford, 1973-78. Author of five volumes of poetry. One of the most significant contemporary British novelists since the publication of *Hurry On Down* (1953), to *The Pardoner's Tale* (1978). First Creative Fellow of Brasenose College, Oxford, 1971-72, and President of the Johnson Society, Lichfield, 1976-77; James

Tait Black Memorial Prize and Heinemann Award for his biography, *Samuel Johnson* (1974).

EDWIN MORGAN

Born Glasgow, 1920. Distinguished Scottish poet, critic and academic. Titular Professor of English, University of Glasgow. Writes poetry in Scots and English, from *The Vision of Cathkin Braes*, 1952, to *The New Divan*, 1977. His works include translations from Anglo-Saxon, Russian and Italian, and he has a masterly range of forms and themes, including concrete and visual poems and opera librettos.

STEPHEN MAXWELL

Stephen Maxwell was born in Edinburgh in 1942 but grew up in Yorkshire. After graduating in Moral Sciences from Cambridge University in 1963, he worked for a year as a trainee journalist in Sheffield before going to the L.S.E. to study international politics. After graduating M.Sc. with distinction in 1965, he interrupted work on a Ph.D. thesis to spend a year as junior Research Associate of the International Institute for Strategic Studies, London.

In 1967 he joined the London branch of the Scottish National Party and after a further year of postgraduate work at the L.S.E. he was appointed Lecturer in International Politics at Sussex University, but resigned in 1970 to take up an appointment as Research Fellow of the Royal Institute of International Affairs at Edinburgh University.

In 1973 he became full-time Press Officer for the S.N.P. Between 1975-78 he was a Lothian Regional councillor and in 1977-79 was vice-chairman (Publicity) for S.N.P. and director of the S.N.P.'s Assembly referendum campaign. He is a founder-member of the S.N.P. '79 Group.

He was a contributor to *The Radical Approach* (Palingenesis 1976) and *Power and Manoeuvrability* (Q 1978), and is co-editor of *The Nordic Model: Studies in Public Policy Innovation* (Gower, July 1980). In addition, he has been a frequent contributor to a range of Scottish journals including *Scottish International* and *Q*.

NEAL ASCHERSON

Neal Ascherson was born in Edinburgh in 1932. He has spent much of his life as a foreign correspondent, mostly for *The Observer*. From 1975 to 1979 he was specialist writer for *The Scotsman* on Scottish politics.

OWEN DUDLEY EDWARDS

Reader in History at Edinburgh University. Born Dublin 1938. Married Barbara Balbirnie Lee 1966. Three children. Publications include: *Celtic Nationalism* (with Gwynfor Evans, Ioan Rhys and Hugh MacDiarmid), *Scotland, Europe and the American Revolution* (co-editor with George Shepperson), *P. G. Wodehouse* and, most recently, *Burke and Hare*. Journalist and broadcaster. Member of Scottish National Party. Currently writing a book about Conan Doyle for Mainstream Publishing.

VALDA TREVLYN

Born 1906 in Cornwall. She met MacDiarmid in London at the beginning of the 1930s and they were together for close on fifty years. She is proud of being Cornish and thanks God, despite her long stay in Scotland, that she is not Scots, and doubly thankful that she is not English.

P. H. SCOTT

Born in Edinburgh, where he followed the traditional path of High School and University. He worked abroad for many years, but remained involved in Scottish affairs. He is a frequent contributor to *The Scotsman*, Blackwood's and *The Economist*, and other periodicals, mainly on Scottish literary and historical subjects. His publications include *1707: The Union of Scotland and England* (W. & R. Chambers).

A. C. DAVIS

Born in Darnick — 40 miles north of Langholm. A graduate in English of Edinburgh University. Worked in Scotland and abroad for the British Council, latterly as its representative, Scotland. Organising secretary of the Saltire Society 1974-79. Former member of the editorial board of the *New Saltire* and *Scottish Review*.